INCEST

A BIOSOCIAL VIEW

This is a volume in

STUDIES IN ANTHROPOLOGY

Under the consulting editorship of
E. A. Hammel, University of California, Berkeley

A complete list of titles appears at the end of this volume.

INCEST

A BIOSOCIAL VIEW

JOSEPH SHEPHER

Department of Sociology and Anthropology
University of Haifa
Mount Carmel, Israel

With a Foreword by Edward O. Wilson

ACADEMIC PRESS

A Subsidiary of Harcourt Brace Jovanovich, Publishers

New York   London

Paris   San Diego   San Francisco   São Paulo   Sydney   Tokyo   Toronto

ACADEMIC PRESS, INC.
111 Fifth Avenue, New York, New York 10003

United Kingdom Edition published by
ACADEMIC PRESS, INC. (LONDON) LTD.
24/28 Oval Road, London NW1   7DX

Library of Congress Cataloging in Publication Data

Shepher, Joseph.
    Incest: a biosocial view.

    (Studies in anthropology)
    Bibliography: p.
    Includes index.
    1. Incest. 2. Biosociology. 3. Socialization.
4. Incest--Israel--Case studies.   5. Collective
settlement--Israel--Case studies. I. Title.
II. Series: Studies in anthropology (Academic Press)
GN480.25.S52 1983   306.7   81-6552
ISBN 0−12−639460−1

PRINTED IN THE UNITED STATES OF AMERICA

83 84 85 86   9 8 7 6 5 4 3 2 1

To my extended family, who carry my inclusive fitness,
and to my tiny village in the lower Galilee,
where most of these ideas were conceived.

CONTENTS

11 Conclusions   175

FOREWORD

From Sophoclean drama to psychoanalysis, incest is a brooding presence that pervades man's self-interpretation. If any trait universally characterizes human nature, it is the incest taboo. From the horror of its abrogation have grown complicated myths and rituals and some of our most compelling and enduring literature. Like submariners in a primitive bathyscaphe, Freud and other psychoanalytic theorists have descended into the unconscious in a search for the taboo's origins and true meaning. Theorists in anthropology have looked to the need for family cohesiveness and social alliances as the prime movers. To a large degree the taboo has defeated all such attempts to understand it.

Recently, however, the incest taboo has begun to make sense as a more overtly biological phenomenon. As Edward Westermarck first suggested in 1891, the basis of the taboo may be simpler and more straightforward than conceived in the psychoanalytic and anthropological models. In essence, inbreeding at the level of brother–sister or parent–child drastically increases the incidence of homozygosity and genetic defects. Any psychological barrier to incest, any inborn propensity to mate beyond the circle of closest relative, will convey a reproductive advantage. All other things being equal, individuals who have a genetic propensity to avoid incest, by whatever means, will contribute more healthy offspring to the next generation than those who lack the propensity. It follows that if Darwinian natural selection has been operating for long periods of time, we can expect to find the propensity to be widespread in human populations. In a phrase, the incest taboo, or more precisely the array of incest taboos displayed by human beings, is the consequence of Mendel's laws of heredity combined with the advantage that results from the maintenance of genetic diversity.

Not only does the inborn propensity exist, it appears to be enabled by an equally simple rule in psychological development. As Joseph Shepher shows in this important and carefully documented book, the mechanism in at least the case of sibling incest avoidance is a kind of negative imprinting that results in sexual indifference to individuals who live in close domestic proximity when one is a young child. Myths, rituals, and great literature can be, and very likely are, the splendid cultural outgrowths of this psychobiological primary force.

The incest taboo has an added importance in the present ferment that characterizes human sociobiology and the social sciences. Because of the apparent relative simplicity of the selection force and epigenetic rule, the biological origins of the behavior are more tractable to analysis than is the case for most other forms of human social behavior. And because the epigenetic rule in the case of sibling incest is so powerful, the sibling taboo can be made a paradigm in the analysis of the translation from individual behavioral development to cultural patterns. In other words, this phenomenon might serve the social sciences in the way *Drosophila* chromosomes or sea urchin eggs serve biology.

The author brings to the subject a rare understanding of both biological theory and the real world of ethnographic data. His book will not be the final word on this important set of phenomena, but I believe it to be more important than previous works on the subject in pointing the way to rigorous analysis and ultimate, deep evolutionary understanding at all levels of biological and social organization. If so much as a single human behavioral phenomenon can be comprehended with anything approaching this degree of completeness, the effects on the social sciences will surely be revolutionary.

EDWARD O. WILSON
HARVARD UNIVERSITY

PREFACE

Many eminent anthropologists, among them White, Lévi-Strauss, Schneider, and Fox, have considered the study of incest to be at the core of anthropological theory. This book surveys all the important theoretical approaches to the problem, focuses on the sociobiological theory of incest, and compares this theory with the others.

Despite the considerable literature on incest that has accumulated over the last 100 years, to my knowledge no single volume has ever been devoted to summarizing all the theoretical approaches to incest and to synthesizing them in light of one theory. Many books contain important contributions to the theory of incest, but these contributions are wrapped in empirical research and usually contain scant theoretical analysis. Indeed, of all the books with "incest" in the title, I can think of only one possible exception: Robin Fox's 1980 collection of his 20 years of theoretical essays on the subject.

To the extent that I emphasize theoretical analysis, I believe this book fills a gap in the literature. However, it is also an effort to present for validation a new and controversial view: the sociobiological theory of incest. This view is of relevance to both the behavioral and life sciences. Its relevance for anthropologists, sociologists, and psychologists studying the problem of incest is obvious. What may not be obvious is the book's relevance for biologists. One of the theoretical arguments I make is that the existence of culture does not lead to the exemption of *Homo sapiens* from the evolutionary process. Instead, it creates a coevolutionary process, of which the evolution of incest avoidance in human beings is the simplest, yet most instructive, example.

The first chapter of the book introduces the reader to the problem of incest.

The second and third chapters are devoted to the sociobiological theory in general and to important methodological issues. Chapters 4–6 survey the theories and empirical findings that led to the sociobiological theory of incest. I present the theory itself in Chapter 7. Chapters 8–10 outline and examine the main theories of incest from the past 100 years. Finally, Chapter 11 summarizes the theories and synthesizes them in light of the sociobiological theory.

This work grew out of several years of research in Israel under the direction of the late Yonina Gerber-Talmon, who drew my attention to the strange phenomenon that kibbutz children reared together never marry each other (Talmon, 1964). Being myself a kibbutz member, I had the opportunity to investigate the specific system of kibbutz socialization. My doctoral dissertation (Shepher, 1971a, 1971b), written under the guidance of Lionel Tiger and Robin Fox at Rutgers, was devoted to the problem of incest avoidance. My colleague, Frank R. Vivelo, and I wanted to publish a Reader of Incest Theories, but we pleaded in vain for its publication. Though we received many compliments, no one wanted to assume the laborious task of requesting reprint permission for 70 articles. I asked the advice of David Schneider, whose unpublished paper I wanted to include in the Reader. His answer was "Write a book of your own, it would have more value than a Reader."

E. O. Wilson, who was host at Harvard, where I spent a sabbatical in 1978, encouraged me in the project. His advice as well as personal contact with Robert Trivers, William Hamilton, Irven De Vore, Mel Konner, John Whiting, John Hartung, Sarah Blaffer Hrdy, and Jon Seger at Harvard proved invaluable in helping me contend with the many problems involved in writing this book.

Several colleagues read different parts of the manuscript and kindly commented on shortcomings: E. O. Wilson, W. D. Hamilton, Sarah Blaffer Hrdy, Pierre Van den Berghe, David M. Schneider, Yakov Gluck, and Dov Porat. I am greatly indebted to all of them.

My research assistant, Shoshana Shadmi, contributed materially to the process of writing with important comments on the intelligibility and readability of the text.

Special thanks are due Tswiah Ekstein and David Bukai of the Research Authority of the University of Haifa, who effectively administered the secretarial tasks relating to the preparation of the manuscript.

Finally, I am grateful to Academic Press and E. A. Hammel, who overcame the great handicap of 6000 miles distance between New York and Haifa and brought this work to successful completion.

1

INTRODUCTION

R Yohanan said in the name of R. Simeon ben-Yehozadak: "By a majority vote, it was resolved in the upper chambers of the house of Nitza in Lydda that in every law of the Torah if a man is commanded: 'Transgress and suffer not death' he may transgress and not suffer death, excepting idolatry, incest and murder"

—SANHEDRIN
Babylonian Talmad (74/a)

Geschrieben steht: "Im Anfang war des Wort!"
Hier stock ich schon! Wer hilft mir weiter fort?
Ich kann das Wort so hoch unmöglich schatzen,
Ich muss es anders übersetzen,
Wenn ich vom Geiste recht erleutet bin.
Geschrieben steht: "Im Anfang war der Sinn."
Bedenke wohl die erste Zeile.
Dass deine Feder sich nicht übereile!
Ist es der Sinn, der alles wirkt und schafft?
Es sollte stehn: "Im Anfang war die Kraft!"
Doch, auch indem ich dieses niederschreibe,
Schon warnt mich was, dass ich dabei nicht bleibe.
Mir hilft der Geist! Auf einmal seh ich Rat
Und schreib getrost: "Im Anfang war die Tat!"
—Goethe
Faust I, 1224–1237

["In the beginning was the Word"—thus runs the text.
Who helps me on? Already I'm perplexed.
I cannot grant the word such sovereign merit,
I must translate it in a different way
If I'm indeed illumined by the Spirit.
"In the beginning was the Sense" But stay!
Reflect on this first sentence well and truly
Lest the light pen be hurrying unduly!
Is sense in fact all action's spur and source?
It should read: "In the beginning was the Force!"
Yet as I write it down, some warning sense
Alerts me that it, too, will give offense.
The spirit speaks! And lo, the way is freed,
I calmly write: "In the beginning was the Deed!"]
(The Arndt translation)
1976 New York W. W. Norton)

1

As an undergraduate student of sociology, I was perplexed by the distinctions made between human universals and human particulars. Taught Parsonian structural–functional sociology, I wondered how my teachers could claim a certain trait as a human universal and delve immediately into the peculiarities of various cultures. It seemed enough to declare, for instance, that families occur in every society and then to take up the fascinating differences among Nayar, Tiwi, and modern Western families. The more I learned about human societies, the more I wanted to know why families are universal but not, say, soccer teams or corporations producing stereo equipment. I wanted to know what caused the difference between universal and particular traits and why we neglected to study it. Why did we not even consider the variability of traits among humans a universal itself and examine it with other universals? I was more interested in what was *common* to all humans than in what *separated* them.

Once in a while, a student would point out that a given individual difference might distort the integrity of a social form or cultural trait. The professors agreed, explaining, however, that "the individual" belongs to the frame of reference of psychology and hence is out of bounds to sociologists. Their reaction was somewhat more harsh if a student raised the possibility that a biological variable might be responsible for some form of behavior. The prototype of sociological research was Durkheim's (1952) *Suicide*, in which the author eliminated every biological or psychological cause and demonstrated triumphantly that a social variable like suicide depends only on other social variables such as anomie. The basic unit of sociology, the learned social action, inexorably bound the individual to the social group from birth to death.

The human individual somehow got lost: Individual behavior was seen as a variable dependent on social institutions and on cultural norms. Social institutions and cultural norms, on the other hand, were described as being different from society to society, from culture to culture. What, though, if individuals in different cultures behave in a similar, or even identical, way? Does it mean that the cultural norms of different societies are also identical? Yes and no. Human universals do exist, but the identical norms are formulated differently in each culture. Hence, people encounter human universals through their own culture.

Incest prohibition is such a universal, and I encountered it through my own culture—Judaism. In 1935 in Budapest, when I was 13 and preparing for my bar mitzvah, I learned the basic principles of Judaism and read the quotation from the Babylonian Talmud that appears at the beginning of this Introduction. Our rabbi explained that the three worst sins a Jew can commit are idolatry, murder, and incest. "You should die rather than commit those sins," he enjoined, although he did not explain what the sins were. I understood only two of them. Idolatry, the technical term for conversion, had occurred among Hungarian Jews who hoped to save themselves from persecution by converting. I still remember my family's horror at the mention of a convert. The second sin, murder, was also very real to me then. But the third, incest? I understood neither the Hebrew nor the Hungarian term. I went to the dictionary: Sexual intercourse between members of the same family: mother and son, brother and sister, father and daughter. My emotional reaction was one of ridicule and disgust; my intellectual reaction was that there must be some mistake! Idolatry or murder are things that people *do* because they gain or at least think they gain from them. But incest? Who would be so idiotic and disgusting? I returned to the rabbi with my question, but in Budapest in 1935 no rabbi or teacher or parent would talk with a 13-year-old boy about such a matter. When I grew up, they told me, I would understand.

In the seventh gymnasium, 4 years later, I found the explanation in Sigmund Freud's (1950) *Totem and Taboo* and *The Three Contributions to the Theory of Sex* (1910). How naive I had been! I had never thought about incest because I had successfully suppressed those sexual wishes, relegating them to my unconscious. I tried unsuccessfully to recall my father's fierce reaction to my infantile sexual love for my mother. I watched out for symbolic dreams and *Fehlleistungen* that would reveal my unconscious longings . . . and failed.

The basic dispute in incest theory is between Freud and Westermarck. Freud thought that people want to commit incest and because incest is not good (the reasons are immaterial at this point) it therefore had to be *prohibited*. Westermarck, on the other hand, thought that people do *not* want to commit incest, that incest is not good and is *inhibited*. As a youngster of 13, I had agreed with Westermarck; at 17, I agreed with Freud. The scientific world sided with Freud. Sir James Frazer's ironic comment, which Freud used to discredit Westermarck's argument, appeared again and again: If incest avoidance is instinctual, why prohibit incest?

The dispute went deeper than the question of inhibition versus prohibition; it represented a dispute central to the behavioral sciences: the nature–nurture controversy. Inhibition, or as Westermarck first termed it, *instinct* comes from within, from nature: it is "in the beast." Prohibition, on the other hand, is received from culture and has to be learned. Does humanity necessarily imply culture? Is there an uncrossable breach between humans and other animals, or is the transition gradual and continuous?

Here we touch on a basic question about humanity. Are humans the product of evolutionary processes like all other forms of life on earth? If so, has culture nonetheless exempted us from the laws of evolution? Does culture allow us to obey completely different laws, or —as we would like to believe—have we learned so that our culture is the only determinant of our personalities and, ultimately, our destinies. Or, does our culture itself comply with basic patterns and limits on our nature which have evolved over millions of years?

From time to time, new points of view have appeared in the study of incest. Lévi-Strauss introduced the idea of a bridge between nature and culture, as he held that a universal phenomenon cannot be merely cultural. Many scientists have realized that not all incestual dyads can be analyzed by identical methods. Whatever their disputes, most scientists have agreed on the central importance of incest regulations. In them, Malinowski saw the maintenance of the social order through the family, Freud the basis of human morality and religion. White argued that incest regulations are the source of human cooperation and thereby the basic glue of economic and political institutions. Lévi-Strauss declared the incest taboo to constitute the "basic rule" and to be the source of reciprocity and exchange.

Historically, anthropologists, many of whom contributed to incest theory, began by assuming that incest was universally prohibited. In seeking to answer why this was so, they assumed that without the prohibition, incestuous relationships would be the rule. Many anthropologists believed that people understood the harmful results of incest and hence rejected it. Others believed that people had to be restrained or coerced into avoiding incest. In my opinion, the avoidance of incest preceded both external coercion and intellectual understanding. First came the deed, in Faust's phrase. The prohibition itself—that is, the word, the sense, and the force—came later.

Two methodological problems have plagued those studying incest: the limited opportunities for empirical research and the universality of the basic variables. Empirical research into human behavior is not easy under the best of circumstances; it is more difficult if the research topic is associated with human sexual practices; it becomes all but impossible when research focuses on a tabooed behavior like incest. A partial solution lay in cross-cultural research because it admitted of ethnographic data, of "culture" as the unit of research, and of counting cultures with the characteristics under investigation. But cross-cultural research did not solve the problem because both the dependent and the independent variables were universal. If researchers wanted to explain the origin or function of the incest taboo (the dependent variable) by the "obvious" causative factor, the family (the independent variable), they could not find a society without the incest taboo or the family.

I have been fortunate enough to have conducted empirical research, if not on incest per se, then certainly on incest-like behavior. I will describe my research in detail in Chapter 5, but a few sentences are in order here. I investigated kibbutz adolescents and adults and found that those who are reared together between birth and 6 years neither have premarital sex together nor marry each other. Although these behaviors are not tabooed, they do not occur. In the kibbutz, cosocialized children are not relatives and yet exhibit the same behavior we find among blood siblings. My study thus let me eliminate, once and for all, the family as a possible independent variable. In this way, the kibbutz affords a kind of "natural laboratory" from which we can draw fresh conclusions about incest avoidance.

Thus, my research represented a partial way out of the methodological deadlock—partial, because it dealt only with one incestual dyad, that of siblings. In this work I shall extend this breakthrough.

First, I set out my basic theoretical framework (Chapter 2) and deal with some important methodological questions (Chapter 3). Then I survey those works that paved the road to an integrated biosocial view of incest (Chapters 4–6). Chapter 7 presents the biosocial view of incest. I consider this chapter to be the decisive contribution of this work. Chapters 8–10 surveys the classic theories of incest. Finally, in Chapter 11, I try to integrate the different points of view. Such an integration may help man's ages-old striving to understand himself.

Thus, the book has a dual aim: the presentation of a sociobiological view of incest and a comprehensive survey of the theoretical literature on incest. This literature, dispersed over hundreds of books and articles, has never before been systematically surveyed. Readers who do not accept my assumptions or my methods may nonetheless benefit from this survey and remain free to choose among the theories presented.

A complete survey of incest theories would require at least three volumes. I have omitted the early evolutionists like Morgan, Starcke, Kohler, MacLennan, and Lubbock because of their limited influence on the central theorists. I did not include "strange" theories, like those of Durkheim, Briffault, and Lord Raglan, again because of their lack of influence on other people's thinking. Also excluded were studies of incest that confine themselves to one culture (Radcliffe-Brown on the Andaman Islanders, Evans-Pritchard on the Nuer, or Leach on the Lakher) despite some important observations made. Ultimately, of course, I have included what I consider important, and as such my choice is debatable.

Biosocial theory proposes many hypotheses, and this book presents evidence for only some of them. Evidence for the rest will come with hard work. In fact, as I attempt to show, biosocial theory obliges conscientious social scientists to reexamine many of their assumptions. They will certainly be forced to accept or reject this powerful new theory; to ignore it becomes more difficult every day.

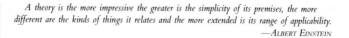
A theory is the more impressive the greater is the simplicity of its premises, the more different are the kinds of things it relates and the more extended is its range of applicability.
—ALBERT EINSTEIN

2

THE BIOSOCIAL VIEW

Although many excellent books have introduced sociobiology (e.g., Barash, 1977, 1979, Caplan, 1978; Gregory and Silvers, 1978; Clutton-Brock and Harvey, 1978; Ruse, 1979; Alexander, 1979; Barlow and Silverberg, 1980), a short summary of the basic tenets of the theory seems necessary before we begin to analyze the specific question of incest. Sociobiology is a comprehensive theory of the evolution of social behavior; as such, it deals with the whole animal world starting with colonial microorganisms and invertebrates and ending with man (Wilson, 1975). However, because this book deals with incest as a human problem, I shall limit this summary to human sociobiology.

The basic assumption of human sociobiology is that humans are part of nature. The human body consists of the same materials, organized along the same principles, as the body of any other living organism. Its composition reveals that we resemble more closely organisms in the animal kingdom than in the plant kingdom or than monera (bacteria and algae), protista (mastigophora and other protozoa), or fungi. As part of the animal kingdom, we are classified among the primate order of the class of mammals. This classification may be self-evident to the biological taxonomist but it is usually forgotten by the social scientist.

Like all species, humans have evolved and continue to do so. *Homo sapiens sapiens* is a rather recent species in the hominid family. The evolutionary route

7

that led to the emergence of *Homo sapiens sapiens* is still hotly debated among experts. Johanson and Edey (1981) propose the following sequence:

Australopithecus afarensis, a hominid with mixed pongid and hominid traits, is the ancestor of two genera: *Australopithecus* and *Homo*. It existed between 3 and 3.7 million years ago. Its population evolved into two branches: *Australopithecus africanus*, the oldest fossil of which dates back 2.7 million years ago, and *Homo habilis*, dating back 2.2 million years ago. The first branch evolved into *Australopithecus robustus*, a specialized type that became extinct around 1.2 million years ago. *Homo habilis* evolved into *Homo erectus*, which spread from Africa to Asia and Europe and was the direct ancestor of *Homo sapiens*, whose oldest fossils go back 400,000 years. The taxon *Homo sapiens sapiens* was given to the Cro-Magnon man, who lived around 30,000 years B.P.

Many paleoanthropologists argue that the genus *Ramapithecus* which existed in the Myocene period (14 million years ago) possessed some hominid traits. Johanson and Edey, however, consider the gap of 10 million years between *Ramapithecus* and *Australopithecus afarensis* to be a "black hole," as is the gap of 800,000 years between *Australopithecus afarensis* and *Homo habilis*. Other authors offer alternative family trees (e.g., Leakey and Lewin, 1977; Brace, 1979; Campbell, 1976).

When did hominids evolve symbolic culture, a trait peculiar to the species? On this point the authorities are divided: Some think that *Australopithecus* used language and had social rules; others postpone the acquisition of these cultural markers to *Homo erectus*. But regardless of when culture appeared among us, our manufacture and use of tools, our symbolic language, and our invention of social rules *did not exempt* us from the realm of nature. We used elements of culture in adapting to the natural environment, in extending the human habitat, and, increasingly, in transforming it. (We are not the only animal to do so, but we do it more thoroughly and successfully than ants, termites, or beavers.) The point is that acquiring culture did not change the biological reality: We remain mammals and primates.

Like other organisms, humans have undergone natural selection, and our genetic fitness, expressed in the environment by differential reproduction, created specific gene pools for specific human populations. To this process, culture would add a powerful new factor, the sociocultural. This sociocultural factor would enter the already very complex interaction between our genetically predisposed behavior and the environment (and, in many species, the social environment). Individuals—and therefore populations—continued to reproduce differentially, and so certain genotypes appeared more frequently than others. Some human populations, and the cultures their behavior expressed, became extinct; some flourished, changed, and endure. None of use can look back and state exactly or even approximately the relative weight of the factors in our equation: the genetic, environmental, and sociocultural (although Alexander, 1979, and Lumsden and Wilson, 1981, are more optimistic). Was the decline of the Roman Empire and the ascent of the Germanic tribes of the *Volkerwanderung* a consequence of differences in genetic fitness, changes in the mediterranean climate, sociocultural vigor pitted against exhaustion, or a hopelessly complex interaction of many such factors?

Natural selection operates mostly at the level of the individual who carries genes and transmits them to other individuals. Populations merely offer the investigator a convenient macrocosm for watching this interaction among individuals. Genes are directly responsible for morphological changes in the individual organism. One's eye color, for example, is determined by the genetic contribution of one's ancestors. If we find uniformity of eye color in a population, we are safe in ascribing it to that population's gene pool. What, then, makes us search for explanations for uniformity of behavior within a population's culture? Learning that Orthodox Jews do not eat pork, we do not look for a gene that renders pork unpalatable (although we know that genes do govern taste). No, we turn to the *Pentateuch* instead and find there the prohibition against eating pork. Yet, if we find uniformity of behavior throughout an entire species, we can hardly ascribe this uniformity to culture, for *culture is variability par excellence; it cannot cause universals*. Universals exist *in spite of culture*.

The logical conclusion must be that genes are the ultimate source of universal behaviors. This conclusion sounds fantastic, unacceptable: a gene for family formation? a gene for hierarchy? a gene for a sense of justice? No one can prove the existence of such genes. But we do not require biologists to prove the existence of, say, the honeybee's gene for waggle dancing. If a honeybee waggle dances, everyone accepts this behavior as species specific and genetically inherited; nobody searches for a single waggle-dancing gene. But let anyone argue that some human behavior, say, territoriality, is biologically predisposed, and people start challenging "Is there a *gene* for territoriality?" There is certainly no *single* gene determining territoriality. We know that even the most simple morphological traits are not determined by one gene but by the interaction among many genes, and this is especially true of behaviors that result from a complex coordination of different systems (neural, neuro-hormonal, muscular) within the animal. But there is probably a constellation of genes that predisposes human animals to feel very uncomfortable if they cannot delineate a territory that is relatively unavailable to other human beings and access to which requires permission. People in every culture strive for this territorial exclusiveness. Westerners live in homes that are closed and private.

But what about Africa's Nyae Nyae Bushmen, who can hardly be said to have "houses"? They have vulnerable shelters and fires easily blown out by the wind. Even so, this vulnerable shelter is private, and "avoidance of entering somebody else's shelter indicates that the !Kung do hold shelters as a symbol for demonstrating reserved behavior [Marshall, 1976:250]." Van den Berghe (1978) has described reserved behavior in a modern recreational area. Even in concentration camps, prisoners' bunks became private "territories" to be defended against trespassers.

Another problem that arises when we talk about predispositions is that of uniformity. Critics of biosocial anthropology rely heavily on "exceptions," arguing that exceptions prove that a trait is cultural. But, here again, more is expected of biosocial anthropologists than of biologists. Biological predisposition does not result in uniform behavior among animals, without symbolic culture, let alone among the human species. Any journal of ethology will demonstrate that genomes create patterns of significant frequency in behavior. Thus, for instance, Loy (1971) found among rhesus monkeys in Cayo Santiago a significant correlation between increasing age of females and increasing dominance of their male sex partners. This correlation is far from being absolute (.60), but we accept that the rhesus monkeys did not develop a specific culture within which higher ranking males were attracted to older females. We can also find exceptions to human territorial behavior. Thus, Houriet (1971) describes a commune on the West Coast of the United States whose members decided for ideological reasons to be "open"—that is, not to claim any territorial rights, either for the settlement as a whole or for any of its houses. The commune rapidly disintegrated, but it had for a time overcome biologically predisposed territoriality by cultural means.

EPIGENETIC RULES

What are those biological predispositions? If the assumption is true that the ultimate source of human universals is to be found in the genes, then one has to explain how uniformities in genes come to be expressed in human universals. Genes are DNA sequences that regulate the building of proteins. Some are structural, building the organs of the body. Others are regulatory, directing the different phases of the organism (development, adjustment to environmental stimuli, internal organization). All these functions are accomplished by means of biochemical reactions.

Behavior, as we have seen, is the result of a complex interaction among different systems of the body: neural, neurohormonal, and muscular. Many expressions of behavior in higher organisms, in general, and in humans, in particular, are learned. Learning is the result of interaction between different individuals. Behavior patterns acquired through learning, however, belong to the realm of culture; therefore—so the argument goes—they cannot be explained by biological variables. Yet, as Crook (1980:10) aptly puts it: "Studies of the natural constraints on learning suggest that what is learnt, and when, is probably under a genetic surveillance so that learning, does not normally occur outside of an evolutionary stable strategy." (See also Gould and Gould, 1981.) Although no behavior patterns can occur without involving the organism, some patterns are under genetic surveillance more than are others.

This genetic surveillance of learning takes the form of *epigenetic rules*. Lumsden and Wilson (1981:7) define epigenetic rules as "genetically determined procedures that direct the assembly of the mind, including the screening of stimuli by peripherial sensory filters, the internuncial cellular organizing processes and the deeper processes of directed cognition. The rules comprise the restraints that the genes place on development (hence the expression 'epigenetic') . . . ."

The plasticity of learning, therefore, is not infinite. In certain spheres of social life, we are directed to prefer certain cultural traits (culturgens, in Lumsden and Wilson's phraseology). These take the form of biased ethno-graphic curves. Thus, for instance, the logical possibilities of the number of mating partners in a human mating system are four: one male–one female (monogamy), one male–more females (polygyny), one female–more males (polyandry), more males–more females (polygynandry). A survey of human mating systems will, however, reveal a very uneven distribution of mating patterns among the existing human cultures: Polyandry and polygynandry are very rare; polygyny is normative in more than 80% of the cultures, monogamy in less than 20%. The epigenetic rule behind this biased ethnographic curve is the asymmetry of parental investment between males and females. Although all four patterns can be learned by any individual, very few cultures teach even two of them.

THE IMPORTANCE OF REPRODUCTION

The human species is subject to evolution. Evolution is a sequence of changes in organisms. Natural selection is the process by which organisms that are more adapted than are others will survive and thus leave more progeny than will competing organisms. Genetic fitness, or leaving more progeny, puts reproduction at the focus of the evolutionary process. Reproduction, however, is a broader concept than sex. Among higher organisms, reproduction includes not only sexuality but the socializing of offspring so that they can reach sexual maturity and reproduce. Reproduction also includes competition, which creates dominance systems, and nesting behavior. Economic life and the proper distribution of scarce resources may also be a precondition of reproduction.

Biologists see the behaviors within reproduction quite clearly. They see the recurrent relationships among fights over feeding and nesting territories and reproduction. But in human behavior the connections are obscured; culture has elaborated every aspect of reproductive behavior. Indeed, now that humans have effective methods of birth control, we sometimes assume that reproduction, once a central component, has become almost negligible. Yet evidence shows repeatedly that reproduction remains of central importance (Alexander, 1979).

Studies of the social life of hunter-gatherers amply demonstrate a correlation between success in hunting and gathering, and social status and reproduction (Chagnon and Irons, 1979). The correlation may be less clear in other cultures, but reproduction remains central. A culture must be transmitted by a living population in order to "survive," to develop, and change. A culture preserved only in archaeological remnants or other records has actually died; it is stagnant and calcified. A culture may be abandoned by one population and taken over by another, but a carrier population is a precondition for a living and developing culture.

INCLUSIVE FITNESS AND KIN SELECTION

Dawkins (1976) talks about living bodies as "survival machines" in which genes "choose" to be carried, a rhetorical technique that emphasizes how genes carry life and assure its continuation. Genes that imbue their bearers with traits or behaviors that allow the bearers to survive and reproduce will themselves survive. As such, the individual is the basic unit of the evolutionary process, although the individual may not actually reproduce. Individuals may also promote the reproduction of a close relative who bears some of their own genes. By renouncing reproduction and promoting that of a relative, the individual performs an *altruistic act*. According to Hamilton (1964), altruistic acts expand the idea of "fitness," which Darwin used to describe only the individual's differential reproduction, into *inclusive fitness*. The idea of altruism also expands the concept of selection in that natural selection may operate not only at the level of the individual but at the level of a group of kin bearing a proportion of identical genes: that is, *kin selection*. Hamilton's theory can be readily applied to the nonhuman animal world. The logic of kin selection is especially conspicuous in the social organization of certain insects (see Wilson, 1971; Hamilton, 1972; Trivers and Hare, 1976). But does the theory apply to humans?

KINSHIP ALTRUISM (NEPOTISM):
THE NUCLEUS OF HUMAN SOCIALITY

Altruism in humans is primarily nepotistic, that is, favoring the relative to the stranger and the closer relative to the more distant. This tendency is universally present, but there are exceptions: Peace Corps volunteers, Albert Schweitzers and Florence Nightingales, the Shaker community which has survived for over 200 years even though members sever ties with their biological relatives and substitute devotion to "brothers" and "sisters" in the Shaker community. The Albert Schweitzers of the world are, of course, a tiny minority, and the Shakers are one culture in many hundreds. Most individuals in most cultures are nepotistic.

In most preindustrial societies, nepotism is obvious: One is culturally obliged to favor one's relatives over strangers. Although some cultures insist on normative favoritism toward either patrilineal or matrilineal kin, day-to-day behavior contradicts the norms. For example, Gary Witherspoon discusses *the cultural dimension* of kinship analysis in *Navajo Kinship and Marriage* (1975). Witherspoon concludes that even in the matrilineal Navajo society, "the Navajo father is related to his children by both kinship and affinity [p. 34]." The father is an affine to his children by the very fact that he maintains sexual relations with the mother, herself the central kinship link. The kinship of father and children comes about *because* actual (reproductive) behavior contradicts the cultural norm which states that in a matrilineal society children cannot be related to their father. The opposite case, relationship of children to mother in a patrilineal society, is more obvious still: No cultural definition can conceal, distort, or negate the stubborn fact of maternity. In most patrilineal societies the child's relationship with maternal relatives is very important and very warm (Homans and Schneider, 1955). Van den Berghe (1979) argues convincingly that there is no contradiction between inclusive fitness theory and unilinear descent.

In industrial societies, economic and political activity often obscure relationships based on kinship. But even the strongest social sanctions cannot stop people from preferring their own relatives. In Israel, children of university faculty and administration do not pay university tuition. In the United States, some students admitted to prestigious medical schools have parents who have made donations to the university in question. Certain subcultures in the United States, such as Jews, Italians, Chinese, and Japanese, are even more overtly nepotistic.

Humans have an interesting tendency to use kinship terms when really strong cohesion and altruism are called for. *Brother, sister, father,* and *mother* are common terms in churches, sects, armies, and revolutionary movements, especially in times of emergency. Stalin was called "The Father of the Peoples of the Soviet Union" during World War II.

Because basic forms of altruistic behavior are learned first of all in the family, nepotism has not only evolutionary (phylogenetic) but also developmental (ontogenetic) logic. The individual expands altruistic relationships outward from the family to include other friends and, later, mate(s). The closer a relationship grows, the more closely the individual likens it to family relationships. Cultures tend to expand kinship terms and relationships in fraternities and sororities (which are certainly not limited to American colleges), blood brotherhoods, peer groups, religious orders, monasteries, and youth movements, all of which emulate the altruistic among relatives. This tendency may supplant family ties in certain cases. The early kibbutz and the youth movement within which founders were educated constituted a deliberate revolt against biological families. "We have burnt our bridges behind us," the youngsters sang, preferring camaraderie to family. But this fervor lasted only a generation; then family inexorably returned (Tiger and Shepher, 1975; Shepher, 1977). The Masai sever the family ties of young males for a certain period but renew them after the males have made the transition to their new age groups. Several other pastoral societies exhibit similar patterns (Eisenstadt, 1956). Yet nepotistic altruism is not the only form of altruism in human or even in nonhuman animal societies.

RECIPROCAL ALTRUISM

Trivers (1971) asked whether nepotistic altruism was the only form of altruism in the animal world. How can altruistic behavior directed at a nonrelative (conspecific or cross-specific) animal evolve? He argued that if a pair of altruists is symmetrically exposed to altruistic situations so that each can benefit from reciprocally altruistic behaviors, a reciprocal altruism can spread in a population. Trivers's animal examples included cleaning symbioses among aquatic animals and warning calls among birds. He especially emphasizes human reciprocal altruism and indicates that the main problem accompanying this altruism is cheating. The solution to the problem of cheating is to be found in the psychological system underlying human reciprocal altruism, as well as in culturally evolved, complex regulating systems. We shall see later the central importance of reciprocal altruism in the development of the human social order.

MATE SELECTION AND PARENTAL INVESTMENT

If kin selection is such a powerful factor and reproduction so central, mate selection must be very important too. It profoundly influences the future of one's genes. In mating, the parents each contribute half their genes to the genetic whole of their offspring. The combination with a mate who has a dominant, deleterious gene may doom the offspring. A mate who is a heterozygote with respect to the same recessive deleterious gene that the partner possesses, may produce a disabled offspring, or no live offspring at all. These risks are difficult to detect, and some, still at the genetic level, are not detectable at all.

Individuals do not select mates solely for reasons of genetic health. Because the intent of mating is reproduction, mate selection also depends on the partners' implied judgment of their mates as parents. As Trivers (1972) has theorized, how much each parent invests of itself in the pair's offspring determines their sexual strategy. The mate with the larger investment limits the other. Also, the mate with the larger investment usually finds a partner; the mate that invests less usually must struggle for a partner.

Differences in parental investment start with the relative size of sex cells. Usually the female sex cell is much larger than the male (in humans the ratio is approximately 1:50,000). In animals with internal gestation the female harbors the embryo for a long period. In mammals, internal gestation requires enormous energy from the mother. The female also carries out parturition, lactation, physical care, and defense of the offspring.

Among mammals, therefore, the investment of the two parents is usually very unequal: Females invest more and limit the males who fight among themselves for the right to mate. The investment of the male is relatively low, sometimes limited only to contributing sex cells. In such cases, the female has only one "problem," genetically speaking: fitness of the mate. She will mate with any male that triumphs over his competitors. As Symons (1979:23) put it: "The most reproductively successful males are those who gamble and win; sexual selection favors calculated risk taking in male competition."

Another factor to consider is how the sexes benefit genetically from mating with more than one partner. The female ordinarily will not produce more offspring by mating with more than one male. But the male can hope for offspring from every female he impregnates. The general tendency among mammals is toward polygyny. Monogamy and polyandry are rare (Daly and Wilson, 1978).

As I have shown elsewhere (Shepher, 1978), human fathers invest quite heavily in their children. As this tendency evolved, the human female developed two important criteria for selecting a mate: genetic health and future paternal investment. The male's parental investment can be further subdivided into (a) fidelity, the male's persistence in supporting the female and her offspring; and (b) his ability to support them with food, shelter, and defense, an ability which may be a result of genetic health but which may be independent of it.

The human male has a sexual strategy similar to the female's, but the criterion of his partner's parental investment is less important. Although the male wants a female who will invest properly in his offspring, he may at least assume that her early investment is so great as to prevent her neglect or abandonment of a child—her loss would be too great. In contrast, because the male's initial investment is lower, males are deserters more often than females. Females can sometimes get a second male to invest in a first male's offspring. The male's low initial investment even lets him look for other females to impregnate.

But polygyny among humans is limited. Because the ratio of males to females tends to favor males at birth only slightly (and sex ratio diminishes increasingly with age), polygyny is unlikely to develop unless one or more of the following three conditions is present:

1. Measures that effectively upset the sex ratio, such as systematic male infanticide, male sterilization, or warring which kills off many young males
2. Measures that prevent a considerable percentage of males from marrying (e.g., celibacy or long military service)
3. Measures that confine marriage to older males and younger females

Polygyny will occur under these conditions. But it is also limited because even under such conditions not all males can be polygynous at the same time. The males will tend to control each other's polygynous tendencies unless the balance of power and dominance is radically upset. Kings, rulers, and chiefs are entitled a disproportionate number of females. Similarly, male slaveowners mate with female slaves and leave many male slaves without mates. Hypergyny may also be cultivated with higher castes absorbing females from lower castes (Dickemann, 1979). Such lower caste females marrying upward can hope to have sons who have the chance to mate polygynously and leave many grandchildren for their mothers. (For a sophisticated analysis of certain forms of polygyny, see Hartung, 1982.)

Females, with a high initial investment, are ordinarily expected to select a mate very carefully (Symons, 1979). The female and her relatives express this carefulness in all sorts of behavior. Usually the female (or her parents or brothers) will favor a local mate whose qualities are well known or easily checked. If the future mate comes from another place, he may perform bride service to achieve familiarity. The opposite case, that of a bride serving at the home of the bridegroom, is extremely rare (see Wolf, 1968). Males are more prone than females to look for a mate far from home. Another related behavior is coyness among females, which is the norm in many societies. Even in societies where premarital sexual intercourse is quite free, females are expected to be cautious in choosing husbands because reproduction is almost always limited to marriage. In some cases when a young female is not considered careful enough to choose a mate, her parents or brothers act on her behalf.

The female's coyness and cautiousness elicit behavior from the male that reveals whether he is likely to support or desert her as a mother with offspring. Fidelity and continued support are ordinarily easier to predict than genetic health. Moreover, a male who seems genetically very healthy may be a very poor provider. Such a situation may prompt a female to cuckold a rich and powerful male by secretly siring her offspring by a young, athletic male—a recurrent model of female adulterous behavior. Recent primatological research, however, reveals that female reproductive strategies are more flexible than were previously considered (Hrdy, 1981).

For long periods, the female tends to prefer nurturing her existing offspring—protecting her investment as it were—to starting another child. Even when she can get pregnant again, she must choose between nurturing the children she has and those yet unborn. In that choice is the nucleus of a conflict between parents and offspring to which I shall later return.

Inclusive fitness and parental investment can only explain so much. The human ability to abstract symbolically has sometimes taken bizarre forms. Take the famous case of Nayars (Gough, 1959), among whom the criteria of genetic fitness and paternal investment have been separated. Females were not coy at all and, at least according to the social norms that existed in the eighteenth and nineteenth centuries, could choose as many lovers as they wanted from their own or higher castes. Unfortunately, we have no good data on the actual number of males each woman chose. Paternal investment by both the *vir* (the man who was officially married to the female) and the *genitor(s)* (her lovers) was minimal: token gifts and payment to the midwife. Neither husband nor lovers lived in the household of the woman and her offspring, nor did they contribute to their economy. The sociological role of father, or *pater*, went to a woman's brothers and/or maternal uncles. Uncertainty about biological fathers being as pronounced as it was, a woman's brothers and maternal uncles were, on the average, much more closely related to her offspring than any other male. The exceptional behavior of the Nayar female has to be explained; it probably stems from the fact that Nayars were a warrior caste among whom paternal investment was problematic. We need also to study the whole body of literature on polyandric, materilinear–uxorilocal, and matrifocal societies as well as societies with high frequencies of extramarital and premarital relations among females (see Kurland, 1979; Greene, 1978).

Modern Society

We encounter more problems whem we investigate modern societies, in which sexual intercourse has been deliberately separated from reproduction. This separation may be contributing to a declining fertility rate. Westoff (1978) predicts a constant decline in fertility in modern societies (by projecting the average number of births a woman might expect in her lifetime from the rates of a specific year). Although Westoff admits that similar predictions had proved low in the past, he enumerates several profound and irreversible social changes that decrease fertility: the growing number of working women, the rising divorce rate and falling remarriage rate, and the increasing cohabitation of unmarried males and females.

The separation of sex and procreation undermines my argument. If there are no children, there is no reason to worry about genetic health or parental investment! If sex is for recreation rather than procreation, people will concentrate on sensual pleasure. The more the better, and the more pleasurable the better. We could expect one immediate result to be the "androgynization" of men's and women's sexual strategies. Women should become sexual adventurers, like men; both sexes would experiment with partners according to the "pleasure principle." Males would be at a disadvantage because women can achieve several orgasms more easily than men. There would no longer be much sense in contracting marriages; personal independence and lack of commitment would probably heighten erotic tension. Once a mutually satisfying sexual relationship were worked out, we would expect it to endure until one person grew bored, at which point both would switch to other partners. Because most people would act according to these standards, a norm would gradually crystallize that was hostile to monogamy.

This scenario may remind the reader of Aldous Huxley's (1932/1969) *Brave New World*:

> "But every one belongs to everyone else." he [His Fordship Mustapha] concluded . . . [p. 26]
> "But seriously," she said, "I really do think you ought to be more careful. It's such horribly bad form to go on and on like this with one man. . . . Four months of Henry Foster, without having another man—why, he'd [the Director of Hatcheries and Conditioning] be furious if he knew. . . " [p. 27].

Or take the hymn of promiscuity:

> Orgy-porgy, Ford and fun,
> Kiss the girls and make them One.
> Boys at one with girls at peace;
> Orgy-porgy gives release [p. 56].

It is unclear how far we have moved toward this utopia. We have no good demographic research to tell us how many people live that way. We do not know, for example, how many of the 23% of the population of the United States who are females 14 years or older are living in a brave new world and how many are waiting to get married. Mere journalistic evidence indicates that in large metropolitan areas, especially on the East and West coasts, some economically independent females are promiscuous (Constantine and Constantine, 1973). As of yet, we have no indication that childbirth and the nuclear family are giving way to promiscuity and infertility.

Many factors encourage the advent of Huxley's utopia. We cannot yet artificially incubate a human fetus, but people are working on it. It is true that there is support for zero population growth and, if Westoff (1978) is correct, negative population growth may soon occur. In industrial societies, childlessness proves an enormous economic boon for the individual family. Thus governments of many industrialized nations have begun fighting declining fertility with cash allowances and tax relief. For example, in East Germany, where the death rate in 1975 was higher than the birth rate, a family could get $10,000 interest free loan and pay it back by having three children (Westoff, 1978).

Yet the long view reveals that the general tendency in the United States and Great Britain has been a constantly increasing rate of marriage between 1890 and 1960. The change over the next 15 years may prove ephemeral (Historical Statistics of the U.S. 1970; Second Abstracts of British Historical Statistics). Similar tendencies can be found in other modern societies at least through 1970 (U.N. Demographic Yearbook). Moreover, the descending fertility rates may in fact conceal a change in individual reproductive strategies. Although the rate of children born to each 1000 married mothers decreased continually between 1910 and 1970 in the United States, we must also ask how many of those children reached sexual maturity. Note that these data represent children born to married females. The number of children born in the United States to unmarried females grew from 11 per 1000 in 1945 to 24 per 1000 in 1970. This tendency continues: Kitagawa, 1981, estimates the birth ratio for unmarried women per 1000 population to be 14.8 and to be 24 per 1000 unmarried women between the ages of 15 and 44 in 1976 (see also Herzog, 1966). The increase in children born to unmarried females somewhat narrows the fertility gap between 1910 and 1970.

In short, although population fertility declined dramatically from 1910 to 1970, an individual new sexual strategy may have emerged: Fewer children are born, but a higher proportion reach sexual maturity (Table 2.1; see also Robinson, Woods, and Williams, 1980, for a somewhat different analysis).

We can ask a rather different question at this point: Why, despite the profound social effects of hormonal birth control, do most members of the species still want to reproduce and enact sexual strategies that evolved in response to the exigencies of parental investment? Alongside social norms preferring permissive sexuality and low fertility in some sections of the population, we see also pressures to increase fertility. Thus, O'Neal (1977) has found postmenopausal females in a metropolitan population exerting considerable pressure on their daughters and sons "to make them grandmothers."

Nonetheless, it cannot be denied that hormonal birth control has affected sexual strategies. The question of how people react and adjust to the new situation has to be answered by interdisciplinary research involving biologists, psychologists, sociologists, and demographers (see Tiger, 1975).

Table 2.1
Fertility and Offspring Reaching Sexual Maturity in the United States.

	1910	1970
Number of children born per 1000 married women	2870	2360
Estimated number of children who reached the age of 24+	2430	2300

Source: U.S. Department of Commerce, *Historical Statistics of the United States*, 1975, p. 54.

PARENT-CHILD AND SIBLING CONFLICT

Given that males and females have different sexual strategies, can we also expect differences in strategy between parents and children?

Because husbands and wives—or mates—are less closely related to each other than parent and offspring (except in case of incest), we should expect that differences in strategy between parent and offspring would be less pronounced than among mates. But there *are* differences and even conflicts (Trivers, 1974). We have already discussed how a female usually has to decide between investing in offspring already born and those unborn. Sometimes the dilemma is especially cruel. A !Kung woman who has a baby before the usual interval between births (3–4 years) commits infanticide (Howell, 1976:147; Marshall, 1976:156–166).

The child's strategy is to survive and to take as much as possible from its mother's investment until it becomes independent. We can expect children to resist any weakening of the mother's investment in them, and in fact, weaning and sibling rivalry are problems throughout the mammalian world. Expressed somewhat differently, a child "is related" to itself by a factor of 1 in that it "shares" all of its own genes. A child is related to its full sibling only by one-half. But the mother is related to all her children by the same one-half, and so her interest lies in bringing them all to maturity. She therefore will discourage any egoistic, competitive behavior among her children which might jeopardize any of their chances of reaching maturity and she will pressure her children to act altruistically toward each other. Because she governs the resources her children need, she is usually successful. People learn first to behave altruistically toward their siblings and later extend their love, protection, and care to other, more remote "brothers" and "sisters." The mother who gets her children to behave altruistically toward their siblings mutes their conflict with her as well. This learning process puts the only child at a disadvantage.

Personality problems among only children are well known to psychologists and educators.

The father who invests less in his offspring than does the mother experiences less conflict with them. But the conflict is there. It appears later on, if and when the children's reproductive success depends more heavily on the father and his resources than on the mother. Sometimes the conflict is straightforward and unequivocal. In many pastoral societies, a son's reproductive success directly depends on receiving enough cattle from his father or other agnatic kin. But if the father wants a wife at the same time, a wife for whom he must pay in cattle, the conflict between father and son grows sharp and clear. Conflict with a daughter might erupt over choosing her bridegroom if she might be interested in the prospect's genetic health and her father is more concerned with questions of economic ability. Both sons and daughters may clash with their father over when to marry (i.e., mate), over how long parents should invest in their child's education (ultimately the economic basis of establishing a family in modern societies), or over how much parents should invest in the requisites for a successful courtship such as clothing, access to a car, cash, and so on.

Of course, conflict between parents and children combine with sibling conflict, especially as resources are usually limited. Rules of inheritance, for instance, flourish when conflict is imminent. Hartung (1976, 1982) tried to explain fathers' common preference for sons as inheritors by the fact that fathers transmit Y chromosomes only to their sons. Also, because females with their high parental investment universally have better chances to find a mate than do males (most traditional societies have no spinsters, and in modern societies unmarried males always outnumber unmarried females), fathers may favor sons as heirs. So also do mothers, especially in polygynous societies (Hartung, 1982). The inherited wealth may enhance the son's chance of mating and producing grandchildren for the donor of the wealth. A father's interest would lie in bestowing wealth on his son and looking for a son-in-law whose own father was calculating along the same lines.

AGGRESSION AND SOCIAL ORDER

Conflict, however, usually produces aggression. We have evidence of war from every century of recorded human history and certain scant evidence from earlier periods as well (Bigelow, 1969). Aggressive behavior is universal among primates and other mammals. Humans are not always aggressive, and we must reject the notion that humans have an aggressive "instinct." Yet we can assume that humans possess a biological predisposition to behave aggressively under certain conditions. Like all universal human behavior, aggression is the outcome of a complicated interaction between biological predisposition and the physical and social environments. Aggression may be triggered by the physical environment, as illustrated by the Bedouin saying: "If the *chamsin* [a dry, hot desert wind which produces daytime temperatures of 110 and nighttime temperatures of 100] lasts more than 7 days without stop, and the Bedouin kills his wife, he cannot be tried." (See also Edholm, 1978:48, and Briggs, 1975:111.) Threats, discrimination, or oppression in the social environment or a combination of physical and social factors may also prompt aggression.

Culture modifies aggression, sometimes provoking and sometimes inhibiting it. Culture produces atomic bombs and gas chambers, but it also tends to reduce the number of deadly clashes between individuals. Our first lessons in altruism teach us to love our siblings, to overcome our aggressive tendencies toward these, our first competitors. The injunction, "Love they brother as thyself," is symbolically extended to "Love thy neighbor as thyself."

The origin of social order is one of the main questions of sociological theory (Eisenstadt and Curelaru, 1976). Alexander (1979) reanalyzed the question in sociobiological terms. His main argument is that human societies, in their effort to cope with the problem of social order, have to find a balance between nepotistic-kin altruism and reciprocal altruism. Rules of group living, rules of just distribution of resources, legal systems that pinpoint the procedures for dealing with "cheaters," and religious and ideological belief systems make up the main components of the social order. These developed differentially in bands, tribes, chiefdoms, and nation states because of the different relative weights assigned kin altruism and reciprocal altruism.

SUMMARY: THE BIOSOCIAL VIEW OF CULTURE

In presenting my views, I have chosen only what I will need to elucidate the problem of incest. Yet biosocial theory is powerful enough to shed light on every sphere of human activity. Some of the more recent books—for example, Wilson (1978), Tiger (1979), Alexander (1979), and Crook (1980)—take up the biosocial basis of religion, law, ethics, political order, consciousness, and philosophy. Even from the few points I have ventured, we can offer a biosocial view of culture.

Culture is the species-specific adaptation of the human. It has evolved biologically; it follows basic biological predispositions or epigenetic rules, and certain forms of behavior result that are statistically more frequent than others. Culture can sometimes create patterns that contradict the epigenetic rules, although such deviations are limited in extent and are comparatively short lasting.

Alexander (1979) formulized this view as follows: "Culture would represent the cumulative effects of what Hamilton (1964) called inclusive-fitness-maximizing behavior (i.e., reproductive maximization via all socially available descendant and nondescendant relatives) by all humans who have lived. I regard this as a reasonable theory to explain the existence and nature of culture, and the rates and directions of its change [p. 68]."

People react to extrinsically caused changes in culture by changing their strategies so as to use culture to their own advantage. Cultural changes involve a positive feedback between novelty and needs. this is a much more rapid evolution than genetic evolution. These two basic forms of evolution constantly interact; under certain conditions, very stable cultural forms can be considered as part of the environment to which the human organism has to adapt genetically (Lumsden and Wilson, 1981:295).

The constant interaction between biological and cultural evolution has been the subject of some very challenging contributions: Richerson and Boyd (1978), Wilson (1978), Durham (1979), Alexander (1979), Crook (1980), Lumsden and Wilson (1981), Webster and Goodwin (1982). This literature makes it clear that if we do not understand human nature, we cannot properly understand human culture.

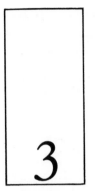

In general, though words are among the important objects of human consideration, it is not true that all propositions are about words. Most propositions are about objects like the sun and the stars, the earth and its contents, our fellow creatures and their affairs, and the like; and the implication between propositions, which is the subject matter of logic, has to do with the possible relations between all such objects. It is only as words are necessary instruments in our statements or expression of a proposition that logic must pay critical attention to them, in order to appreciate their exact function and to detect errors in inference.

—M. R. COHEN and E. NAGEL
Logic and Scientific Method (1934)

3

INCEST: CONCEPTS, DEFINITIONS, AND ISSUES

During the past 100 years, many scientists have concerned themselves with the universality of incest prohibition. These authors have used many concepts, defining them differently and investigating the problem along various dimensions. Consequently, they have come up with numerous different answers, often prompting fierce controversies. As an identical set of questions could not be agreed upon, discussion focused on the divergent answers.

Hence, it is necessary to clarify concepts, definitions, and issues before presenting the biosocial view of incest and comparing it with the most important alternative theories.

DEFINITIONS

We must begin by agreeing on what *incest* itself connotes. Let us compare the three most widely used definitions of incest:

Incest is illicit sexual relationship between persons within degrees of consanguinity excluded from such relationship by socially determined regulations.

—Reo Fortune
Encyclopedia of the Social Sciences, Vol. 2, 1953:620

Incest may be defined as heterosexual relations between members of the nuclear family, and by extension between family members beyond the nuclear family.

—David M. Schneider
Gould and Kolb, 1964:322

Incest is the infraction of the taboo upon sexual relations between any two members of the nuclear family except husband and wife, that is, between parents and children or any sibling pair.

—Margaret Mead
International Encyclopedia of the Social Sciences, Vol. 7, 1968:115

Let us investigate the components of these definitions:

The following points emerge from Table 3.1:

1. Fortune and Mead do not distinguish between heterosexual and homosexual relationships explicitly; Schneider limits the relationship to heterosexual ones.
2. Fortune and Mead tie incest to sociocultural regulations; Schneider does not.
3. Fortune includes in the incestuous category every consanguine relative so defined by the social regulations; Schneider distinguishes between core relationships and extensions; Mead precisely includes only nuclear family members.

It is not easy to choose among these definitions. All are associated with important methodological questions:

1. Should we consider all sexual relationships or sexual intercourse only? Sexual relationships may include kissing, hugging, stroking. If we consider them incestuous, then hardly any nuclear family is without incestuous relations. It would be better to agree that incest is sexual intercourse.

2. Should we include all sexual intercourse or only heterosexual? Here our decision depends on our theoretical approach. If, for instance, we think that the function of incest regulations is to maintain social order in the nuclear family, then homosexual intercourse must be included because it would impair the harmony of the nuclear family no less than heterosexual intercourse. If, however, we think that incest regulations arose to prevent inbreeding, then we can neglect homosexual intercourse which, being sterile, does not produce inbreeding. In searching for the right theory, we cannot reject homosexual intercourse a priori.

TABLE 3.1
Comparison of Three Definitions of Incest

Components of definition	Fortune	Schneider	Mead
Character of relationship	Sexual relationship	Heterosexual relations	Sexual relations
Qualifications of social control	Illicit by socially defined regulations	Open	Infraction of taboo
Participants of the relationship	All consanguine relatives so defined by regulations	Members of the nuclear family and by extension members of family outside nuclear family	Any two members of the nuclear family except husband and wife

3. Schneider's open definition does not tie the concept of incest to prohibitions, taboos, or any other socially defined regulations. But the word *incest* etymologically entails the notion of prohibition: It comes from the Latin *incestus* which means 'unchaste' and connotes illicitness. In those languages of Europe where the term for *incest* is not derived from Latin, it frequently includes the concepts of blood, contamination, or shame, again connoting illicitness: German: *blutschande*, Danish: *blodskam*, Swedish: *blodskam*, Czech: *Krvesmilstvo* (*krv* = blood), Hungarian: *vérfertőzés* (contamination of blood).

The fact that the word *incest* incorporates the notion of illicitness is perhaps somewhat problematic if I argue that prohibitions are only one form of regulations by which intercourse between close relatives is rendered rare. Löffler (1972:332) distinguishes between the German words *inzest* and *inzucht*, the latter meaning 'inbreeding'. I could accept Loffler's distinction, but it would oblige me to use the word *inbreeding*, which in population genetics, has a very broad connotation. I could also use the term *intrafamily mating*, but that would create additional problems: First, I would always have to specify "except husband and wife," and, more seriously, I would be assuming the existence of a family—specifically a nuclear family. Most of the problems of incest research stem from an assumption of the ubiquitous coexistence and interdependence of the family and incest prohibitions. I shall show that in order to explain incest regulations we must first reject this assumption. We will therefore keep the term *incestuous*, but we should bear in mind the logical problems in its usage.

4. We come now to the complicated question of participants in the sexual

intercourse. Here I tend to support Mead's exact definition, but she insists on membership in the nuclear family. Let me postpone solving the problem of the interrelationship between nuclear family and incest, and focus on clarifying incestuous dyads (assuming that only two people participate in sexual intercourse).

Including all dyads in the concept of incest is not sufficient. We have to distinguish among them. Let me illustrate the importance of such a distinction with the three basic incestuous dyads—mother–son, father–daughter, and full siblings. In the first of these dyads, the male partner is younger, the female partner is older; the male partner is a child, the female partner a parent. In the father–daughter dyad, the composition is the opposite: The male partner is older and parent, the female partner younger and the child. In the third dyad, either the male or the female may be older, and, in the rare case of twins, they may be the same age. In all sibling cases, both are children and share a social role (of the child) but differ in gender. In the parent–child dyads, partners share neither social role nor age group. These differences are summarized in Table 3.2. Of course the same distinctions can be made with other dyads.

Count (1973:150) includes all possible relationships—even autoerotic—in the formula in Table 3.3. The problem with Count's otherwise clear presentation is that he assumes the following:

1. The mother's husband is the father of the mother's offspring.
2. The husband's wife is the mother of his offspring.
3. The brothers and sisters are both uterine (having the same mother) and agnatic (having the same father).

These assumptions, however, do not always hold.

First of all, as we have seen, there is a basic "asymmetry" in reproduction. Whereas the male's indispensable contribution is his semen, which can be transmitted to the female by the relatively brief act of sexual intercourse (or, in the case of artificial insemination, even without it), the contribution of the female includes a 9-month pregnancy, childbirth, and, in most human cultures, a period of lactation which may last up to several years. Consequently, maternity is easily recognizable and publicly observable; its juridical existence is very rarely contested. Yet, because sexual intercourse is almost always a private act, witnessed only by its participants, uncertainty about paternity has been known throughout human history. The famous juridical contest in the Bible (Kings I, 16–28) is exceptional, as compared with innumerable paternity suits.

TABLE 3.2
The Distinctions among Different Incestuous Dyads

	Sex	Status—Parent–Child axis	Status–Age axis
Mother–Son	Different	Different—female parent, male child	Different—female old, male young
Father–Daughter	Different	Different—male parent, female child	Different—male old, female young
Siblings	Different	Identical—both male and female children	Different or identical—either male or female older

We can therefore expect that uterine relatives are more surely identifiable than agnatic relatives and can extend Count's matrix to include all possible relationships within the nuclear family, biological consanguinal or not. We can include agnatic and uterine siblings, adopted children, stepfathers, and stepmothers. In Table 3.4, I distinguish seven different terms for relationships among family members who have sexual intercourse. I use the term *incest* in cases where I assume that all societies would consider the relationship incestuous. In cases where the intercourse would be considered incestuous in some but not all societies, I used the term *classificatory incest* (a term used in extranuclear relation, too).

This rather extensive table illustrates that the number of "incestuous" relationships possible between biologically related mates represents a small minority of the total number of possibilities—only 17%. There are, on the

TABLE 3.3
Several Relationships within the Nuclear Family

	HF	WM	(BS)1	(BS)2	(DS)1	(DS)2
HF	Autoerotic	Legitimate	Homosexual	Homosexual	Incestuous	Incestuous
WM		Autoerotic	Incestuous	Incestuous	Homosexual	Homosexual
(BS)1			Autoerotic	Homosexual	Incestuous	Incestuous
(BS)2				Autoerotic	Incestuous	Incestuous
(DS)1					Autoerotic	Homosexual
(DS)2						Autoerotic

Note: In order to emphasize the possibility of homosexual incestuous relationships Count uses two brothers-sons and two Daughters-sisters. (HF refers to husband-father, BS to brother-son, WM to wife-mother, and DS to daughter-sister.)

TABLE 3.4
Several Relationships within the Nuclear Family—Including All Possible Genetic and Role Variables

	HF	HF̄	H̄F	WM	WM̄	W̄M	Ba	Ba	Bu	Bu	Bau	Bau	Za	Za	Zu	Zu	Zau	Zau	Bad	Bad	Zad	Zad
HF	ae	hs	hs	leg	leg	leg	hs (in)	hs (in)	hs (in)	hs (in)	hs	hs (in)	in	in	(in) leg	(in) leg	in	in	hs (in)	hs (in)	(in) leg	(in) leg
HF̄		ae	hs	leg	leg	hs	hs (in)	hs (in)	hs	hs	hs (in)	hs (in)	imp	imp	imp	imp	imp	imp	hs	hs	hs	hs
H̄F			ae	imp	hs	hs	hs (in)	hs (in)	hs	hs	hs (in)	hs (in)	hs	hs	hs (in)	hs (in)	hs	hs	hs	hs	hs	hs
WM				ae	hs	hs	leg	leg	in	in	in	in	in	in	leg	leg	in	in	hs	hs	leg	leg
WM̄					ae	hs	(in)	(in)	imp	imp	imp	imp	imp	imp	imp	imp	imp	imp	(in)	(in)	(in)	(in)
W̄M						ae	leg	leg	in	in	in	in	hs	hs	leg	leg	hs	hs	leg	leg	hs	hs
Ba							ae	(in)	hs (in)	hs (in)	hs (in)	hs (in)	hs (in)	hs (in)	leg (in)	leg (in)	hs	hs	hs (in)	hs (in)	hs (in)	hs (in)
Ba								ae	hs (in)	hs (in)	hs (in)	hs (in)	(in)	(in)	leg	leg	hs	hs	hs (in)	hs (in)	leg (in)	leg (in)
Bu									ae	hs (in)	hs (in)	hs (in)	in	in	in	in	in	in	hs (in)	hs (in)	leg (in)	leg (in)
Bu										ae	hs (in)	hs (in)	in	in	in	in	in	in	hs (in)	hs (in)	leg (in)	leg (in)
Bau											ae	(in)	in	in	in	in	in	in	hs (in)	hs (in)	leg (in)	leg (in)

	Bau	Za	Za	Zu	Zu	Zau	Zau	Bad	Bad	Zad	Zad
Bau	ae	in	in	hs (in)	hs (in)	hs (in)	hs (in)	hs (in)	hs (in)	leg (in)	leg (in)
Za		ae	hs	in	in	leg (in)	leg (in)	leg (in)	leg (in)	leg (in)	hs
Za			ae	hs	hs	in	in	leg (in)	leg (in)	leg (in)	hs
Zu				ae	hs	hs	hs	leg (in)	leg (in)	leg	hs
Zu					ae	hs	hs	leg (in)	leg (in)	leg	hs
Zau						ae	hs	leg (in)	leg (in)	leg	hs
Zau							ae	in	in	leg (in)	hs
Bad								ae	hs	hs	lcg (in)
Bad									ae	hs	leg (in)
Zad										ae	hs
Zad											ae

Key: ae, autoerotic; hs, homosexual; leg, legitimate; ill, illicit; in, incestuous; (in), classificatory incest; imp, impossible; HF, husband of children's mother and father of them; H̅F, husband but not father; HF̅, father but not husband; WM, wife–mother; W̅M, wife but not husband; WM̅, mother but not wife; BaZa, agnatic siblings; BuZu, uterine siblings; BauZau, agnatic and uterine siblings; Bad, Zad, adopted siblings.

31

other hand, many forms of classificatory incest. Thus, intercourse between a male and his wife's daughter by a former mate constitutes classificatory incest: It can be defined as incestuous, but it can also be considered legitimate (although this is rarely the case). Similarly, intercourse between a man's wife and his son by another woman can be defined as incestuous (as in the case of Reuben and Bilha in the Bible [Genesis 35:22]), but, again, it can be considered legitimate.

We have to distinguish among dyads according to the following criteria: (a) heterosexuality or homosexuality; (b) the degree of genetic relatedness or consanguinity between mates in the dyad; and (c) the degree of severity of social reaction to the transgression. Our matrix would thus be considerably simplified, as seen in Table 3.5. Within the cells we can designate the severity of social reaction to the transgression, a dependent variable. (It is hard to imagine how social reaction could be an independent variable: how, for instance, the social reaction could cause homosexuality or genetic relatedness.)

This new matrix will be very helpful in our investigation of the different theories. Because genetic relatedness proceeds in an ordinal scale, if incest regulations have something to do with genetic relatedness, then the severity of reaction to the transgression should reflect such relatedness. If, however, incest regulations are completely, or even largely, independent of genetic relatedness, then degrees of severity ought to be distributed in the squares of the matrix independently of both heterosexuality versus homosexuality and degree of genetic relatedness.

But, as we have seen, relatedness can be putative and we can subdivide each cell accordingly: In the upper-left-hand cell we can compare the social reaction to sexual intercourse between full siblings with the reaction to sexual intercourse between adopted siblings.

All this raises the following dilemma: If I do not decide on a definition, I preclude the possibility of intelligent communication with my readers. If I do decide on one, I may close the door on certain theoretical approaches. Thus, for instance, if I accept the definition, "Incest is heterosexual intercourse between persons whose genetic relatedness is 1/4–1/2," I exclude from my inquiry every theoretical approach except one without presenting evidence that would justify such a narrow definition. If, on the other hand, I accept Fortune's definition I have to cover an endless variety of rules without being able to distinguish between ubiquitous patterns and rare curiosities. Thus, although I tend to accept the first definition, I shall refrain from letting it limit my inquiry. I hope that my readers will concur with my choice of definition after they have

TABLE 3.5
Distinctions among Incestuous Dyads according to Homosexuality versus Heterosexuality, Genetic Relatedness, and Social Reaction to Occurrence

	GR 1/2	GR 1/4	GR 1/8	GR 1/16	GR 1/32	GR 0
Heterosexual dyads						
Homosexual dyads						

Note: GR (genetic relatedness) 1/2 — mother–son, father–daughter, full siblings
1/4 — aunt–nephew, uncle–niece, half siblings, grandparent–grandchild, double cross cousins
1/8 — all first cousins
1/16 — all first cousins once removed (Bodmer and Cavalli-Sforza 1976:365)
1/32 — second counsins

followed my line of inquiry. Until then, I ask the reader to keep in mind the questions I have enumerated. (For similar problems of definitions, see Meiselman, 1978.)

Before continuing, I must emphasize the difference between sexual intercourse—my topic—and marriage. Marriage always implies the intension of sexual intercourse, but sexual intercourse can take place with or without marriage. Marriage as a social and juridical contract includes legitimized sexual intercourse, and if that intercourse does not take place, it is almost universally sufficient grounds for dissolution of the marriage. In some cases, as among the Nuer (Evans Pritchard, 1951), two women can marry, but the marriage is clearly a juridical tool for ascertaining the rights of inheritance of the women and for arranging sires for their offspring—the inheritors of the women's property.

Sexual intercourse is a biological act present in all animal species with internal fertilization. Marriage is a socially and culturally defined act and confined to humans. There are monogamous pairs in the animal world, but they do not abide by rights, duties, and sanctions. Marriage can only be prevented and prohibited by social and cultural means; sexual intercourse can be prevented and inhibited by biological and/or biopsychical means as well.

REGULATIONS OF INCESTUOUS INTERCOURSE

No matter how one defines incest, no one would contest the empirical generalization that behavior resulting in incestuous relationships *is not random*, that is, it is *somehow* regulated, and not necessarily by sociocultural norms. We will use the term *regulation*, therefore, to indicate any mechanism that renders incestuous intercourse relatively rare.

We could call these incest regulations "negative assortative mating" in that however broadly we define the category of incestuous dyads, matings within them are always less frequent than matings not within them. How this relative infrequency is achieved is an empirical question we must deal with. Behavior can be limited by a variety of means. Clearly, physical limits are one means: Few people jump higher than 7' 4½", not because it is forbidden to do so, but because most people are physically incapable of it and are not motivated to make the attempt. Cultural limits are another means: Interspecific sexual intercourse is severely discouraged, and is rare in the majority of cultures. But bestiality is not necessarily rare because it is prohibited. Infrequency of behavior can result from a range of causes:

1. The behavior can be *prevented*. Prevention may be internal or external. Thus, the writer is prevented from running 100 meters in less than 10 seconds because of his inferior physical condition. Most Israeli males are prevented from having sex with Tahitian women because of the great distance that separates them.

2. The behavior can be *inhibited*. Inhibition is more or less fixed in an animal's neuropsychic system. Memory, for instance, can be inhibited, as in the well-documented tip-of-the-tongue (TOT) phenomenon (Brown and McNeill, 1966). Our aggression may be inhibited (Lorenz, 1960, 1966). Learning processes can be inhibited (Lawrence, 1968), as can creativity. How these inhibitory mechanisms work is not clear, although certain simple inhibitors of the senses and in the central nervous system have been studied (Granit, 1963; Elkes, 1968). Inhibitions may be biologically programmed and species specific. The turkey hen attacks every animal that approaches her nestings, but the auditory signals of the chicks inhibit her aggression. Sometimes inhibitions are culturally induced. An Orthodox Jew who has internalized the prohibition against eating pork may vomit in reaction to transgressing the prohibition.

3. The behavior can be *prohibited*. Prohibitions are cultural rules which may appear in all forms of social norms. Norms are usually classified according to their width of application and the severity of the social sanctions against transgressors. We can classify norms very generally as in Table 3.6. Thus, for instance, in most modern societies there is a diffuse norm of returning found (lost) objects to their original owner or to the police; transgressors usually receive mild social sanctions. On the other hand, transgression of the specific

TABLE 3.6
Social Norms according to Width of Application and Social Sanctions against Transgressors

	Sanctions	
Application	Severe	Mild
Specific		
Diffuse		

norm obliging Catholic priests to abstain from marrying may be severely sanctioned.

The causes for infrequency of behavior are not mutually exclusive. Thus Israeli males are prevented from marrying Tahitian females not only by geography but also because Polynesians are not Jewish. Even if the author wanted to prepare himself for the next Olympics to run 100 meters in under 10 seconds, his doctor would certainly forbid it. We are probably nearly all internally inhibited from having sex with corpses, but necrophilia is nevertheless strictly prohibited by society.

When all three causes may be operating to limit the frequency of a certain form of behavior, we face two important new questions:

1. What is the relative weight of each cause? Is prevention more important that prohibition? Inhibition more important than prohibition? Prohibition more important than both?
2. Which cause came first? What chain of causation produced the (empirical) reality we now observe?

In order to answer the first question with respect to incest, we must be able to separate the three causal factors. We must find situations in which incestuous behavior (a) is prevented but neither inhibited nor prohibited; (b) is inhibited but neither prevented nor prohibited; and (c) is prohibited, but neither prevented nor inhibited. If we find that one causal factor is more important than the other two is suppressing incest, we will weight it accordingly.

We must first clarify our use of *prevention* and *inhibition*. When we speak of prevention, we are not talking about total physical prevention (as with a critical number of erythrocytes, short of which physiological existence is impossible) but of situations that create low probabilities of occurrence. Thus, to use our former example, Israeli males might mate with Tahitian females, but the probability is low. The same is true of inhibitions, biopsychological mechanisms that create a pattern of low probability of occurrence in a population. Bestiality is probably inhibited (as are all interspecific matings in nature), but does have a low probability of occurrence.

The job of finding situations in which the three causal factors are completely separated is not easy. First of all, we confront the alleged ubiquity of incest prohibitions. Yet Van den Berghe (1979) has argued that not all human societies have a horror of incest, a sentiment that usually accompanies a taboo. In many societies incest is considered ridiculous rather than horrid or heinous. Moreover, as Van den Berghe pointed out, it remains to be seen whether prohibition of incest or other kinds of sexual intercourse (homosexuality, bestiality, necrophilia, etc.) substantially affect their rate of incidence. Thus there are societies in which there are no taboos at all on homosexuality but in which homosexuality remains rare. In order to avoid this trap and to avoid falling back on the sterile disputes of the first half of the century, we must accept the following points:

1. The surest way to rule out prohibitions is to investigate animals, especially primates, because it is generally accepted that animals do not have social or cultural prohibitions. Thus, if we find that mother–son sexual intercourse is rare in animal species, we must ascribe this fact to either inhibition or prevention, or both, but not to prohibition. Animal material is therefore essential to our argument.

2. Unlike sophisticated rational prohibitions, inhibitions and preventions are more simple. I shall explain this later.

THE USE OF ANIMAL DATA

The legitimacy of using animal data in dealing with humans may be obvious to an evolutionary biologist but less so to a social scientist. Many writers have ineptly applied mammalian and primate data to human behavior (e.g., Ardrey, 1961, 1966, 1970, 1976; Morris, 1967, 1971). Today it is possible to construct a set of parameters for arguing from animal to human behavior (Larsen, 1974):

1. It is advisable to use functional analogies only for heuristic purposes. Thus, for instance, if a male monkey "presents" to a dominant male, it would be a mistake to see in this behavior the roots of human homosexuality. But it would be acceptable to use the analogy for

heuristic purposes, that is, to find out why the signal for submission takes a female posture.

2. It is advisable to use as homologies only evolutionarily stable traits throughout the primate order or even the entire mammalian class. Thus the mother–offspring bond can be used in inferring from animal to human because it is a stable trait throughout the mammalian class.

3. It is also advisable to confine oneself to those traits, even homologous traits, that remain stable in humans, at least at the hunter-gatherer level. Thus not all primate mating systems are present in hunter-gatherers, whereas male dominance is stable in primates and invariably present among hunter-gatherers (Wilson, 1975).

4. The argument from animal to human does not have to be restricted to analogies and homologies. It can extend to surprising contrasts. An evolutionarily stable trait in primates that is "suddenly" absent in humans might be equally more illuminating than any present homologue. As an example, female estrus is a stable primate trait, but it is absent in humans, and the explanation of this radical absence might contribute greatly to our understanding of humanness.

5. In evolutionary arguments, we have to point out the mechanisms, processes, and conditions under which certain traits persisted and others disappeared.

In generally accepting the mechanistic axiom, we do not imply that nature works with the precision of a machine. On the contrary, nature brings about statistical probabilities in behavior. Among certain birds, for instance, which feed on insects a mechanism evolved which deters them from eating certain poisonous wasps. Their phylogenetically inherited mechanism is triggered by the sight of yellow and black stripes. Not everything with yellow and black stripes is poisonous or vice versa, but the mechanism creates a high probability that the birds will not eat poisonous wasps. There is even some waste in the mechanism: The birds might miss some nonpoisonous species with black and yellow stripes. Sometimes, too, a mechanism becomes outdated, atavistic, and dysfunctional. Jonas (1976) argues that human angina pectoris is the vestige of a mechanism that was very adaptive during the scavenging phase of human evolution. Because the great cats do not touch corpses, Jonas assumes that hominids evolved a mechanism which, through sudden vasoconstriction, stopped the heartbeat for a short period and thereby assured escape from the predator. This is a somewhat farfetched hypothesis, but if it is true, it indicates that a once functional mechanism has a dysfunctional vestige.

Moreover, nature's strategies are situational; they depend on the interaction of the organism with the environment. Evolution predisposes the animal to act, or to refrain from acting, in a certain way in situations that are routine in its life. But even the most characteristic situations are neither ubiquitous nor everlasting. There are always exceptions, and even in the most stable environments there are always changes. Biological predispositions only create high probabilities of behavior.

Most behavior patterns are activated by releasing mechanisms in the environment. Lorenz and Tinbergen's famous experiments in 1937 proved that ducklings are genetically predisposed to crouch at the sight of a certain overhead silhouette. Because the silhouette can take many forms, ducklings later learn to fear only a specific form of silhouette and reacted to it by crouching (Wilson *et al.*, 1973:553).

Let me summarize our discussion to this point:

1. In defining incest, the only component we must agree upon at this stage is that incest is *sexual intercourse* between members of the nuclear family. I leave open the questions of homosexual versus heterosexual intercourse and the range of people included in the (nuclear) family.

2. I shall use the terms *incest, incestuous intercourse,* and *behavior* with the understanding that they connote sociocultural prohibitions, but I do not limit my inquiry to the sociocultural sphere.

3. I use the term *regulation* to denote any mechanism that renders incest rare: inhibitions, preventions, and prohibitions.

4. To separate inhibitions, preventions, and prohibitions, I accept the careful use of animal data in cases where the absence of rarity of incestuous intercourse certainly must be ascribed to inhibitions or preventions.

Now we turn to three questions posed in earlier writings: origins, persistence, and functions. .

ORIGINS

Origins are causes of change in individual behavior. In looking for the origin of incest regulations, we logically assume that at some stage of our evolution such regulations did not exist and that something created them. This something is the origin of incest regulations.

Although some authors have addressed the danger of confusing origins and functions (especially Aberle *et al.*, 1963, and Coult, 1963), most have assumed that incest prohibitions originated because they benefited the family or society as a whole. For such a process to have taken place, the family or society as a unit must have preceded the prohibitions. But this is hardly plausible. Although *family* has many definitions, most of its students agree that it is a group based on a system of four double roles—father-husband, mother-wife, son-brother, daughter-sister. Such a system must itself be the result of certain cross-sex regulations, or the role sets are dubious. Thus, if a son mates with his mother, he becomes a son-husband to his mother and a father-brother to his son or daughter by his mother. The only role sets that can be assumed to precede, and therefore potentially to cause any incest regulation are those of mother–offspring and uterine brother–sister. All others are based on cross-sex mating regulations, whether those regulations are of biological origin (such as monogamy and the expulsion of sexually mature offspring in some birds or mammals), or cultural origin (such as incest prohibitions). Bearing this important modification in mind, we can look for origins of behavior that have resulted in incest regulations.

A second set of fallacies proceeds from the assumption that individuals act for the good of society or that society creates social norms for its own good, independently of its members, and then compels them to act accordingly (e.g., that if it is good for a society that its members marry outside of it, then either individuals will realize the good and act accordingly or the society will enact a norm or law to coerce them). But social groups or societies, of course, consist of individuals; they certainly cannot be assumed to precede or preempt individuals. (We do not imply by this that sociology is useless. Regularities in ways that individual actions are organized into a system are legitimate topics for study. Furthermore, once a social norm results from individual actions, it thereafter influences individual motivations.) Leyhausen paraphrased the origin of the social norm in an animal fable:

> One very cold night a group of porcupines were huddled together for warmth. However, their spines made proximity uncomfortable, so they moved apart again and got cold. After shuffling repeatedly in and out, they eventually found a distance at which they could still be comfortably warm without getting pricked. This distance they henceforth called decency and good manners [quoted by Wilson, 1975:257].

Human personal distance, like that among porcupines, begins with the individuals. When we are dealing with origins, we cannot a priori assume "for the good of the society" as a cause.

What we have to look for, then, are the causes of change in the behavior of individuals. Once most individuals in a social group have similarly modified their behavior in response to a common factor (for instance, change in climate), a social norm may result.

Behavior constantly changes. It comes into being, changes, even disappears. Explaining how incest regulations came into being will not suffice; we have to explain why they persist. One can try to prove that monotheism was caused by pastoral adaptations. But when Jews and Moslems ceased to be pastoral peoples, monotheism continued. Some behavior patterns may persist through sheer inertia. Wearing cuffs on trousers probably was an imitation of an English courtier over 100 years ago who folded his trouser legs to keep them from getting muddy and wet. Although the custom has no necessary function (and is even dysfunctional in that pants cuffs collect dirt), it has persisted in Europe and America. To change a norm requires energy, and if the change is not crucial—that is, the norm itself is neither very beneficial nor deleterious to the majority of individuals—the norm will persist by sheer inertia.

A specific form of persistence by inertia occurs in ritualization. After a social pattern has been functional for a while, it may continue to exist even when it has ceased to be functional. The bar mitzvah ceremony of the Jews was once probably as functional as any other pastoral initiation rite and probably originally included the ceremony of circumcision (see Exodus 4:24–26). The bar mitzvah persists among modern urban Jews in spite of having lost most, if not at all, of its original functions. Yet, in most cases, behavior persists because it satisfies individual important needs. Most initiation rites persist because they strengthen the individual for role changes.

A behavioral pattern may also be completely accidental in origin but continue because it proves beneficial to most individuals. The origin of the use of fire was quite possibly accidental, but it proved so important that its use continues to this day.

Function is a concept that the social sciences borrowed from biology. In biology, function designates the contribution of an organ to an organism. Lungs and gills have the function of oxygenating the blood. In the social sciences, function designates the contribution of a behavioral pattern to the maintenance of a social group. In other words, functions are considered results of behavior. Merton (1949:21–83) warned against a too easy application of the concept and pointed out that functions may be intended (overt) or unintended (latent). This distinction should hint at the distinction betwen origin and function. If in the sociocultural sphere we have a latent function, we also have an example of the distinction between the intention of the creator of the pattern (the origin) and the unintended results of that pattern (function). Thus, a government, concerned with the potential dangers of inflation and wanting to prevent citizens from overspending, may launch a campaign explaining how over-spending causes rising prices. The result might be that people, fearing price rises, rush out and spend, which pushes prices up. The origin here was the need to curb inflation, the function was in fact to strengthen it.

Functions may, of course, coincide with origins. At the level of conscious will, such identity is common. A salesman who wants to convince a client to buy merchandise uses certain patterns of behavior, and, if he succeeds in getting the client to buy, the origin of the behavior and its function coincide.

It is harder to distinguish between function and persistence because, unless persistence is inert, function causes persistence. Sometimes we witness persistence without knowing either the origin or the function: The hymen persists as a biological feature in the human female without any apparent function (and I was unable to find anything on its origin). Although distinguishing among functions, origins, and persistence is problematic, the

TABLE 3.7
Variables in Incest

Dyads	Regulatory mechanisms	Origins	Persistence	Functions
Mother–Son	Prevention			
	Inhibition			
	Prohibition			
Brother–Sister	Prevention			
	Inhibition			
	Prohibition			
Father–Daughter	Prevention			
	Inhibition			
	Prohibition			

Note: The table can be extended to include more dyads.

distinction will prove helpful when we deal with theories of the origin of incest regulations.

Table 3.7 includes all the variables I shall use in my own analysis. These variables can also serve as criteria in my survey of the literature and in my critique of different theories.

Having presented in the theoretical framework and analyzed important methodological questions, I have now to describe the long road that led to the biosocial view of incest. I shall survey the work of Edward Westermarck, the Finnish anthropologist whose seminal work more than 90 years ago can be considered the first biosocial analysis of incest. Then I shall devote a separate chapter to two empirical investigations that verified Westermarck's thesis. Lastly I shall survey the work of many scientists who inclined toward the biosocial view and of a few who explicitly identified with this view.

All those authors undoubtedly inspired my own thinking. Yet it would be false to limit the intellectual origin of my thinking to them. I have also learned much from those who rejected the biosocial approach, and whose work will be presented after the exposition of my own view.

4

> *If we want to find out the origin of marriage, we have to strike into another path, the only one which can lead to the truth, but a path which is open to him alone who regards organic nature as one continued chain, the last and most perfect link of which is man. For we can no more stop within the limits of our own species, when trying to find the root of our psychical and social life, than we can understand the physical condition of the human race without taking into consideration that of the lower animals. I must, therefore, beg the reader to follow me into a domain which many may consider out of the way, but which we must, of necessity, explore in order to discover what we seek.*
>
> —EDWARD WESTERMARCK
> The History of Human Marriage (1891:9)

EDWARD WESTERMARCK

Westermarck stands nearly alone in his belief that incest is instinctually avoided. A few others—Hobhouse, Lowie, and Ellis—accepted the idea, but none elaborated on it or adduced real evidence in its support. Westermarck presented his theory of incest in the first edition of *The History of Human Marriage* (1891), where he devoted two chapters (14 and 15) to it. Thirty years later, he expanded the book to three volumes (1921). The chapters devoted to incest (19 and 20) take up more than 150 pages and form a considerable part of the second volume. Although Westermarck was repeatedly attacked by leading anthropologists, he stood behind his ideas until he died. His late papers were published in 1934 as *Three Essays on Sex and Marriage.*

Westermarck was considered the enfant terrible of European social science at the turn of the century. Coming to London in 1887 from the University of Helsingfors, Finland, to work on his doctorate, Westermarck jumped into the stormy sea of academic inquiry into the human family and its origin. In the second half of the nineteenth century, many books appeared on the topic (Backhofen, 1861; Tylor, 1870; Giraud-Teulon, 1874; Lubbock, 1874; Maine, 1874; Morgan, 1977; Engels, 1884; Spencer, 1915, Starcke, 1889). Westermarck took up residence in the library of the British Museum and started reading voraciously. He completed a manuscript in less than 2 years, presenting parts of it as his doctoral thesis to the senate of the University of Helsingfors. He had familiarized himself with Darwinian theory and met

Darwin's colleague and the codiscoverer of evolutionary theory, Alfred R. Wallace. Wallace read the manuscript and agreed to introduce it to the English public. Published by Macmillan in 1891, the book caused general uproar in the English academic world and attracted the attention of scientists in Europe and America.

No doubt Westermarck was, like most of his contemporaries, an "armchair" anthropologist. Although 9 years later he would undertake fieldwork in Morocco which would last several years and result in numerous books and articles, when he began writing he had had no anthropological education at all, such education being completely unknown in Eastern Europe. Having studied literature and philosophy, he probably did not feel limited to any specific discipline.

Westermarck's basic theoretical framework is Darwinian. He claims that marriage and the family evolved as natural selection channeled the human male to invest heavily in his offspring. "Marriage and the family are thus intimately connected with each other: it is for the benefit of the young that male and female continue to live together. Marriage is therefore rooted in family, rather than family in marriage [1891:22]." But perhaps most distressing to his contemporaries were his three chapters attacking the hypothesis of primeval promiscuity. He likened Backhofen, Morgan, Engels, Spencer, MacLennan, and the whole classificatory-system school to the emperor without clothes. Westermarck revealed the fallacy in the widely accepted notion that early humans had lived in promiscuous bands from which first "matriarchy" and later "patriarchy" evolved. He demonstrated convincingly that the human mating system centers on the pair bond, even if it appears as polygyny or polyandry. Westermarck's 90-year-old arguments fit astonishingly well with what we know today. His criticism of the naive evolutionary school of Backhofen and Morgan quickly prevailed among European and American anthropologists; not so his theory concerning the origin of incest.

Westermarck, like many of his contemporaries, did not distinguish between sex and marriage. Setting out to explain the prohibition of marriage among kin, he says: "The horror of incest is an almost universal characteristic of mankind, the cases which seem to indicate a perfect absence of this feeling being so exceedingly rare that they must be regarded nearly as anomalous aberrations from a general rule [1891:290]." He enumerates marriage prohibitions that are much broader than incest prohibitions, assuming that when marriage is forbidden intercourse is also. He states that in "primitive society" marriage prohibitions are much wider than in modern society. Yet he does realize that incest prohibitions cannot be deduced from exogamous marriage proscriptions because "it is a noteworthy fact, generally overlooked by anthropologists, that besides these prohibitions arising from the clan system and, naturally, applying only to the mother's relations, there is, as it seems everywhere, a law which forbids the marriage of persons near of kin [1891:300]."

> Whatever observations may have been made, the prohibition of incest is in no case founded on experience. Had the savage man discerned that children born of marriage between closely related persons are not so sound and vigorous as others, he would scarcely have allowed this knowledge to check his passions. Considering how seldom a civilized man who has any disease, or tendency to disease, hesitates to marry an equally unhealthy woman, it would surely be unreasonable to suppose that savages have greater forethought and self-commmand. But even if we admit that man originally avoided marriage even with near kin from sagacious calculation, and that he did this during so long a period that usage grew into law, we do not advance a step further. All the writers whose hypotheses have been considered in this chapter, assume that men avoid incestuous marriages only because they are *taught* to do so. "It is probable," says Mr. Huth, "that, if brothers and sisters were allowed to marry, they would do so while yet too young." But though law and custom may prevent passion from passing into action they cannot wholly destroy its inward power. Law may forbid a son to marry his mother, a brother his sister, but it could not prevent him from desiring such a union if the desire were natural. Where does that appetite exist? The home is kept pure from incestuous defilement neither by laws, nor by customs, nor by education, but by an *instinct* which under normal circumstances makes sexual love between the nearest kin a psychical impossibility. An unwritten law, says Plato, defends "as sufficiently as possible" parents from incestuous intercourse with their children, brothers from intercourse with their sisters: ["nor does even the desire for this intercourse come at all upon the masses"] [1891:318–319].

In Chapter 15, Westermarck introduces his innovation: the *instinct* that under normal circumstances makes sexual love between close kin a physical impossibility is not a product of kinship per se. An instinct, he maintains, cannot distinguish between kin and nonkin. After citing examples of incest between siblings and mothers and sons who had been separated and then reunited, Westermarck states:

> What I maintain is, that there is an innate aversion to sexual intercourse between persons living very closely together from early youth, and that, as such persons are in most cases related, this feeling displays itself chiefly as a horror of intercourse between near kin.
>
>   The existence of an innate aversion of this kind has been taken by various writers as a psychological fact proved by common experience; and it seems impossible otherwise to explain the feeling which makes the relationships between parents and children, and brothers and sisters, so free from all sexual excitement. But the chief evidence is afforded by an abundance of ethnographical facts which prove that it is not, in the first place, by the degrees of consanguinity, but by the close living together that prohibitory laws against intermarriage are determined [p. 321].

Thus incest among close kins is instinctually avoided because of proximity rather than kinship. He presents ethnographic evidence of incest in the nuclear family and exogamous marriage prohibitions. He argues that marriage between parallel cousins is usually forbidden and that between cross cousins permitted because the former usually live together whereas the latter do not. In this, Westermarck creates difficulties for himself by positing instinctive incest avoidance as well as explicit prohibitions of those relationships stemming from cohabitation. As we shall see, Westermarck's adversaries attacked this apparent contradiction. Westermarck summarized his argument as follows:

> The hypothesis here advocated can, I think, account for all the facts given in the last chapter. It explains how the horror of incest may be independent of experience as well as of education; why the horror of incest refers not only to relations by blood, but very frequently to persons not at all so related; why the prohibitions of consanguineous marriages vary so considerably with regard to the prohibited degrees, applying, however, almost universally to persons who live in the closest contact with each other; and why these prohibitions are so commonly extended much farther on the one side, the paternal or the maternal, than on the other. The question now arises: —How has this instinctive aversion to marriage between persons living closely together originated [1891:334]?

Westermarck might have stopped there and gone on to consider other problems of human marriage, but he asked what the Darwinian theory of evolution compelled him to ask: How and why did this instinct evolve?

Earlier in Chapter 13, Westermarck had dealt with the "law of similarity," or what modern sociologists would call the "law of homogamy," which states that people tend to marry or mate among people who resemble them culturally, ethnically, religiously, and in class or caste membership. So Westermarck asked why men did not take this tendency to its logical extreme and marry or mate with their own sisters, mothers, or daughters. His simple answer: "The similarity must not be *too* great."

Relying heavily on Darwin and Wallace, Westermarck explains the hazardous consequences of inbreeding (which he erroneously called "interbreeding"). He concludes:

> It is impossible to believe that a law which holds good for the rest of the animal kingdom, as well as for plants, does not apply to man also. But it is difficult to adduce direct evidence for the evil effects of consanguineous marriages. We cannot expect very conspicuous results from other alliances than those between the nearest relations— between brothers and sisters, parents and children. And the injurious results even of such union would not necessarily appear at once. Sir J. Sebright remarks that there may be families of domestic animals which go through several generations without sustaining much injury from having been bred in-and-in, and the offspring of self-fertilized plants do

not always show any loss of vigour in the first generations. Man cannot, in this respect, be subjected to experiments like those tried in the case of other animals, and habitual intermarriage of the very nearest relations is, as we have seen, exceedingly rare [1891:339].

The rest of the chapter is devoted to evidence from botany, zoology, anthropology, and sociology. Westermarck summarizes his argument synthesizing origin, mechanism, and function:

Taking all these facts into consideration, I cannot but believe that consanguineous marriages, in some way or other, are more or less detrimental to the species. And here, I think, we may find a quite sufficient explanation of the horror of incest; not because man at an early stage recognized the injurious influence of close intermarriage, but because the law of natural selection must inevitably have operated. Among the ancestors of man, as among other animals, there was no doubt a time when blood-relationship was no bar to sexual intercourse. But variations, here as elsewhere, would naturally present themselves; and those of our ancestors who avoided in-and-in breeding would survive, while the others would gradually decay and ultimately perish. Thus an instinct would be developed which would be powerful enough, as a rule, to prevent injurious unions. Of course it would display itself simply as an aversion on the part of individuals to union with others with whom they lived; but these, as a matter of fact, would be blood-relations, so that the result would be the survival of the fittest.

Whether man inherited the feeling from the predecessors from whom he sprang, or whether it was developed after the evolution of distinctly human qualities, we do not know. It must necessarily have arisen at a stage when family ties became comparatively strong, and children remained with their parents until the age of puberty, or even longer. Exogamy, as a natural extension of this instinct, would arise when single families united in small hordes. It could not but grow up if the idea of union between persons intimately associated with one another was an object of innate repugnance. There is no real reason why we should assume, as so many anthropologists have done, that primitive men lived in small endogamous communities, practising incest in every degree. The theory does not accord with what is known of the customs of existing savages; and it accounts for no facts which may not be otherwise far more satisfactorily explained.

The objection will perhaps be made that the aversion to sexual intercourse between persons living very closely together from early youth is too complicated a mental phenomenon to be a true instinct, acquired through spontaneous variations intensified by natural selection. But there are instincts just as complicated as this feeling, which, in fact, only implies that disgust is associated with the idea of sexual intercourse between persons who have lived in a long-continued, intimate relationship from a period of life at which the action of desire is naturally out of the question. This association is no matter of course, and certainly cannot be explained by the mere liking for novelty. It has all the characteristics of a real, powerful instinct, and bears evidently a close resemblance to the aversion to sexual intercourse with individuals belonging to another species [1891:352–353].

A classical group selectionist argument appears in the first part of this quotation: Consanguineous marriages are detrimental to the species, and therefore an instinct has evolved to prevent them. But in the western Europe of 1891, Mendel's work, done in the 1860s, was still unknown—a situation which was to persist until the first decade of the twentieth century. Westermarck does not mention Mendel in his first edition, although 30 years later, in the fifth edition, he says: "Baur denies that all degeneration phenomena connected with self-fertilization and inbreeding can be explained by a *Herausmendeln* of recessive types [1921:376]." The German pun refers to the elimination of individuals that are homozygous to deleterious recessives.

During those 30 years Westermarck was heavily criticized. In response, he not only strengthened his ethnographic data but prepared a powerful counterattack. I will review some of the important disputes.

Westermarck believed that Sir James Frazer, in his monumental *Totemism and Exogamy* (1910), and later Sigmund Freud in *Totem and Taboo* (1913), misconceived the origin of legal prohibitions. Many forms of human behavior are both instinctually avoided and prohibited. Westermarck mentions two examples: bestiality and parricide.

Westermarck also takes issue with the criticism mady by Frazer and others that the instinctive avoidance theory cannot account for extensions of the incest taboo. He argues that the extensions alone prove that he is right, that one must take into account the "law of association." Once sexual relations between close relatives were recognized as rare and intolerable, prohibitions were added to prevent the few exceptions which occurred when consanguinity and common residence did not completely overlap. Incest prohibitions were extended to anyone who was a close relative. If a cousin were called "brother" or "sister," marriage with him or her was forbidden according to the law of association. But because many of these classificatory close relatives did not live together and felt no inhibition, prohibitions grew more important.

In his fifth edition, Westermarck also drops the words *instinct* and *instinctual* in favor of the term *innate aversion*. As he explained in a later article (1934a:40), he did so chiefly to avoid useless controversy about the term *instinct*.

Although for almost 30 years Westermarck was largely ignored or criticized, nonetheless others did take up the possibility of an instinctive horror of incest. Thus, one of the fathers of British sociology, L. T. Hobhouse, wrote in his *Morals in Evolution* (1912):

> Is the horror, then, of incest instinctive? The usual objections to this view are based on a misunderstanding of instinct. It is said that the horror is not universal, and that the objects to which it is directed differ widely in different peoples. But many instincts in the animal kingdom fail in universality and are modifiable in their application. And, as we have seen,

what is instinctive or hereditary in human nature becomes more and more a feature of character, a tendency or disposition to feel or act which obtains its actual direction from experience, and especially from education and social tradition. Hence, to say that the horror of incest is instinctive is merely to say that there is in it something rooted in the character which the average man inherits, but it still remains to determine what that something is and to understand how it can be developed in such a variety of ways [pp. 147–148].

Although Hobhouse mentions Westermarck and borrows ethnographic data from him, he does not borrow Westermarck's explanation for incest avoidance. Lowie, one of the most influential cultural anthropologists, also settled on an instinctual explanation. In his famous *Primitive Society* (1920/1949), he writes:

It is not the function of the ethnologist but of the biologist and psychologist to explain why man has so deep-rooted a horror of incest, though personally I accept Hobhouse's view that the sentiment is instinctive. The student of society merely has to reckon with the fact that the dread of incest limits the biologically possible numbers of unions. He must further register the different ways in which different communities conceive the incest rule. For while parent and child, brother and sister, are universally barred from mating, many tribes favor and all but prescribe marriages between certain more remote kindred. That is to say, while the aversion to marriage within the group of the closest relatives may be instinctive, the extension of that sentiment beyond that restricted circle is conventional, some tribes drawing the line far more rigorously than others [p. 15].

Lowie does not mention Westermarck at all. In later writings, apparently under pressure from his colleagues, he abandoned the idea of an instinctual aversion and considered incest regulations "primeval cultural adaptations [1933:67]"; "the horror of incest is not inborn, though it is doubtless a very ancient cultural feature [1940:232]."

SUMMARY

Westermarck dealt with origins, functions, and persistence. He distinguished the mechanisms of inhibition (which he sometimes called "instinct" and sometimes "innate aversion"), prevention, and prohibition and discussed their dynamics, but he did not distinguish between sexual intercourse and marriage nor did he investigate the mechanisms in different dyads.

Hobhouse concentrated on origins, Lowie on both origins and functions, but both treated the problem of incest only marginally.

It would take a whole treatise on the sociology of knowledge to explain why Westermarck's ideas did not prevail for more than half a century. The strange case of the kibbutz provides a test of Westermarck's ideas, and it is to this strange case that we shall turn to in the next chapter.

5

The best opportunity for the use of hypothesis testing is on the occasion of the "natural experiment." The difficulty with the use of hypothesis in field studies is the inability to determine causal relationships with any definiteness, since most of our measures are not taken with respect to systematic changes in some ascertained independent variable. Now, a natural experiment is a change of major importance engineered by policy makers and practitioners and not by social scientists. It is experimental from the point of view of the scientist rather than of the social engineer. But it can afford opportunities for measuring the effect of the change on the assumption that the change is so clear and drastic in nature that there is no question of identifying it as the independent variable, at least at a gross level.

—DANIEL KATZ
Research Methods in the Behavioral Sciences (in Festinger and Katz, 1953:78)

THE KIBBUTZ AND THE SIM-PUA: FOOLING MOTHER NATURE

As I indicated in the introduction, one of the main methodological problems in incest research originated in the assumption that incest is prohibited in order to safeguard the nuclear family or to prevent its social isolation. Family served as an independent variable, incest prohibitions as a dependent variable. It was, however, impossible to find a society without family or without incest prohibitions. The two variables were inseparable.

The cases of the kibbutz and the sim-pua represent two social situations in which people behave as though they were members of a family, but are not. In each case, sexual relations between members are avoided, in spite of the fact that nobody forbids such relations. On the contrary, such relations are normatively favored in both societies.

The theoretical significance of the investigations of these two situations lies in this fact: If people who are not family members avoid social relations in spite of the normative freedom (in the case of the kibbutz) or even positive pressure (in the case of sim-pua), it is not the existence of the family that is essential in the etiology of the avoidance. What is essential is the situation.

Each of the two cultures is totally independent. The kibbutz is a modern, planned, collectivistic community in Israel. The sim-pua is cultivated in a traditional peasant society in Taiwan. The probability of cultural diffusion is practically nil. Then, too, the social situations are completely different. Different cultural arrangements produce the same result—that of bringing together unrelated children under quasi-family conditions. Van den Berghe dubs the two cases "culture fooling Mother-Nature."

The Kibbutz: Collective Education

Kibbutzim are communal villages in Israel. The first kibbutz was founded in 1910 by eastern European Jewish immigrants to Palestine who were disenchanted with Jewish life in the Diaspora and with the social structure of the east European Jewish village, the *stetl* and its religious, stern, patriarchal family. They wanted a new form of life in their new country, and under the influence of Biblical study, populism, and Marxism, they experimented with degrees of communality in the years before and after they emigrated. Palestine presented a harsh environment: underdevelopment, medieval technology, and the inimical social environment of both older Jewish immigrants and native Arabs. The immigrants, seeking a collective solution, combined ideology and reality to create the kibbutz, the most successful and most persistent commune of the twentieth century. From the first kibbutz, founded by fewer than a dozen youngsters in 1910, there developed 250 kibbutzim, with a population of over 120,000 (Shepher, 1977; Tiger and Shepher, 1975).

After long experimentation, the kibbutz succeeded in crystallizing a specific form of education. Because the second generation of kibbutz members had to be socialized so that as adults they would find collective life "natural," virtually from birth children were educated in peer groups of six to eight. Although the children were nursed by their mothers, they were socialized by a trained nurse who was appointed by the kibbutz education committee. Children met with their parents for 2 hours each afternoon at their parents' apartment and then returned to the children's house where they were put to bed either by their parents or the nurse.

I have elsewhere described the collective socializing process in detail (Shepher, 1971b:51–104; Tiger and Shepher, 1975:159–165). What is important to the topic at hand is that when the second generation came of age in the 1940s, kibbutz members perceived that these second generation adults were not sexually interested in each other. Kibbutz members did not ascribe any special significance to the phenomenon. To them it was "obvious" and "natural" that children reared like *siblings* would not develop sexual interest in each other. Although kibbutz people are extremely conscious of the social pecularities of their way of life and have written voluminously about it, to my

knowledge none has dealt with this avoidance phenomenon. Social scie
however, took note.

In the early 1950s, a sudden interest in the kibbutz awakened among
American Jewish academics. Perhaps because of the establishment of the State
of Israel in 1948 and the prominent role of the kibbutzim in the War of
Liberation, a group of young Jewish social scientists went to do research on the
kibbutzim (E. Rosenfeld, H. Rosenfeld, Faigin, Spiro, and Diamond). The
kibbutz seemed to challenge major sociological and psychological theories: The
kibbutz claimed to be a classless society, yet in 1948 Davis and Moore had
published a famous article claiming a classless society to be functionally
impossible. The kibbutz challenged accepted psychological truths in its claim
that mother and child can be separated without harm to the child. Melford
Spiro and his wife visited a kibbutz to which they gave the pseudonym Kiryat
Yedidim. In one of his books, *Children of the Kibbutz* (1958), Spiro describes the
avoidance phenomenon:

> An important characteristic is that the couple is never comprised of individuals who
> have grown up together in the kibbutz. Students who have always been members of the
> same kevutza [educational peer group] have never been known to engage in sexual
> behavior with each other [pp. 338–339].
>
> There are two aspects of sabra [second generation kibbutz member according to Spiro's
> usage] sexuality that require comment. The first concerns the choice of sexual partners—
> whether for intercourse or for marriage. In not one instance has a sabra from Kiryat
> Yedidim married a fellow sabra, nor to the best of our knowledge, has a sabra had sexual
> intercourse with a fellow sabra. If in the light of additional data the latter part of the
> generalization be rendered false, I would be highly confident of the validity of its
> following reformulation: in no instance have sabras from the same kevutza had sexual
> intercourse with each other [p. 347].

Spiro did not study many second generation children as adults. Although the
kibbutz he studied had been founded in 1921, for a long time childbearing had
been discouraged because of problems with economics and security. During his
year-long stay, only a few of the second generation were in their 20s, and so
Spiro concentrated mainly on high school students: "They are attracted to each
other but *ex hypothesi*, they have repressed this attraction, and have, thus,
precluded its expression. If this interpretation is correct it would explain why,
despite their claim of mutual asexual feelings, they insisted on the abolition of
the mixed showers while in the high school [p. 348]."

Spiro was not very secure about his data or his conclusion, and his evidence
for repression is meager indeed. Spiro quotes an "atypical" and "most
extroverted and uninhibited" male who denies he is not attracted to second

generation females. A typical female native admits to Spiro that she is not interested in native males, but Spiro "had the definite impression" that she would have welcomed feeling attracted. Hence Spiro's evidence is too flimsy, and it is unclear why the second generation should have repressed their sexual feelings, for no one had ever prohibited them, as Spiro himself points out (1958:220).

Rabin (1965) investigated collective education by studying 24 infants, 38 schoolchildren, 30 adolescents, and 31 young adults from an unspecified number of kibbutzim and comparing them with *moshav* children (a moshav is an agricultural cooperative based on individual production and consumption but on cooperative purchasing and marketing; see Ben-David, 1964; Weintraub et al., 1969). Rabin's main concern was the personality development of collectively versus individually reared children, and he touches on the incest problem only marginally:

> It may well be that the modesty that develops is in the service of defense against the instinctual drives that are intensified during adolescence. Despite the "freedom" with respectd to viewing the body of the opposite sex, kibbutz taboos and prohibitions in regard to sex play and sexual contacts are strict and unrelenting. These taboos apply primarily to members of the peer group with whom the contact is continuous for many years. The taboos are not unlike the brother sister taboos in the conventional family. It is probably due to this fact there are few marriages between members of the same group in the kibbutz. Such "incestuous" relationships are avoided by marrying outside the group, often into another kibbutz or by importation of a spouse from the city [p. 33].

Rabin attributes the peer group exogamy to a taboo, although he presents no evidence for such a taboo. Rabin mistakes the discouragement of sexual intercourse before high school graduation for a taboo specific to the peer group and confuses this discouragement of intercourse (with any partner) with discouragement of childhood sexual activities. In the federation where Rabin worked, adolescent sexual intercourse is forbidden, but childhood sex is neither interfered with nor forbidden.

Bettelheim (1969) also deals with incest in his analysis of sexual modesty:

> From infancy on everything would be open about sex and the body. Nothing would be hidden as shameful.
> Actually such arrangements lead to sexual stimulation. This forces one either to act upon it — as occurs typically among children who share life together very "openly" under slum conditions—or leads to early and far-reaching sex repression, and thence to the development of a deeply puritanical attitude toward sex. But kibbutz children have little option. Because they are not only asked to be "natural and open" about their bodies, it is expected that this will make them "pure" about it. That is, they should not only not have sex, but should not even desire it.

In fact, it is precisely because these boys and girls have always shared a bedroom with each other and have showered together, that they have been sexually stirred by each other, felt ashamed, and been forced to suppress what they felt. Not just (as the literature suggests) because these others are their "siblings": Repression does not work all that neatly. Nor is it because of the reason they give when asked why they do not fall in love with or marry one of those they grew up with. They say, and kibbutz theory holds, that one does not fall in love with the person one sat next to on the toilet, as a child; an explanation that has also entered the literature.

It is not because of the sitting on the toilet together, but because of the sexual feelings thus aroused, of which the youngsters are made to feel guilty (and hence ashamed). It is because of the feelings one had to suppress about oneself as others watched one sitting on the toilet, or masturbating (or wanting to), or having an erection, or menstruating. It is because of those other feelings one had to suppress too—feelings one had about the other as one watched him or her eliminating or masturbating (or wishing to), or having an erection, or menstruating—not to mention those other instinctual behaviors that characterize children's "polymorphous" sex play. [This quote is reprinted from Bettelheim, B. *Children of the Dream.* Copyright © 1969 by Macmillan Publishing Co., Inc. pp. 236–238.]

Bettelheim, like Spiro, uses the explanation of repression: Toddlers sitting together on the toilet were sexually aroused and ashamed of it. Yet Bettelheim offers no evidence for who made the children feel shame or guilt; Spiro might have been of help on this point. For example "There is not one instance in the entire sample of a nurse's interference in the sexual activity of the children [1958:220]."

The first Israeli to focus her research on our problem was also the founder of scientific social research in the kibbutz. Talmon (1964) investigated 3 well-established kibbutzim out of a sample of 12 which were representative of the kibbutzim in one federation. The 3 kibbutzim selected for Talmon's study were the only ones with sizable populations of second generation individuals of marriageable age. Talmon studied 125 married couples and collected statistics on their marriage patterns. The data on premarital sexual relationships were "scantier and less reliable than our data on marriage," according to Talmon. In essence, they revealed that "we have not come across even one love affair or one instance of publicly known sexual relations between members of the same peer group who were cosocialized from birth or through most of their childhood. A small number of love affairs occurred between members of different peer groups [p. 493]." Talmon states that there was absolutely no sign of any taboo on marriage between members of the second generation; such unions could even have been considered preferable.

Talmon presented a typology of marriage patterns based on the social distance between the mates' original social circles. She devoted the rest of the article to social–functional and psychological–motivational explanations for the phenomenon. She concluded that the social functions of second generation exogamy were the following:

1. To recruit new members
2. To check the emergence and consolidation of large and powerful kinship groups
3. To link subgroups of the kibbutz and bridge the gap between generations
4. To weaken the solidarity of the peer group in adulthood
5. To weaken an emerging stratification system
6. To link distinct communities
7. To revitalize relations with the youth movements
8. To bridge the gap between kibbutzim and other sectors of society

But, as Talmon acknowledged, "listing the beneficial or dire consequences of an institutional pattern from the observer's point of view does not in itself account for the actors' attitudes and behavior [1964:449]." Talmon enumerated certain institutional mechanisms that could account for attitudes and behaviors among the second generation adolescents or adults: (a) regional secondary and vocational schools; (b) youth movement activities; (c) training groups in the kibbutzim; (d) ideological seminars and refresher courses.

All these mechanisms may include potential mates with values acceptable for second generation adolescents. But even more important in Talmon's article is the explanation of why individuals act out the institutional pattern of exogamy. The socialization process produces in them the following values:

1. The perception of a difference between the communal sphere of the peer group and the private sphere of the family
2. A lack of erotic feeling shown between the sexes within the peer group
3. A turning to sexual and family life for intimacy and privacy
4. A need for individuality
5. A need to balance loyalty to parents and to revolutionary ideology

Talmon added a warning: "These results are tentative and should be viewed with great caution [p. 495]."

When I began my research, I knew that I could investigate the premarital sex among adolescents on only one kibbutz. But I did have the opportunity to collect data on the marriage patterns in the three large kibbutz federations covering 97.5% of the second generation adults in the movement (the remaining 2.5% lived in religious kibbutzim, for which no data were available). I knew the methodological difficulty I faced: Marriage is based on sexual intercourse, but not vice versa. Although I had reliable data on marriage from 211 kibbutzim, I had reliable data on premarital sex from only one. However, I noted that the patterns of premarital behavior on the kibbutz I studied (which I called "Ya'ara") were similar to the patterns of marriage there. The marriage patterns in Ya'ara, in turn, resembled those on other kibbutzim. I could thus assume that patterns of premarital behavior on all kibbutzim were similar to those in Ya'ara. This line of reasoning was the best solution to the methodological problems inherent in the fact that premarital sex is private and clandestine whereas marriage is formal, public, officially recorded.

The data on premarital sex among 42 second generation adolescents and adults in Ya'ara revealed not a single case of erotic behavior between children reared in the same educational group (*kvutza*). There was one case of heterosexual activity between second generation individuals reared in different peer groups, the male being 4 years older than the female. In cases of boys or girls joining a peer group at later ages (rather than being born into it), heterosexual attraction to peer group members was intense and preferred to other relationships. This indicated that the deterrent factor is neither the lack of age difference nor the number of potential mates in the small group.

Marriage at Ya'ara revealed the same pattern. No one married within the peer group. There were no marriages between peer groups either, except one case in which the male had joined the kibbutz at the age of 7. Most marriages were to partners outside the kibbutz, either from other kibbutzim or from the cities. The similarity between the patterns of premarital sex and marriage in Ya'ara was complete.

The investigation of marriage patterns across the entire sample involved computer analysis. The computer found marriages between natives and ranked them by age differences of the spouses. Couples differing by 2 years or less were considered potentially members of the same peer group given that the age range in a peer group never exceeds 2 years. I found 20 such couples in each of the three federations and sent their names to each federation's Institute of Sociological Research to learn whether the couples had been socialized in the same peer groups. Most of the couples came from different peer groups on the same kibbutz. But 14 couples came from the same peer group and were distributed among the federations as follows: Federation I—4 couples; Federation II—4 couples; and Federation III—6 couples. To these couples I sent personal letters. Their responses were revealing. Some quotations follow.

The response from 109411 and 109412 was:

> *We want to answer your questions because it is intriguing to belong to the special "quartet" of 1054 couples.*
>
> *Concerning your questions: until the third grade of elementary school we were not together at all. Our peer groups were joined at that time and we were together from the third grade until the Mosad junior high. My wife left to go abroad with her parents and spent one and a half years away.*

Thus the couple had not been in the same peer group in early childhood; when they were 8 or 9 years old their peer groups were merged, and they remained together for 4 or 5 years.

Couple 0109103 and 0109104 write:

> *Before we answer your questions here are some facts. My wife was born in kibbutz 7 but left with her parents to settle in Haifa at the age of three. In the second grade at the age of seven, her family joined our kibbutz, and since then we have been together.*
>
> *. . . N. B. at the age of nine I told my wife that we would marry when we grew up. She paid no attention to my announcement . . . During the years of our schooling we played cat and mouse and quarreled a lot. We rediscovered each other when we went into the army, and we married upon completion of our service.*
>
> *An interesting detail: On our kibbutz there are three men who successfully completed the pilot's training course in the air force. All three married girls from their own peer group, girls with whom they had grown up from childhood until the end of the Mosad [high school].*
>
> *With best wishes.*

This interesting case describes another marriage to a kibbutz-bred partner. (The "interesting detail" provoked me to inquire further—see Shepher, 1971b.)

Couple 0215041 and 0215042 write:

> *We are sorry to disappoint you, but there was an error in your survey. We are not at all from the same peer group [kitah]. My husband was educated in an older group, and there is one year's age difference between us. Before the ninth grade (age 14 to 15) our two groups had no contact.*
>
> *With regards.*

Couple 0210051 and 0210052 write:

> *Here is the information you asked for. My wife and I first met in fourth grade when we were nine years old (Kibbutz 10 was founded by two kibbutzim after the*

split in Kibbutz Meuchad). From then until we went into the army we were in the same group and did not leave the kibbutz for more than two weeks.

This, then, is another marriage of peer group members who met during middle childhood.

The third federation presents more interesting cases. Couple 0308145 and 0308146 write:

> *We were not together in either the infants' nor the toddlers' house. At the age of four we were together in kindergarten. It had three age groups and twenty six children altogether. We were together in school. One of us left the kibbutz with his parents for half a year during kindergarten.*
>
> *With regards.*

This is an interesting case. During their first 4 years the couple was not socialized in the same peer group. They were together in kindergarten for about 1½ years along with 24 other children divided into three different age groups.

In contrast, 03026013 and 03026014 write:

> *We were together in both the infants' and the toddlers' house. After age three our groups were separated. There were two separate kindergartens in the kibbutz, each with about fifteen children. We were together again in school. Neither of us left the kibbutz for any considerable period.*

This couple was together during the first half and separated during the second half of their first 6 years.

The 14 borderline cases are summarized in Table 5.1. Of the 14 borderline cases, there were only 5 in which the spouses had been in the same peer group at any time before 6 years of age; and, of these, none had been socialized together during all 6 years. Thus there was not a single case in which spouses born on the same kibbutz had been socialized together without interruption. (Complete data on 2769 married couples in 211 kibbutzim appear in Shepher 1971b:142.) The marriage patterns in all the kibbutzim resemble those from Ya'ara: no marriages within peer groups. My hypothesis had been substantiated. But what did the data mean, and how could we explain them?

We seem to have a strong case for Westermarck's instinctive avoidance theory. In a large population from all over Israel which shared a system of socialization, there were no marriages between people who had been continuously reared together for their first 6 years. This avoidance and aversion could not be attributed to prohibition or taboo. My fieldwork proved what

Table 5.1
Summary of Borderline Cases: Quasi-Intra-Peer-Group Couples

	Infancy 0	Toddler 1 2 3	Kinder-garten 4 5	6 7	Elementary school 8 9 10 11 12 13	14	High school 15 16 17 18
A				--			
B							
C				--			
D					were in separate peer groups		
E							
F							
G							
H							
I							
J							
K			--				
L		·····························⟩·······························					
M			--				
N	············		··				

Note: ---- = uninterrupted cosocialization; .... = interrupted cosocialization.

Spiro and Talmon had thought: There is no marriage between second generation kibbutzniks yet there is no taboo against such marriage. On the contrary, evidence showed that such marriages were preferred by parents and other members of the kibbutz, mainly because both spouses, having been reared on the kibbutz, would be less likely to settle elsewhere. Nor is childhood sex play between peer group mates punished by parents or teachers, even if it turns into genital manipulation. Here is an excerpt from my field notes:

> From the gemulon [house of the weaned] on the children spend twenty-two out of twenty-four hours of the day with peers. They do almost everything together: eating, using the pot and later the toilet, bathing and playing. Bodily contact between any two children, but especially between heterosexual pairs, is frequent. I have no evidence of counted instances of bodily contact between children, and it is possible that heterosexual contact seems to me and to my informants more frequent than homosexual contact only because it is more frequently mentioned by the metaplot [babies' nurses] and parents. There is no intervention either from the metapelet [sing], or from the parents or any other adult. In the peuton [literally, the house of small ones], where cribs are replaced by beds, it sometimes happens that a boy is found in the bed of a girl or vice versa. There is no reaction by the metapelet to the children involved, and her remark to the parents is a joking one.
>
> Metapelet: "I found Yehoram in the bed of Timna this morning!"
> Father of Yehoram: "He begins quite early! I am going to tell Dan [Timna's father] that we are going to be related."

Fox tried to explain (1962:132) the extinction of sexual attraction among the peer group members as the result of negative reinforcement. He surmised that the sexually excited children could not find relief in climax and were therefore severely frustrated. But the children engaged in sexual play from early childhood until latency. Instead of seeming to suffer from these encounters, the children seemed to enjoy them and therefore to indulge in them repeatedly.

My data fit Thorpe's (1964) widely accepted definition of imprinting. Imprinting is confined to a certain critical period and must be triggered by a set of factors in the environment. Here we have critical period, early childhood, and the tactile relationships of the children constitute the environmental circumstances. Once imprinting is accomplished, it is extremely stable and probably irreversible. Indeed, we did not find peer group mates marrying even in their second or third marriages. Imprinting itself is complete by the age of 6; the sexual avoidance does not appear until the age of 14 or 15. Moreover, imprinting is a supraindividual learning of the broad characteristics of the species. Although in a uniformly controlled situation like the kibbutz movement we find no exceptions, this fact alone does not constitute proof for Thorpe's fourth requirement (a broad characteristic of the species). Since my data were published in 1971, I have come across only one instance of disagreement with either my data or my interpretation. Kaffman (1977), although admitting that the sexual revolution has not done away with self-imposed exogamy, claims that "the suggestion of absolute sexual abstinence within the group is less than exact [p. 216]." He quotes "undisguised reports" from adolescents which state that there is no sexual indifference, avoidance, or incest aversion between boys and girls of the same group. He explains the rarity of enduring romantic relationships and marriages within peer groups in this way:

1. The groups are small, usually no more than sixteen youngsters, so that the variety of choices is limited in comparison with the possibility of finding a partner outside the group. Further, since girls mature earlier, the likelihood of finding a partner within one's own nuclear group is limited.
2. Psychologically speaking, it is difficult to reverse initial imprintings of habits, attitudes, and expectations as to the roles played by peers raised in the same group from infancy.
3. The familiarity of the relationships within the peer group in the course of day-to-day living, although not precluding sexual attraction to peers, is not conducive to the encouragement of the illusions, excitement, and mutual idealization that are such important elements of romantic love. Most adolescents who fall in love are carried away by an exciting wave of romance and idealization of the loved one. Years of common daily routine and everyday intimacy hardly seem helpful to the development of romantic expectations and blind passion [p. 216].

But his explanation is faulty. First, even under conditions of random mating, a certain, albeit low, percentage of matings within peer groups would occur, but none have been found. (For instance, assuming that five consecutive age groups are the population of random mating and that each group has four males and four females, then the expected percentage of marriage within peer groups would be 16/4000, or 4%.) Moreover, girls do marry partners of their own age and even younger when mating is exogamous. Kaffman's second point seems to strengthen my argument and weaken his. His third point is contradicted by many cases of marriages within peer groups between partners reared together after the age of 6. If the decisive factor were the impediments of daily contact to romantic love, then 12 years of daily contact should suffice to destroy any romantic paradise. Livingstone (1980) supports Kaffman's doubts. Bixler (1981b) finds serious mistakes in Livingstone's arguments: "This dismissal of their [Shepher and Wolf's] work should be treated lightly, except by analysts of *non-sequiturs* [p. 274]."

THE SIM-PUA MARRIAGE

A social arrangement completely different from that of the kibbutz provides another "natural experiment" yielding evidence for the Westermarckian hypothesis explaining the avoidance of sibling incest. In a series of publications (Wolf, 1966, 1968, 1970; Wolf and Huang, 1980), the anthropologist Arthur P. Wolf presented the case of the sim-pua marriage.

Wolf conducted ethnographical research among the Hokkien-speaking Chinese peasants in the village of Hsiachichou in northern Taiwan. He found three main forms of marriage here, as well as in southern mainland China: the patrilocal type, the uxorilocal type, and the sim-pua type. The uxorilocal marriage is rare, practiced in cases in which a bride's family has no sons and the bridegroom goes to live in their house. In this type of marriage, as in the patrilocal type, the couple meet each other as adults. Wolf designates those types as "major" marriages. The sim-pua (little bride) marriage, on the other hand, starts with the adoption of a future bride. Usually she is under the age of 3, sometimes under the age of 1. The future parent-in-law rear the little girl together with their son, her future husband.

> From the time the girl enters the family, she and the boy are in contact almost every hour of every day. Until seven or eight years of age they sleep on the same tatami platform with his parents; they eat together and play together; they are bathed with the other children of the family in the same tub; and when they work or study, they work in

the same fields and study in the same school. At the age of ten or eleven, when they become aware of the implications of their jural status, they may attempt to avoid each other, but this is not socially required of them. "It is just because they are embarrassed." So far as the society at large is concerned, they are free to behave as though they were siblings until they are designated husband and wife [This quote and subsequent quotes are reprinted from Wolf, A. P. "Childhood Association, Sexual Attraction and the Incest Taboo: A Chinese Case." *American Anthropologist* 1966, 68:884, American Anthropological Association].

When the children come of age, they are married in a short and inconspicuous ceremony, which usually takes place on the eve of the lunar New Year. The head of the family tells his son and his adopted daughter-in-law that, henceforth, they are husband and wife. The couple's reaction can be characterized as extremely reluctant:

> I asked my informants to describe the couple's reaction. One old man told me that he had to stand outside of the door of their room with a stick to keep the newlyweds from running away; another man's adopted daughter did run away to her natal family and refused to return until her father beat her; a third informant who had arranged minor marriages for both of his sons described their reactions this way: "I had to threaten them with my cane to make them go in there, and then I had to stand there with my cane to make them stay." These are exceptional rather than typical cases, but as evidence they carry a special weight. Most of the people I talked to had heard of at least one instance of a father's beating his son and adopted daughter to make them occupy the same bedroom. When I asked whether they had ever heard of this happening in the case of a major marriage, they just laughed [This quote and subsequent quotes are reprinted from Wolf, A. P. "Childhood Association and Sexual Attraction: A Further Test of the Westermarck Hypothesis." *American Anthropologist* 72:508 American Anthropological Association].

Wolf carefully eliminates possible sociological explanations for the couple's reluctance to consummate the marriage. He scrutinizes, and rejects, five explanations (1966:887–888):

1. The rejection of the sim-pua marriage is a subcategory of a more general rejection of the overweaning parental authority.
2. Sim-pua marriage has a lower social status than the "major" patrilocal type.
3. By marrying sim-pua, the young people miss the opportunity to play a central role in an important ceremonial event.
4. The "major" marriage has some important material advantages compared with the sim-pua marriage.
5. The "major" marriage has important strategic advantages compared with the sim-pua marriage by creating alliances of social and economic significance.

His conclusion is that the cause of the couple's reluctance lies in the sphere of sexuality: The youngsters are not attracted to each other sexually. He provides extensive evidence for this conclusion.

Because parental coercion usually overcomes the couple's reluctance and the couple eventually assumes marital life, the lack of sexual attraction—Wolf hypothesized—will result in frequent extramarital relations. Wolf investigated the hiring of the services of prostitutes by males married in the different patterns of marriages. He found that males married in the sim-pua form are more prone to visit the "dark rooms" than are husbands married in the other forms (Table 5.2). The difference is significant at the .01 level $(df = 2; \chi^2 = 9.1)$. Wolf found the same difference when he investigated the husbands' neglect of wives for concubines (Table 5.3). The difference is significance at the .001 level $df = 2; \chi^2 = 17.66)$ (computed from Wolf, 1966:886).

Although extramarital relations are quite common among the Chinese married males, they are extremely rare among the Chinese married women. From a nearby district Wolf gathered data about female extramarital relations; the data are shown in Table 5.4.

TABLE 5.2
The Use of Prostitutes in Hsiachichou, by Marriage Patterns

	N visiting "dark rooms"	N not visiting "dark rooms"	Total N
Virilocal marriage	10	60	70
Uxorilocal marriage	4	22	26
Sim-pua marriage	11	12	23
Total	25	94	119

Note: The term *virilocal* is used instead of the outdated patrilocal.

TABLE 5.3
Concubinage in Hsiachichou, by Marriage Pattern

	N living with concubines	N not living with concubines	Total N
Virilocal marriage	3	67	70
Uxorilocal marriage	2	24	26
Sim-pua marriage	8	15	23
Total	13	106	119

TABLE 5.4
Female Adultery in Northern Taiwan, by Marriage Pattern

	Sim-pua marriage	Major marriage
Total number of women	127	159
Number involved in adultery	42	18
Percentage involved in adultery	33.1	11.3

Source: Wolf, 1970:512.

The same tendency showed in two other indicators. Wolf hypothesized that if sexual attraction was lacking, sim-pua marriages will end in divorce more often than will major marriages. He also posited that the fertility of sim-pua marriages will be considerably lower than that of the major marriages. His findings were as follows: Of the sim-pua marriages, 24.2% ended in divorce and separation, in contrast to 1.2% of the major marriages; the fertility of women married in the sim-pua pattern was about 30% lower than that of women married in the major pattern (Wolf, 1970:511, 513). Wolf succeeded in acquiring the household registration records of a part of northern Taiwan from 1905–1945. These records, kept during the Japanese occupation on 1478 families, again showed that sim-pua wives were 30% less reproductive than other wives (Wolf and Huang, 1980).

Thus the evidence seems to be overwhelming. Nevertheless, some questions arise when we read Wolf's psychological explanation of the sexual aversion:

In a review of instinctive behavior and reproductive activities, Frank Beach notes that "male mammals often fail to copulate in an environmental setting previously associated with punishment. Dogs that have become 'neurotic' as a result of experimental treatment are slow to respond to estrous females presented in the room where the experiments were conducted, but the same males mate readily in the kennel" (Beach 1951:408). These findings suggest the possibility that the very fact they are socialized together may account for the mutual aversion of persons who have grown up in the same family. The socialization process inevitably involves a good deal of punishment and pain, and children who are socialized together must come to associate one another with this experience. While mammals such as rats and dogs identify their environment primarily in terms of its physical characteristics, men ordinarily think of their surroundings largely in terms of the people with whom they associate. It is thus not unreasonable to suppose that experiences in the context of the family will be generalized in terms of the concept of the family.

This thought can be pursued one step further. Children who grow up as members of the same family are not only socialized together, they are also socialized relative to one another. Simply because a child's social world is largely made up of his parents and siblings, it is usually in relation to these people that he learns to control his impulses. His parents may tell a child not to hit "other people," but it is for hitting a parent or a sibling that a child is most frequently punished. It can be argued that a child will learn to anticipate punishment and pain in many situations involving the use of a family member for the satisfaction of strong natural impulses. Regardless then of whether the parents punish a child for sexual approaches to other members of the family, his experience should have the effect of teaching him that it is dangerous to satisfy certain impulses with respect to a family member. We need only to assume that such natural impulses as sex and aggression have a common subjective component that can serve as a basis for generalization. Because all human societies demand that children learn to control strong aggressive impulses toward other members of their family, we might expect people everywhere to exhibit an aversion to the possibility of satisfying sexual desires within the family [Wolf 1966:892–893].

Besides the fact that the two explanations do not fit together very well, neither fits the kibbutz case. In the collective educational system, the use of physical punishment is very rare. No differences were found between peer groups reared by strict and liberal nurses. Kibbutz children avoid each other erotically when they reach adolescence, although they are not reared in a family and no sexual approaches are ever punished. Yet Wolf was aware of the research on the kibbutz case and even quotes Fox (1962), Talmon (1964), and Spiro (1958) in his 1966 paper.

More important, however, is the lack of data on the ages of the cosocialized couples. In his 1968 paper, Wolf quotes a missionary who had described her visit to a Christian school in the city of Foochow in 1879. The lady met an 8-year-old boy who carried a baby girl in his arms and asked him whether the baby was his sister. The shy boy did not answer, but his brother did: "She is his wife." If the negative imprinting hypothesis is correct, I would assume that the boy had no problems in consummating his marriage.

Had Wolf possessed data on the ages of the cosocialized children, he might have been able to account for considerable variance in his evidence. The 52% of the males and 67% of females married in the sim-pua manner who did not have extramarital relations may be assumed to have differed considerably in age (by more than 4 years) from their mates, like the 8-year-old boy and his baby wife. Sim-pua marriages reduce fertility, Wolf argues, in some regions by as much as 40% (Wolf, 1968:865). How, then, can we explain the very high fertility of the Taiwanese population? Wolf had analyzed the marriages between 1905 and 1925. Assuming that the average Chinese girl did not bear her first child before the age of 15, we can see what happened to the Taiwanese population after 1920. Between 1920 and 1935, it grew from 3,655,308 to 5,212,426, an average annual natural increase of nearly 3% (*Encyclopaedia Britannica*, 1959, Vol. 9, p. 521).

All this indicates that only an unknown proportion of the sim-pua marriages fit the pattern described by Wolf. Presumably, these were cases in which the spouses were cosocialized during the critical years of negative imprinting. The result is sexual aversion or indifference in adulthood. In several Australian aboriginal cultures, prospective wives are reared by their husband's families. Because of the considerable age difference between the spouses, no problems of sexual aversion arise (Hart and Pilling, 1960).

SUMMARY

We have seen how two culturally defined social situations created two natural experiments in which a nuclear-family-like pattern was simulated beyond the limits of the nuclear family of consanguinity. The simulation "fooled Mother Nature." The result was as though the boys and girls in the kibbutz peer groups and the bride and groom in the sim-pua marriages were real siblings. When these children reach adolescence, they become sexually indifferent to each other. They cannot accept each other as mates and look elsewhere for sexual partners. This happens despite the fact that endogamous marriages are highly appreciated in the kibbutz, and that in Taiwan heavy social and cultural pressure is exerted on the couple.

The theoretical significance of these natural experiments is enormous. Sibling incest is preculturally avoided by a biopsychical mechanism. This mechanism is triggered by a statistically prevalent social situation characteristic of the species. Westermarck was right—at least in the case of sibling, incest.

Thus the basic question becomes: Why, by and large, don't human beings like it much? *why, in the vast majority of societies, do they take* some *trouble, however vague, to discourage incestuous unions, even though most human beings are probably not going to indulge in such unions? Why we do not like murder much is perhaps obvious: but why should we not make love with those we love most? At the least, the notion makes us uneasy—but we might sanction it for a privileged few of favored caste; at worst, it fills us with horror.* Unease and avoidance *seem to be the common denominators—not fierce desire held in check by even fiercer sanctions or lust reined in by the power of taboo. The universal root phenomenon appears to be* the ease with which it rouses our unease.

—ROBIN FOX
The Red Lamp of Incest (1980:8–9)

6

CONTRIBUTIONS TO THE DEVELOPMENT OF THE SOCIOBIOLOGICAL THEORY OF INCEST

In this chapter, I shall survey the contributions of scientists who during the last 25 years have asked questions relevant to the biosocial view of incest. Many of these researchers would probably protest if I called them sociobiologists. Yet, in my opinion, they contributed significantly to the formation of a sociobiological theory of incest. All of them rejected the social-culture variables as definitive causal factors of incest regulations. They criticized the naive functionalism that equated beneficiary consequences with the origin of the incest regulations. They offered different alternatives, and reached the conclusion that people would generally not commit incest even if it were not prohibited. They dared to look at comparative animal evidence; they analyzed demographic data, compared cultures, and tested precultural hypotheses. They predicted that the solution to the question of why prohibitions are needed if incest is avoided to begin with lies somewhere in a coevolutionary process of biological predispositions that direct learning propensities.

Three scientists are omitted from this survey: R. D. Alexander (1974, 1975, 1977, 1979, and n.d.), P. Van den Berghe (1978, 1979, 1980, 1980 [with Mesher], and in press), and R. H. Bixler (1980, 1981a, 1981b, 1981c). Because their thinking is almost identical to my own, discussion of their work is incorporated in the next chapter.

MIRIAM KREISELMAN SLATER:
THE DEMOGRAPHIC EXPLANATION

Miriam Slater's "Ecological Factors in the Origin of Incest" appeared in 1959 in *American Anthropologist*. Although she substitutes the word *ecological* for *demographic*, she was not the first to apply demographics to the problem of incest. Wilson D. Wallis, in a letter to the editor of *The American Anthropologist* in 1950, had criticized Leslie A. White's famous article. Although Wallis's probability calculations were wrong, he showed that in a hypothetical situation of families with six children each, about one-third of the children would have to marry out because of the probable distribution of the sexes. Were the number of siblings per family smaller, the exogamic percentage would rise. Additional factors, such as mortality, the spacing of children, and the birth order of the sexes, further diminish the probability of sibling incest. Wallis reached an important conclusion: "It seems, then, more probable that perception of its advantages led to this prevalent [exogamic] type of marriage [p. 278]."

Slater's work was more sustained and intensive than Wallis's. She criticized the theoretical approach to incest of White, Seligman, and Lévi-Strauss on methodological grounds (see Chapters 8–9 in what follows). By applying the four causes paradigm of Aristotles, she concluded that the four theories failed to explain anything material. By using what she called interaction theory, Slater argued that in the development of a cultural pattern, action comes first, with values later crystallizing around those actions that are usual and common.

The question then becomes what sort of animal would develop an action pattern of mating in which parents and siblings are avoided as mates. The answer: an animal that could not find mates among its parents and siblings because of ecological reasons. Slater turned to the demographic characteristics of primitive humans and found the following common traits: (*a*) a short life span; (*b*) adolescent sterility in females; (*c*) wide spacing between births because of prolonged nursing and inhibition of estrogen by the hormone prolactin during lactation; and (*d*) high infant mortality.

From these facts, Slater constructed two charts. One is based on an age at menarche of 15 years, an adolescent sterility of 2 years, and a lactation period of 3 years. The second is based on an age at menarche of 13 years, no sterile period, and lactation of 2 years. Children are spaced at 4 years in the first and 3 in the second. By assuming a normal sex ratio, 50% child mortality, and an average life span of 35 years, Slater arrived at the plausible conclusion that mother–son incest in the first system is almost impossible and in the second highly improbable. Father–daughter incest can be more common than mother–son. The father might die after having impregnated the daughter, but were the father to die, leaving no one to care for the lactating mother and her offspring, the offspring would die also. Brother–sister incest would depend greatly on the birth order of the sexes. Sibling mating is the most probable of the three incestuous dyads, but it would be far less frequent than exogamy.

In summarizing her argument, Slater claimed that "cooperative bonds were determined by mating patterns, not vice versa [p. 1058]" and that the mating patterns themselves were formed by ecology. (Slater consistently avoids the term *demography*, preferring *ecology*. She ignores the fact that several crucial variables in her arguments—for example, sex ratio—have little to do with ecology.) Slater also included examples from the Comanche and the Tallensi to illustrate how these people consider incest impossible and incredible. Slater's work is important because she introduced and drew attention to the crucial mechanism of prevention.

ROBIN FOX

Robin Fox has devoted almost two decades to incest research. His first article, "Sibling Incest" (1962), was followed by various other publications (1967a, 1967b, 1967c, 1968, 1972), including a book, *The Red Lamp of Incest* (1980), which summarizes and synthesizes his research. Fox's writings reveal a strong attraction to psychoanalysis, an almost apologetic acceptance of neo-Darwinian evolution, and a desire to synthesize theories drawn from Freud, Westermarck, Lévi-Strauss, Marx, Piaget, and Goody. Because the 1980 book covers all of Fox's published work on incest, it will serve as the focus of our discussion.

Fox was intrigued by the apparently unbridgeable gap between Freud and Westermarck, and his 1962 article serves to bridge the gap. Although Westermarck assumed that siblings reared together were uninterested in each other, Freud assumed that they were strongly attracted. Fox explains that this attraction depends on *propinquity* during childhood. Propinquity, he explains, produces aversion; separation engenders attraction. The punishment of transgressors, furthermore, is proportional to the attraction: Strong attraction carries severe punishment; aversion carries lax prohibitions.

Fox presents cross-cultural evidence in support of his thesis. The kibbutz, the

Tallensi, the Pondo, and the Arapesh all support Westermarck's claims. On the other hand, the Apache and the Trobrianders have been shown to confirm Freudian theory, and the Tikopia are a transitional case.

In his 1962 article, Fox explained the inhibition found on the kibbutz by Skinnerian "negative reinforcement," but in the 1980 volume he tends to accept my idea of phylogenetically programmed negative imprinting (Fox, 1980:48). He argues convincingly that different social arrangements trigger different programmed learning abilities in the phylogenetic repertoire of the human being: We are programmed to be imprinted under certain conditions and to feel guilty under other conditions.

Fox asserts that people avoid or prevent incest, and he then turns to an analysis of Freud's primal horde theory. How, he asks, is the "collective mind" transmitted? (I believe I was the first to draw attention to this apparent convergence between Freud and Westermarck; see Shepher 1971b:240–241.) He answers with Chance's (1962) "equilibration" and the evolution of cortical control over lust and rage:

> The young male monkey is moved by several desires: He wants food, he wants to get into the mating game, he is roused to aggression fairly easily. He could simply act these out. He could stalk about in the group and take what food he wanted when he wanted, he could try to copulate with whatever female was in heat, and he could fly into rages and attack the other males who tried to interfere. Anyone who has spent any time with any group of monkeys or apes knows the end result of such a strategy. It is one very unhappy young monkey at best and one dead or expelled young monkey at worst. The older male or males will simply not tolerate him, and he will be attacked and beaten up. The females will reject him, since they are not interested in a potential loser, nor does he fit their notions of a bundle of good genes. His obviously antisocial behavior in such intensely social species will bring him nothing but disaster. Sheer strength and aggression will get him so far, but it has often been observed that the male that is individually the most dominant in this sense rarely ends up as top male in the end. He is more likely to end up as a solitary, unable to make a place for himself in the social/breeding system, thus defeating his own ends. What is the opposite of this? in a nutshell, it is the more intelligent monkey (ape). Or if we do not want to go that far, the more controlled will do [This quote and subsequent quotes are reprinted from *The Red Lamp of Incest* by Robin Fox. Copyright © 1980 by Robin Fox. Reprinted by permission of the publisher, E. P. Dutton, Inc. p. 113].

Fox's application of Chance's equilibration theory to human evolution had several shortcomings:

1. It relied excessively on the mating system among baboons of the multimale system.
2. It neglected the female's part in the evolutionary process
3. It failed to document sufficiently the evolution of neocortical control.

But in his later application, Fox offers satisfactory answers. He presents evidence to the effect that early hominids probably experimented with various mating systems, that female selection was powerful in the evolutionary process, and that recent neurophysiological evidence indicates a complex interaction among amygdala, hippocampus, and cortex. Fox ascribes the conspicuously rapid growth of the brain during the last 2 million years to the equilibration process in combination with the emergence of the hunting-gathering adaptation, the creation and use of tools, symbolic language, and kinship classification. In analyzing one-male and multimale primate social structures, Fox states that humans combined a system of descent (already present in the multimale primate groups) and alliance (present in rudimentary form in the primate harem, dominated by one male).

This idea of descent plus alliance is probably Fox's most important contribution to the study of human evolution. In his earlier writings (1972, 1975), Fox did not explain how this combination evolved, but he does so in his 1980 book, ascribing it to the advent of hunting and gathering, the exchange of vegetable and animal foods between the sexes, and the ordered cooptation of peripheral males (Fox 1980:150–154). Although I essentially agree with this interpretation, it may be unduly complicated. It suffices to say that the combination evolved when the hunting-gathering adaptation forced human males to make greater investment in their offspring. (Although I may earlier have unduly emphasized the role of the pair bond in this process [Shepher, 1978], I still believe that most human males live monogamously or in serial monogamy only reluctantly and they are basically polygynous. When hunting and gathering compelled males to invest more in their offspring and the offsprings' mother, they had to find a way to "regular mate allocation [Fox, 1980:246, footnote 6]," the essence of the alliance–descent combination.)

A final word on Fox's otherwise brilliant and witty book: Although he claims to work within the framework of modern evolutionary theory, he neglects Hamilton, Trivers, and Wilson. Their methods might throw his insights into greater relief and shore them up scientifically. If, instead of trying to create a "universal peace" between such polar opposites as Freud and Westermarck, Lévi-Strauss and Marx, Fox had used the models of inclusive fitness and parental investment, his book would have been even more valuable. But, even so, it is the most important book on incest in the last hundred years.

ABERLE ET AL.: A SYSTEM AND
METHODOLOGICAL BREAKTHROUGH

The group of authors represented in Aberle et al. (1963) was assembled with the explicit purpose of addressing the problem of incest. The original seven scientists—David F. Aberle, Urie Bronfenbrenner, Eckhard H. Hess, Alfred L. Kroeber, Daniel R. Miller, David M. Schneider, and James N. Spuhler—came from five universities and met at Stanford in 1956. (Kroeber died before the report was prepared and did not share authorship.) This impressive group represented several disciplines: anthropology, sociology, psychology, and ethology. Its interdisciplinary nature was itself an important innovation.

The authors raised the basic methodological problem: "There are no criteria save aesthetics and logical consistency for choosing among theories, since there is no possibility of demonstrating that A varies with B, if both A and B are universally and invariably present [p. 254]." There was no way to break the vicious cycle without being reductionistic, a trait their interdisciplinary nature allowed them. They were the first since Westermarck who dared to include animal mating patterns in the inquiry into incest. They, too, criticized the naive functionalism of most existing theories.

> Most of the theories about the incest taboo provided demonstration that in one or in the other sense it is adaptive, and thereby often confuse the question of origin with the question of persistence. It is not logically admissible to assert that a phenomenon has come to exist because it is adaptive: that man grew noses because they support spectacles. It can be said that if something comes into existence which has superior adaptive potential, it is likely to be perpetuated or to spread. The question of the cause of its origin, however, remains unsolved [p. 254].

This stated the authors enumerate six theories:

1. The inbreeding theory (Westermarck, Muller, and Morgan)
2. The socialization theory (Parsons and Bates)
3. The family theory (Freud, Malinowski, and Seligman)
4. The social and cultural system theory (Tylor, Fortune, White, and Murdock)
5. The indifference or revulsion theory (Westermarck)
6. The demographic theory (Slater)

By placing Westermarck in both the categories of inbreeding theory and indifference-revulsion theory, the authors reveal another problem: Westermarck, in contrast to his contemporaries and to later authors, did distinguish between function and origin. He claimed that the origin of the taboo was in the mechanism of indifference and revulsion but that its function was to prevent inbreeding.

The authors set out to criticize the six theories according to three criteria:

1. The adaptive value may be rejected.
2. The adaptive value may be accepted but its identity with origins be denied.
3. The adaptive value may be accepted but the results, because of the incest taboo, may be denied.

The authors accept the inbreeding theory but do not clearly define their grounds for acceptance. They conclude that inbreeding creates biological harm in animals such as humans and reject the counterargument by indicating that cross-cultural differences in the sanctioning of cross-cousin marriages and the interdiction of parallel cousin marriages are irrelevant. But they do not extend their basic criticisms of functionalism to breeding theory and do not explain which mechanisms motivated people toward or away from acting adaptively.

Westermarck's revulsion is dispensed with easily, on the grounds that it contains both logical and empirical difficulties. Here the six distinguished authors fall into the same trap that caught Frazer and Freud: "If something is naturally repugnant, why should it be outlawed by taboo?"

As for Slater's demographic theory, the authors make only one observation: The assumptions concerning the demographic characteristics of early humans require more primatological and archaeological evidence.

The authors then broaden their range to consider animal evidence. This evidence, interestingly enough, parallels Westermarck's aversion argument (and the more recent kibbutz research): Canada and Graylag geese were found by one of the authors, Eckhard H. Hess, to be imprinted against sibling matings, and intergenerational matings were demographically prevented. After reviewing the then scant primate material, the authors concluded:

> The more intelligent, slower-maturing animals living in family groups, where stable attachments are likely, and human beings, who also live in family groups where stable attachments are likely, manifest patterns which limit familial inbreeding: asexual imprinting, intergenerational competition, and the familial incest taboo. We suggest that with the emergence of culture, if not before, relatively stable family groupings in the human evolutionary line required *some* limitation on familial inbreeding. From this inference, alone, however, one cannot predict the familial incest taboo [p. 265].

The authors found three basic forms of incest regulation: inhibition (imprinting), prevention (intergenerational competition), and prohibition (taboo). But they insisted that asexual imprinting does not exist in huma· despite Fox's publication a year earlier (1962) of very convincing mater·

the contrary. The authors also maintained that expulsion of adolescent males in cases where there exists a gap between maturity and full social capacity is unsuitable among humans. Lacking inhibition and prevention, *Homo sapiens* had only one alternative: prohibition, that is, a taboo. They argued that the incest taboo is a cultural phenomenon which, one must assume, emerged along with, or subsequent to, the beginnings of culture.

Thus, according to the authors, there are two ways of solving the issue of mating within the family: institutionalization and taboo. The former would solve the problem of order, the latter would produce further benefits, as by linking families.

The authors made an important contribution, particularly in studying the mating habits of animals, but ultimately they left unresolved the basic problems.

GARDNER LINDZEY

In 1967, Gardner Lindzey published an important paper which supported the evolutionary perspective on incest. In this paper, presented as the Presidential Address of the Seventy-Fifth Annual Convention of the American Psychological Association, Lindzey bluntly declared:

> Very simply the formulation I am advancing argues that the biological consequence of inbreeding is a decrease in fitness. This decrement in fitness is present in all animals, but it is particularly pronounced in the case of man for a number of reasons including his slowness in reaching sexual maturity and his limited number of offspring. Given this lowered fitness a human group practicing incest operates at a selective disadvantage in competition with outbreeding human groups and ultimately would be unlikely to survive. Conversely, a group which prohibited inbreeding (presumably through some form of the incest taboo) would be at an advantage in comparison to groups that permitted inbreeding [p. 1051].

Lindzey's statement is open to attack on a number of grounds. How has natural selection affected groups that prohibited inbreeding compared to groups that permitted it? Did a mutation leading to the prohibition of incest appear in one group and, because of its selective advantage, spread within the group? This is unlikely, because prohibition is essentially a group phenomenon and cannot depend on one individual's genes. For a prohibition to take root, somebody with power must enforce it, and others must comply. Why would man initially prohibit incest? Could he predict its beneficial results on the group? This is a very weak assumption. Lindzey's statement confuses cultural evolution, which is relevant to groups and prohibitions, with biological evolution, which is more relevant to individuals, genes, or very simple behavioral mechanism like predisposition to learn. Lindzey, a great admirer of Freud, did not follow Freud's careful use of the phrase "inherited psychological dispositions" (1913/ 1950:158) as opposed to prohibitions and taboos.

Lindzey devotes most of his paper to proving the maladaptiveness of inbreeding. By viewing prohibitions and taboos as mechanisms that prevent inbreeding from causing harm through natural selection, Lindzey falls into a serious inconsistency. If natural selection led to prohibitions and if, as Lindzey (like many others before him) has stated, "it seems unlikely that there would have been universal selection in favor of such a taboo if there were not rather widespread impulses toward expression of the prohibited act [p. 1055]," then nature contradicts itself. On one hand, it selects incest taboos and prohibitions; on the other hand, it nurtures incestuous impulses. Could two mutually exclusive tendencies evolve simultaneously? Lindzey does not address this apparent contradiction, and claims that, "Again it seems that most of what we know about assortative mating in the human suggests that in the absence of the incest taboo, mate selection within the nuclear family would be a high frequency choice [p. 1056]."

Although Lindzey is correct in assuming that humans avoided inbreeding through natural selection, he errs in assuming that natural selection resulted in prohibitions and taboos. Lindzey also errs in his assumption about mating in the absence of prohibitions, a problem that will be further dealt with in the following chapter. (For a similar criticism of Lindzey, see Fox, 1980.)

N. BISCHOF

In his first paper, "The Biological Foundations of the Incest Taboo," Bischof, a German psychologist, invalidated an old assumption. This assumption, upon which authors such as White and Lévi-Strauss had leaned heavily, was that incest is natural among animals and that the incest taboo is hence a crucial cultural distinction between humans and other animals. Bischof, however, after reviewing the more important writings on incest, came to a different conclusion. He posited the idea of a curve for mate selection. The inverted, U-shaped curve is highest where two lines cross, one line representing the gradient of endogamy and the one line representing exogamy (see Figure 6.1). The X-axis represents the distance between prospective mates in terms of kinship, culture, geography, and physiognomy; the Y-axis depicts a continuum

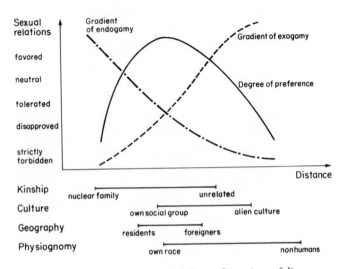

Figure 6.1. Sexual relations and different dimensions of distance.

from strictly forbidden to permissible behavior. The gradient of endogamy illustrates an inclusive "we feeling"; the gradient of exogamy illustrates an exclusive sense of distrust or xenophobia (Bischof, 1972b:9).

Bischof (1972b) bluntly rejects the thesis that incest is characteristic of animals: "In the whole animal world, with very few exceptions, no species is known in which under natural conditions inbreeding occurs to any considerable degree [p. 16]." Among animals that bind, special mechanisms have evolved to prevent or inhibit inbreeding, which in these animals could otherwise be provoked by the physical nearness of blood relatives. These mechanisms include several that Bischof terms "family dissolution mechanisms":

1. Isolation, by which animal's need to bond is thwarted before it matures sexually so that the young animal grows solitary
2. Change of object, by which the need to bond becomes unisexual, a mechanism especially common among sexually immature males
3. Abduction, usually of a young female by a young roaming male
4. Expulsion of the young (usually males, sometimes females) by the adults, accompanied by an emancipated adolescence

Among species where the family does not dissolve—species that do not experience family dissolution—specific ecological conditions suppress sexuality within the family: (a) dominant animals threaten younger animals; (b) sexuality is inhibited through stress and submissiveness; and (c) females rebuff their brothers who attempt to mate with them.

Bischof later elaborated on his idea by classifying the evidence according to the mating patterns of the species in question (Bischof, 1975:43–53). He also mentioned exceptions among domestic and zoo animals, in which instinct has been diverted by breeders and zookeepers. Bischof acknowledged that selection pressure may sometimes let up before incest is completely prevented, but he accepted it as enough that the mechanisms prevented "all too habitual" inbreeding. Turning to humans, Bischof stated that "such mechanisms . . . in the animal species concerned, are integral parts of the genetically fixed instinctive structure, and it would be astonishing if there were not at least rudimentary traces left in man [p. 24]."

As evidence for these mechanisms among humans, Bischof presents the need for emancipation among maturing humans, the evidence of the kibbutz, Taiwan's sim-pua marriage, and Cohen's (1964) monograph on cultural ritualization. He thereby demonstrates how closely cultural norms follow natural inclinations. The function of cultural norms, concludes Bischof, is to safeguard those natural propensities which motivate rather than determine human behavior.

Recently Bischof and his assistants at the University of Zurich have worked on the thesis that prevention operates mainly among females. A computer simulation verified this division of strategies between the sexes—a division predicted by the theory of parental investment (Bischof, personal communication).

MELVIN EMBER

Ember (1975) is exceptional in that he first advances a hypothesis and then tries to test it with cross-cultural data. He hypothesizes that inbreeding theory is the best explanation for the universality of the incest taboo. Seeking a final cause (or basic function) of incest, Ember rejects all alternative theories, especially those that describe effective causes (or mechanisms). Ember's evidence, which prompted him to reject Westermarck's theory, is therefore based on the following assumption: In an endogamous community, where cousins are apt to be reared together, marriages between first cousins would most likely be prohibited, but in an exogamous community they would not be prohibited. But Ember seems to have misunderstood Westermarck on the complementarity of inhibition and prohibition. (Fox [1962] has amply demonstrated the existence of this complementarity.)

Cross-cultural research into the complementarity between inhibitions and prohibitions is very difficult and complicated. In most ethnographies, the relevant variables are absent. Thus the propinquity variable, so essential in proving the presence of sibling incest inhibition, is rarely documented in substantial details. It is all but absent in the description of cousin cases. Ethnographers simply do not describe *everything*. If the theoretical significance of a certain variable is unknown to them or ignored by them, they do not pay attention to it.

Ember's final conclusion—that the incest taboo may have been adopted intentionally in order to assure the greatest chances for reproduction—is extremely naive. Despite the many claims of the harmfulness of incest which appear in mythology (Lindzey, 1967) and in folklore (Burton, 1973), Ember's conclusion is not supported by animal or human evidence. It is possible that in a relatively later phase of hominid evolution an understanding of the harm of homozygosity strengthened the existing tendency to prohibit incest. However, as I hope to show, the inbreeding hypothesis is a hypothesis of a final cause and therefore needs elaboration. Because neither modern nor Pleistocene man behaves according to his long-term interests, something also must have engendered behavior protective of these long-term interests. Ember rejects Westermarck's idea of a mechanism by which prevention of inbreeding is a final cause and childhood familiarity an effective cause. The two are complementary and not mutually exclusive.

                                                            JEFFREY T. BURNHAM

Jeffrey T. Burnham (1975) investigates the inbreeding theory by genetic means. His calculations prove that inbreeding is beneficial in small groups with low genetic load (i.e., a low frequency of harmful recessive genes) because natural selection, by eliminating the lethal homozygotes, actually reduces the population's lethal genes. Because early hominids lived in small, inbred groups in which genetic load was in equilibrium with the degree of inbreeding, avoiding inbreeding had no genetic advantage. Therefore the incest avoidance must have originated elsewhere. In a surprising dialectical switch, Burnham accepts Westermarck's and Freud's theories and explains how in complex and larger populations incest avoidance became necessary again and genetically beneficial. Later on, Burnham added the social benefits of integration and alliance to the theory. Incest avoidance was seen as fitting a universal socio-cultural pattern.

On first sight, this seems to be an elegant and witty argument. Yet, it poses several problems. The evidence is not clear that early hominids (how early?) did live in small inbred groups (how inbred?) with a low genetic load. We can assume that the groups were small from our knowledge of modern hunter-gatherers, but it is hard to accept that because these groups were highly inbred they necessarily had a low genetic load. Incest avoidance preceded humans, although Burnham claims the evidence on this point is "uncertain" (ample evidence appears to have escaped his attention—(e.g., Koford, 1963; Imanishi, 1965; Bischof, 1972; and Itani, 1972). His assumption of low genetic load resulting from the "genetic cleansing" of inbreeding is unsubstantiated. But even if his assumption were correct, how could the individual have complied with this "genetic function"? Arguing for the genetic cleansing function implies group selection and is plausible for cattle breeders or corn geneticists, it is not a plausible explanation of natural selection in humans.

In a population in equilibrium, the number of deaths from deleterious recessives will be constant. But the *individual* who outbreeds will always have more offspring than one who inbreeds, regardless of the genetic load of the population.

PARKER AND OTHERS

A well-documented study by Parker (1976) clearly distinguishes between late *cultural prohibitions* and early *behavioral manifestations*. "Cultural prohibitions" are prohibitions and taboos, and "behavioral manifestations" are avoidance such as preventions and inhibitions. After carefully laying down a theory for combined genetic and cultural evolution from D'Aquili (1972), Parker enumerates the evidence for incest avoidance in human and animal societies. He explains the data by forming two hypotheses: (a) the potential for sexual arousal is somehow linked with the potential for aggressive and assertive reactions; and (b) long and early association is linked to "stimulus satiation" which depresses further sexuality. The copious evidence for the first hypothesis concentrates largely on males. It is highly probable that this mechanism applies to brother–sister and mother–son incest inhibition, but it is not clear how the mechanism works in either sex. Although Abernethy (1974) has described the varying effect of male and female dominance on sexual functioning, such a mechanism must be integrated with parental investment theory to be accepted as a plausible explanation for incest avoidance.

In order to explain the development from avoidance to taboo, Parker embarks on a long survey of the literature on the origin of the family (including a lengthy discussion of Fox, 1972). He explains the development as follows:

> As the cultural way of life became established, additional adaptive pressures arose for this biopsychological tendency to become institutionalized as the incest taboo, because it increased the stability of the family unit, assured wider social alliances, and reduced the number of births to economically immature individuals. The incest taboo is (by definition) a cultural phenomenon and can be explained by cultural events. But like other sociocultural aspects it is "built upon" biopsychological needs, potentials, and propensities of the organism. The meaning or significance of such ontogenetically older needs derived from their integration into a new system-level (i.e., culture) and the (new) functions they fulfill there. Speaking teleologically, culture uses psychobiological potentials for its own purposes and can never be fully explained by the latter. Incest avoidance was certainly not a sufficient condition—it was, however, a facilitating condition. The incest taboo constitutes learned behavior, and as such is subject to principles of learning as is any other cultural item. However, insofar as it is motivated partly by biological propensities of the organism, it is easier to learn because it is subject to additional (aside from cultural) reinforcements from ontraorganismic sources [p. 299].

This explanation is true—as far as it goes. That is, while it is true that sociocultural patterns are (usually) "built upon biopsychological needs, potentials, and propensities of the organism," Parker does not clearly describe the process of this development.

The literature contains other intriguing works. Kortmulder's interesting (1974) paper elaborates on the association between aggression and sex, supplying ample ethological evidence. DeVos (1975) offers cognitive dissonance as the psychological mechanism to explain incest avoidance. Bateson (1978) elaborates on the evolution of sexual imprinting and its final aim: an optimal balance between inbreeding and outbreeding. Schwartzman (1974) supports the inbreeding hypothesis although on the basis of group selection. Frances and Frances (1976) try to bridge the gap between psychoanalysis and evolutionary theory. Finally, Steadman (1978) tries to prove the main motivation behind the inhibition of incest is the wish for more relatives.

SUMMARY

For more than half a century Westermarck's evolutionary approach remained despised and ridiculed. During the last 25 years, however, evidence slowly started to accumulate in its favor. Most of the authors surveyed in this chapter understood the significance of this evidence: Fox, Bischof, Burnham, Parker, and Bateson. Others emphasized the central importance of the prevention of inbreeding: Aberle *et al.*, Lindzey, and Ember. Slater drew attention to the important mechanism of prevention, arguing that actual behavior probably preceded cultural regulations. Most of these authors realized the importance of animal material. Finally, Aberle *et al.* formulated the main methodological problem of universal independent and dependent variables.

Evidence and thinking, research and theory, converged. The route to a synthesized sociobiological theory of incest was paved.

Man is a product of evolution. Much that is puzzling about man can be understood only when man is considered as evolved and evolving. A thorough knowledge of the principles and mechanisms of evolution is therefore a prerequisite for the understanding of man.

—ERNST MAYR
Populations, Species and Evolution (1970:315)

The true Promethean spirit of science means to liberate man by giving him knowledge and some measure of dominion over the physical environment. But at another level and in an new age, it also constructs the mythology of scientific materialism, guided by the corrective devices of the scientific method, addressed with precise and deliberately affective appeal to the deepest needs of human nature, and kept strong by the blind hopes that the journey on which we are now embarked will be further and better than the one just completed.

—EDWARD O. WILSON
On Human Nature (1978:209)

THE SOCIOBIOLOGICAL THEORY OF INCEST

I have presented the relevant aspects of the sociobiological theory and have analyzed the complex problems of definition and dimensions of the concept of incest. I have surveyed the research and theories inspired by biosocial ideas. Now I shall attempt to integrate those ideas in a series of propositions, followed by specific hypotheses. These, in turn, will form the skeleton of my sociobiological theory of incest. The propositions—eight in number—are as follows:

1. Because reproduction lies at the focus of the evolutionary process, incest, a specific case of reproduction, must have been subjected to the evolutionary process.
2. Incest is a special case of mating between relatives, called inbreeding. Every behavior can be advantageous or disadvantageous to the individual's genetic fitness. Close inbreeding is usually harmful in higher organisms. Therefore, it is expected that through evolution close inbreeding will somehow be eliminated or rendered rare in higher organisms, including humans.
3. The degree of closeness of the inbreeding eliminated or rendered rare depends on the costs and benefits of the specific degree of inbreeding.
4. The elimination or "rarification" of close inbreeding is the basic function, and the ultimate cause, of incest regulations. This function is

the result of a complicated coevolutionary process which includes the following phases:

(a) The organism evolves epigenetic rules; that is, genetically determined sets of procedures.

(b) These procedures direct the assembly of the mind so that specific learning patterns develop from social situations that are statistically prevalent in the life pattern of the species.

(c) As a result, behavioral syndromes emerge which inhibit incest, or prevent it, or both.

(d) Because these inhibitions and preventions depend on statistically prevalent social situations, they render incest rare. They do not, however, eliminate it completely. The rarity of incest becomes part of the natural order adapted by humans upon having evolved the capacity of abstract symbolic thinking and communication. The few cases of incest that nevertheless occur are considered abnormal. They are contrary to nature because they are so rare and therefore are prohibited.

(e) Prohibitions are complementary to inhibitions and preventions.

5. The theories of inclusive fitness and parental investment predict different reproductive strategies for males and females. We can thus expect that the coevolutionary process described in (4) will be different in different incestuous dyads: mother–son, father–daughter, and brother–sister.

6. The composite analysis of the costs and benefits of inbreeding and the different sexual strategies lead to the following predictions: (a) There is differential frequency of committed incest in the various incestuous dyads; (b) There is differential opposition of the sexes to incest; (c) There are specific social situations in which incest will occur; (d) There is increasing cultural variability of norms regulating sexual intercourse between partners who are less related than the core incestuous dyads.

7. The coevolutionary process creates the human universal of incest regulations (inhibitions, preventions, and prohibitions), which becomes central in human social life. This centrality assures its persistence mainly because, once established, the universal has very important secondary functions.

8. Those secondary functions are the stability of the family, the strengthening of the process of socialization, prevention of the isolation of the nuclear family, and creation of economic and political alliances.

The Balance of Inbreeding and Outbreeding

Sexual reproduction is only one of the forms of reproduction among organisms. The simplest form is asexual, or mitotic, reproduction, in which the genetic material simply copies itself, and two sets of dividing chromosomes produce two "daughter" cells. In this process the parent organism transmits all of its genes to the offspring. Asexual, or mitotically standardized, offspring have some important advantages over sexual, or meiotically standardized, offspring. They begin life as large organisms, are produced continuously, develop immediately into adults, have low mortality rates, and are exposed to only mild pressure from natural selection—all of which is in contrast to the characteristics displayed by sexually reproduced offspring (Williams, 1975:4). But, if—as is in fact the case—sexual reproduction is almost universal in multicellular animals and plants, it must possess a great advantage: Sexual reproduction promotes genetic variability and therefore, in a changing environment, allows the animal to adapt to the environmental changes (Maynard-Smith, 1971). Conversely, in a constant, unchanging environment, sexually reproduced offspring are at a disadvantage in comparison with asexually reproduced ones. (For a critical reevaluation of the problem, see Maynard-Smith, 1978.)

In sexual reproduction, the genetic material is halved by the process of meiosis in each parent and then recombined at fertilization. Thus each parent transmits only 50% of his or her genetic material and must renounce transfer of the other 50%. Williams (1975) calls this the "cost of meiosis." In fact, the process of combination precedes meiosis in that during meiosis the maternal and paternal chromosomes exchange genetic material, a process known as "crossing over." The resulting variability is formidable. In humans, the number of possible genetic combinations in a single fertilization (without taking into consideration crossings over) is 2^{23}, or 8,388,608. With single crossings over, the number rises to 80^{23}, or 5.9×10^{43}—a truly astronomical number (Stern, 1973:103). This figure, however, is based on the assumption that the parent organisms are completely unrelated to each other, which for humans is virtually impossible.

All human beings are related. With two parents, four grandparents, and eight greatgrandparents, each of us has 2^n ancestors, where n is the number of generations.

Wachter (1980) showed that an English child born in 1947 of wholly English ancestry would have had more than 1,073,000,000 ancestors by the time of the Norman Conquest in 1077, assuming a length of 30 years for a generation. The number exceeds not only the estimated population of England in 1077 (1.1 million according to Wachter, 1980:91), but also the estimated population of the whole world (410 million in the year 1000; Leakey and Lewin, 1977:143). Consequently, this English lad must have had an inbred ancestry; that is, many of his ancestors were each other's relatives.

We are all, therefore, related. But to what extent? Obviously there is a difference in the relatedness of first cousins who marry and the relatedness of two "unrelated" mates whose genetic closeness is unknown, if logically possible. The mating of related individuals results in offspring some of whose genes will be *identical by descent* as against less probable *identical by chance*. The relatedness of individuals is measured by the probability of two genes on any pair of alleles being identical by descent.

As a technical term, *inbreeding* is reserved for cases in which discernible traces can be followed back to common ancestors within two to three generations. An inbreeding coefficient of less than 1/256 in an individual is usually ignored in human genetic analysis.

The Costs of Inbreeding

Falconer (1960:257) points out that the most serious concern about inbreeding derives from the fact that some genes are dominant and others recessive. Dominant genes express themselves in the phenotype no matter what gene is paired on the same locus (the other allele). Thus, for instance, woolly hair or the disease of the nervous system called *dystonia musculorum deformans* are carried by dominant genes and, is transmitted to the offspring by one parent, will show up no matter what gene is transmitted by the other parent.

Let us assume that woolly hair is carried by gene D and there is an allele *d* on the same locus. Offspring types will result as follows:

	Genes transmitted by		Offspring	
	Father	Mother	Genotype	Phenotype
1	D	D	DD	woolly
2	D	*d*	D*d*	woolly
3	*d*	D	*d*D	woolly
4	*d*	*d*	*dd*	not woolly

The first and fourth offspring are called homozygotes (receiving the same gene from both parents); the second and third are heterozygotes (receiving different genes). However, Offspring 1, 2, and 3 are identical phenotypically in that all have woolly hair. Only the fourth offspring will look different. Having woolly hair is not bad, but having muscular dystonia is. Carriers of harmful dominant genes in any form are subject to natural selection—that is, their chances of transmitting their genes to the next generation are lower than those of other animals.

Recessive genes are not subject to the same selection. They affect the phenotype only in homozygotic form. Some types of albinism, for example, and the genetic illness phenylketonuria are carried by recessive genes. If a is a gene for recessive albinism and A the alternative allele, and their frequency is 50% each, the possibilities for offspring will be the following:

	Genes transmitted by		Offspring	
	Father	Mother	Genotype	Phenotype
1	A	A	AA	normal
2	A	a	Aa	normal
3	a	A	aA	normal
4	a	a	aa	albino

For dominant genes, the probability that the offspring will be affected is 75%; for recessive genes, the probability is only 25%. This difference is highly significant: The recessive gene is less exposed to natural selection. That is, natural selection can more easily eliminate harmful dominant than recessive genes from a breeding population because the latter can "hide" in the heterozygous form.

We do not know how many recessive genes are deleterious, but we do know that most of the deleterious genes are recessive, as are most mutant genes (Lerner, 1968; Mayr, 1970; Bodmer and Cavalli-Sforza, 1976; Watson, 1976; Hartl, 1977). Watson (1976:190) explains the recessiveness of a gene by its failure to produce a certain protein, which, in heterozygous form, is produced by the dominant allele on the same locus.

Inbreeding increases homozygosity and hence the chance that a deleterious recessive gene will manifest itself in the phenotype. Jacquard (1974) has shown that in constant full-sib mating, heterozygosity will decline by 19% each generation, and after 10 or 11 generations, 90% of the population will be homozygous. The same process will occur in constant parent–child mating. For half-sib mating, the decrease of heterozygosity would be 11% per generation, and in double-cross-cousin mating, 8%. But in simple first-cousin mating, the decrease in heterozygosity would be slow; even after 50 generations only 38% of the population would be homozygous. Second-cousin mating tends toward equilibrium and would produce a homozygosity only slightly greater (1/53) than would a population with random mating. Li (1962) and Falconer (1976) arrive at the same conclusion.

The most striking observed consequence of inbreeding is the reduction of reproductive capacity and physiological efficiency, a phenomenon called *inbreeding depression* (Falconer 1960:248). Inbreeding depression has been investigated in several animals, using different variables of reproductive capacity and physiological efficiency. Thus, Robertson (1954) found in cattle a 3.2% decrease in milk yield per 10% increase in the coefficient of inbreeding; Dickerson *et al.* (1954), a 4.6% decrease in the litter size of pigs and a 2.7% decrease in their weight; Morley (1954), a 5.5% decrease in fleece weight of sheep and a 3.7% decrease in body weight; Shoffner (1948), a 6.2% decrease in poultry egg production and a 6.4% decrease in hatchability; Falconer (1960:249), an 8% decrease in the litter size of mice per 10% increase in the coefficient of inbreeding. The generally accepted conclusion may be summarized as follows: "Since inbreeding tends to reduce fitness, natural selection is likely to oppose the inbreeding process by favoring the least homozygous individuals [Falconer, 1960:253]"; "In general, the balance of selective forces seems to have favoured out crossing [Maynard-Smith, 1978:139–140]."

Crow and Kimura (1970) and Cavalli-Sforza and Bodmer (1971) showed that if a trait (e.g., size, intelligence, or motor skill) possesses a degree of heritability, then inbreeding will cause a decline of the trait in the population. Thus, inbreeding is harmful in higher organisms. Because of the moral impossibility of experimenting with humans, the evidence for humans is necessarily less than that for animals. It is, however, sufficient to show that inbreeding is harmful. Barrai, Cavalli-Sforza, and Mainardi (1964) show the impact of inbreeding depression on the chest size of men born in the Parma province of Italy between 1892 and 1911. Although chest size may be very important to health, people survive and even reproduce with a relatively small chest girth. However, increased incidence of recessive homozygotes in inbred progeny has been shown to also cause increased mortality. In a careful genetic study conducted in Hiroshima and Nagasaki (before World War II), Schull and Neel (1965) demonstrated an almost linear increase in mortality with the increase in consanguinity between the parents of the children investigated. The slope of this linear function provides some information about the proportion of recessive lethal (causing death) and detrimental (causing severe impairment of health) mutations in a population. This proportion, called *genetic load*, is equivalent to the sum of the proportions of all lethal and detrimental recessives (causing death between birth and reproduction).

Bodmer and Cavalli-Sforza (1976:377) estimated the increase in risk of several diseases among progeny of first cousin matings in different countries. The increase was treated as a function of the estimated number of detrimental equivalent genes. Thus in France, conspicuous abnormalities, they estimated, will occur 3.8 times more often among progeny of first-cousin matings than in the general population; in Italy, severe defects will be 1.9 times higher; in Japan, major morbid conditions will be 1.4 times higher; in Sweden, morbidity will be 2.5 times higher; and in the Unites States; abnormality will occur 2.3 times more often. Comparable data were published by Yamaguchi *et al.* (1970), Stern (1973:495), and Morton, Crow, and Muller (1956).

The highest degree of initial inbreeding can be found in incestuous breedings. A yet higher degree can be achieved if the incestuous mates themselves were inbred, an phenomenon termed *recurrent inbreeding*. Individual pedigrees of progeny from incestuous unions are numerous (Stern 1973:485), but research on larger numbers of such children is rare: Carter (1967) presents data on English children, Adams and Neel (1967) on American, and Seemanova (1971) on Czech.

Carter investigated 13 cases of father–daughter and brother–sister progeny. Three of the children—23% of the cases—died from cystic fibrosis of the pancreas, one from cerebral degeneration and blindness, and one from Fallot's tetralogy (a combination of congenital cardiac defects). One child was severely subnormal and four were subnormal; thus five were debilitated (38%). This leaves only five normal children (38%). If we add the severely subnormal child to those deceased, we come up with a heavy price: Of these progeny, 31% suffered mortality or severe disability.

Adams and Neel (1967) investigated 18 cases. Four of the children died, two were severely debilitated (retardation, seizure disorder, and spastic cerebral palsy), one had a bilateral cleft lip, and three had a very low IQ (70). This leaves eight normal offspring, and a mortality–severe disability percentage of 33%.

By far the most comprehensive study was that conducted by Seemanova (1971), who investigated a sample of 161 Czech children of incestuous unions.

She also used as controls the same mothers in nonincestuous relationships. Of her sample, 2 children were stillborn, 21 died soon after birth, and 4 died somewhat later: altogether a mortality of 17%. Seemanova's description of the surviving children is rather depressing:

> Twelve of the 44 surviving children were severely mentally retarded; in one of these cases, dwarfism was also present, in another congenital cataract, and in a 3rd case deaf-mutism in addition to imbecility. Five had congenital dislocation of the hip, one of these had also Hirschsprung's disease and hypospadias, and microcephaly was present in a second of these cases. One child had congenital heart disease, and in one mucopoly-saccaridosis Sanfilippo was diagnosed. Finally, one child with deaf-mutism and amblyopia occurred in this group of incestuous children [p. 116].

The number of surviving but severely debilitated children is estimated to be 40 (25%). By comparison, the mothers among those investigated also bore 92 children who were sired by unrelated males. The mortality of these progeny was 5.4%, the severe disability 1.8%.

If we combine the child mortality data from Schull and Neel (1975) and Seemanova (1971), the following picture can be presented as seen in Table 7.1. As sad as the death of a child is in human terms, it is of small importance in terms of evolution. Children who die early will not reproduce; neither will children who survive with heavy debilities. If we assume that the ratio of mortality to disability is constant in other degrees of inbreeding, we extend Table 7.1 to include disability, as seen in Table 7.2.

THE BENEFITS OF INBREEDING

Biologists classify living species on a continuum of inbreeding–outbreeding. Certain organisms reproduce by asexual reproduction (agamogenesis)—for example, protozoa, polyps, and some worms. Others reproduce by budding (e.g., many plants and some multicellular animal organisms like hydras). Another form of unisexual reproduction is parthenogenesis, found in several insects. In all these cases, the genetic material of the parent organism is transferred in its entirety to the offspring. The only source of genetic variability

TABLE 7.1
Child Mortality as Related to Consanguinity of Parents

Relatedness of parents	Child mortality (%)	Child vitality (%)
1/32	4.4	95.6
1/16	5	95
1/8	7	93
1/2	17	83

Source: Schull and Neel (1965) and Seemanova (1971).

TABLE 7.2
Child Mortality and Disability as Related to Consanguinity of Parents

Relatedness of parents	Disability (%)	Disability and child mortality (%)	Viability (%)
1/32	6.47	10.87	89.13
1/16	7.35	12.35	87.65
1/8	10.30	17.30	82.70
1/2	24.80	41.80	58.20

is mutation. Logically, these three reproductive systems can be considered as inbreeding (though, semantically, there is a contradiction—because the reproduction is unisexual, there is no "breeding").

Hermaphroditism is probably the transitional system to sexual propagation. Hermaphrodites possess both sperm and ova in the same individual organism. Some hermaphrodites, such as parasitic worms, practice self-fertilization, but most practice cross-fertilization—for example, earthworms, and snails (Curtis, 1970:322).

Unisexualism and hermaphroditism are relatively rare in both the plant and animal kingdoms. Most species have evolved sexual reproduction, and practice different degrees of inbreeding.

One obvious advantage of inbreeding is that more of the parental genes will be transmitted to the offspring (Bengtsson, 1978; Maynard-Smith, 1978:139). A second advantage is associated with kinship altruism. In a group in which individuals are related, altruistic behavior will spread. In social insects, for instance, such altruism is essential. Indeed, we find a high degree of inbreeding in Hymenoptera through the haplodiploid system of propagation. (Wilson, 1971:324; Hamilton, 1972). But the phenomenon is by no means limited to social insects.

Any animal species living in a small group needs a certain amount of inbreeding, mainly because of the difficulty in finding a mate if the other, similar groups are distributed over a large territory. Familiarity may sometimes be identical with relatedness. This is the basis of *assortative mating*, by which animals prefer familiar partners for mating (Wilson, 1975:80). Thus the third advantage contains an ecological factor: coping with the problem of the dispersion of the species in its ecological niche. Such dispersion depends on the availability of resources, the presence of predators, and the energy needed to split groups (i.e., emigration). The degree of inbreeding, therefore, will practically become part of the general strategy of survival (Wilson, 1975; Maynard-Smith, 1978).

A comparison of the well-defined advantages of inbreeding with its disadvantages can only lead to the conclusion that every species has to find a balance between inbreeding and outbreeding. In other words, a species has to define the costs and benefits of its location on the inbreeding–outbreeding continuum, according to the variables of its general strategy of survival. What has to be defined is the degree of inbreeding that is intolerable because its costs outweigh its benefits. In the human case, we can start with an investigation of the highest degree of inbreeding (incest) as compared to outbreeding practices.

Our calculations must take into account the important difference between the two sexes in their strategies of investing in offspring. A female usually cannot profit genetically from polyandry. She can bear only a certain number of offspring, a number limited by her heavy investment in parenthood (large and few sex cells, long pregnancy, lactation), no matter how many males mate with her. On the other hand, a male can profit from polygyny because he can beget offspring with every female he mates with. For the sake of simplicity, I shall fix the number of offspring of every female as two, but any other constant number will give the same results.

Let us start with siblings. A brother and a sister (agnatic and uterine: having the same father and mother) theoretically can choose between inbreeding (incestual) and outbreeding. Figure 7.1 depicts the male's point of view.

Thus, although by mating with his sister the male contributes more of his genes (on average) to an individual offspring than by mating with an unrelated female, he does not gain because he gives up the nephews and nieces his sister might bear in addition to his own offspring. The female loses even more: Because her brother can have more offspring from polygyny, she loses $.25 \times 2n$, where n is the number of her brother's mates. Neither brother nor sister gains from incest, and the sister loses even more if both have the option to mate out. Without that option, inbreeding makes more sense. If, for instance, the sister has no mate, the brother can gain by mating with her even if he has another mate (see Figure 7.2). In such a situation, the male's gain is 1.00. The female's gain is lower (see Figure 7.3). If the brother cannot outbreed, polyandry arises, as seen in Figure 7.4. This represents a loss compared with outbreeding, but, of course, a gain over not mating at all. For the female ego the loss is also slight—$1.5 - 1.25 = .25$.

For brothers and sisters gain is possible only if the sister has absolutely no chance of another mate, and even then her gain is less than her brother's.

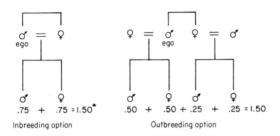

FIGURE 7.1. Brother-sister incest compared with outbreeding option: monogamic situation; male ego.

Let us summarize our findings in Table 7.3. (Note: Outbreeding can be polygynous or polyandrous; the difference is not especially important. Thus in a polygynous society, the male would normally have $2n \times .50$ from his wives + .50 from his sister. If his sister cannot mate, and he therefore mates with her and his own wives, his gain will be 1.00. Conversely, in a polyandrous situation, a male would normally have .75 [one of his own; one of his brother; polyandry is usually adelphic] and .50 from his sister's polyandric marriage, which equals 1.25. He still loses.)

Genetically, then, the gain in brother–sister incest is minimal and limited to situations in which the sister cannot find a mate at all. Even in that situation, the brother gains more than the sister. The situation most conducive to brother–sister incest would be complete isolation, in which neither sibling finds another mate.

In the case of father–daughter incest, the father has already produced offspring according to our assumption (Figure 7.5). Thus, the father will gain considerably, and so will the daughter. We must therefore expect less resistance to father–daughter incest than to brother–sister incest. The daughter's

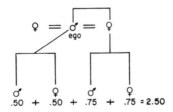

FIGURE 7.2. Brother–sister incest: polygynic situations, male ego.

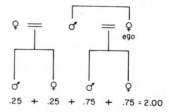

.25 + .25 + .75 + .75 = 2.00

FIGURE 7.3. Brother–sister incest: polygynic situations, female ego.

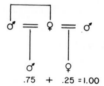

.75 + .25 = 1.00

FIGURE 7.4. Brother–sister incest: polyandric situation, male ego.

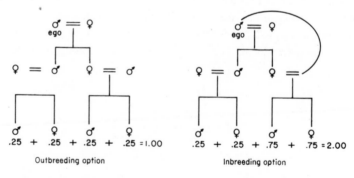

.25 + .25 + .25 + .25 = 1.00

Outbreeding option

.25 + .25 + .75 + .75 = 2.00

Inbreeding option

FIGURE 7.5. Father–daughter incest compared with outbreeding option.

resistance will be greater than the father's, because he has already produced offspring and because she will have to invest heavily in offspring of the incestuous union. High investment means high risk. But this situation is rare. If the father also has another mate, he will have four grandchildren with her and will not gain by inbreeding. Again the situation conducive to incest is comparative isolation.

What about mother–son incest? From the genetic point of view, the mother is in a polyandric situation and because we have assumed she can bear only two children, she will lose (Figure 7.6). (The reader will note that in the case of brother–sister incest, we counted children and, in the case of parent–offspring incest, grandchildren who are also children.) The son loses as well, since in the monogamous situation he will have only one child and no nephews. Thus, on genetic grounds, mother–son incest should be the rarest, brother–sister more common, and father–daughter the most common. We shall see later several mechanisms that assure exactly this pattern. (Note that in the two polyandrous situations, females lose, but less than males. Is it so surprising that polyandrous marriages are so rare?)

We can see that the genetic gain from incest is very dubious. Only for father–daughter incest is there any gain. For other incestuous unions, incest "pays" only in extreme cases of isolation and absence of outside mates.

Does incest pose other advantages? Trivers's parental investment theory claims that the process of choosing a mate is complicated and risky, especially for the human female. Because of her heavy initial investment in the offspring, she must be as sure as possible of two traits in her future offspring's father: (a) that he is genetically healthy, so that her genes will combine with healthy

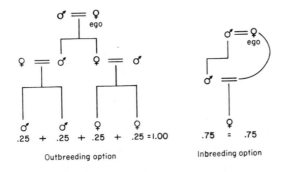

FIGURE 7.6 Mother–son incest compared with outbreeding option.

enough genes to be carried by the offspring to sexual maturity; and (*b*) that he will be both willing and able to invest in her and her offspring.

Certainly, mating with a complete stranger is a genetic gamble. His family is unknown and only his phenotype indicates his genetic health. The well-known person is a better bet. For a group dweller like the human being, living in close contact provided a good way to find out about a future mate's family. It also gave the female a way to learn about her prospective mate's possible degree of investment. The whole process of courtship can be interpreted as devoted to this important inquiry (see Barkow, 1978; Van den Berghe, 1978). Propinquity and relatedness have probably overlapped considerably for most of hominid (including *Homo sapiens*) existence. Moreover, wherever this overlap occurs, we have important advantages for inbreeding. Van den Berghe (1979) showed that most cultural forms of mating (descent ruled, residence rules, preferential cousin marriages) represent cultural regulations aimed at *optimum* inbreeding (see also Van den Berghe, in press).

Another advantage of inbreeding is that is reduces competition among siblings and relatives for mates. When outbreeding depends on a long-distance search for mates, siblings and relatives may find themselves competing for the few available mates. This situation seriously jeopardizes the inclusive fitness of their parents. It is to the parents' advantage, then, to agree to first- or second-cousin marriages, which reduce—although do not entirely eliminate—sibling competition. Parents are not the only partners interested in promoting inbreeding. Usually the whole kin group is involved, especially in unilinear systems. For instance, in patrilineal systems in several pastoral societies, paternal parallel cousin marriage is prescribed in order to keep wealth within the patrilineage (Alexander, 1979).

Cost–Benefit Analysis and
the Evolution of Incest Avoidance

As we have seen, inbreeding can offer certain advantages. Because inbreeding and outbreeding extend along a continuum, we can expect that evolving hominids, through evolutionary trial-and-error, sought the most advantageous balance between inbreeding and outbreeding (Alexander, 1975; Parker, 1976; Bateson, 1978; Bixler, 1981a; Van den Berghe, in press).

Alexander (1977) based his inquiry on outbreeding and devised a model of its costs and benefits (Figure 7.7). (The choice of which concept to focus on becomes to some extent arbitrary.) But his model does not rely on any data. As

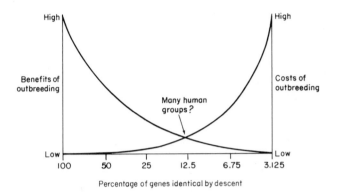

FIGURE 7.7. Cost-benefit analysis of outbreeding. (From Alexander, 1977.)

Alexander wrote, "It is inferred that they [the curves of benefits and costs] tend to balance near the level of first cousins in most human societies [p. 331]." But why there? What are the slopes of the curves based on? I shall try to provide an explanation, constructing a model based on available data (see Figure 7.8).

We have just presented some clear and unequivocal data (see earlier) on the costs of inbreeding. Our tabulations include the results of inbreeding between first and second cousins and the scarce data on the results of incestuous matings. We can combine the data and plot a line for the costs of inbreeding. Because these costs appear as diminishing fitness of offspring, the line will descend from left to right as the mate's relatedness increases. Thus the more closely the parents are related, the less viable their offspring. I am distinguishing here among four curves: (a) child mortality; (b) child disability; (c) the total of (a) and (b); and (d) inferred data on total disability in case of recurrent inbreeding. I do not know of data on results of recurrent inbreeding, but they can be inferred from calculations of homozygosity when it does occur (Falconer, 1960:91).

It is much more difficult to plot the benefits of inbreeding, because they are complex and hardly measurable. Some cases of inbreeding offer genetic benefits or strategic benefits for mate selection. We can calculate the genetic benefits; the percentage of shared genes between parent and offspring will be higher for related than unrelated parents. But other strategic benefits must be studied quantitatively before we can calculate them. We must therefore partially infer the curve of inbreeding's benefits. The two curves cross each other in cases of one-time inbreeding between uncles and nieces and in cases of recurrent inbreeding between first cousins and uncle–niece matings. My diagram ultimately brings us close to Alexander's inference. According to this

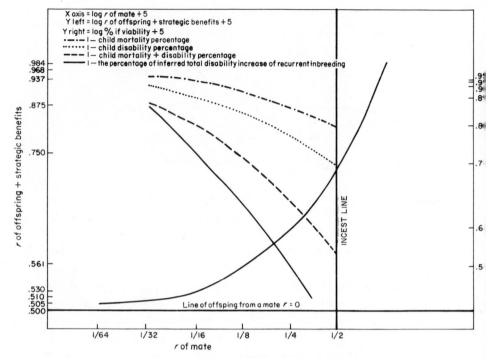

FIGURE 7.8. Costs and benefits of inbreeding.

TABLE 7.3
Comparison between Brother–Sister Incest and Outbreeding

	Situation 1 (monogamic)	Situation 2 (polygynic)		Situation 3 (polyandric)	
	Male and female	Male	Female	Male	Female
Incest	1.50	2.50	2	1	1.25
Normal	1.50	1.50	1.50	1.50	1.50
Balance	0	+1	+.50	−.50	−.25

Note: The assumption in each case is that a female has two offspring. In Situation 2, female has no outbreeding option; in Situation 3, male has no outbreeding option.

model, incest regulations are not arbitrary. Their universality stems from the fact that the price of too close inbreeding is devastatingly high for the individual under normal conditions. Social norms followed the same pattern, just as they have followed behavior shaped by natural selection: The farther we move to the left and unrelatedness, the more societies permit marriage, until we come to second cousins, where the genetic picture becomes irrelevant.

Bengtsson (1978) analyzed the costs of inbreeding avoidance among animals. Because I used the terms *costs of inbreeding* and *costs of outbreeding*, I will apply his argument to my case: humans.

Let us define the cost of inbreeding, I_c, as the probability that the progeny will die or be so seriously debilitated that they cannot breed. The probability that the progeny of inbreeding will survive is $1 - I_c$. Let us further define the costs of outbreeding, O_c, as the probability that the outbreeder will die as a result of his outbreeding strategy (e.g., emigration to look for a mate). The probability that the outbreeder will survive is $1 - O_c$. Let us now assume that only males emigrate, that the sex ratio in the group is 1:1 and that every female can have n children.

The genetic fitness of a male who opts for brother–sister incest may be given by the following model:

$$W_i = nI_c0 + n\,.75(1 - I_c) = n\,.75(1 - I_c) \qquad (7.1)$$

where $W_i =$ the genetic fitness of the inbreeder male
$n =$ the number of children a female can have
$I_c =$ the cost of inbreeding as defined

The genetic fitness of a male who decides to outbreed will be

$$W_o = n\,.25O_c + (1 - O_c)(.50n + .25n) \qquad (7.2)$$

where $W_o =$ the genetic fitness of the outbreeder
$O_c =$ cost of outbreeding as defined

The second equation needs some explanation. The outbreeder risks the probability (O_c) that he will die. Yet even if he does, he will have .25 of his genes in each of his sister's n offspring. If he survives $(1 - O_c)$, he will have n children of his own as well as the n children of his sister.

For inbreeding to be the selected strategy, the following inequality must exist:

$$n \ .75(1 - I_c) > n(.75 - .50 \ O_c) \qquad (7.3)$$

that is, where

$$O_c > \tfrac{3}{2} I_c$$

This means that inbreeding will be the preferred option only if the costs of outbreeding are 1½ times the costs of incest. In the human case, this involves very extreme situations. As we have seen (Table 7.1), the costs of incestuous inbreeding are close to .42.

Thus

$$O_c > \tfrac{3}{2}.42 \rightarrow O_c > .63 \qquad (7.4)$$

Thus, only if outbreeding is extremely risky—that is, there is close to two-thirds chance that the outbreeder will die—will incest be a fitness-rewarding choice.

Incest avoidance is, therefore, an evolutionary stable strategy (ESS) (Maynard-Smith, 1978). How has it evolved?

It is not difficult to imagine the evolutionary process that would produce a mechanism (or mechanisms) to render core incest extremely rare but permit inbreeding among first cousins or more distant relatives. As I tried to show in Chapter 2, behavior results from complex interaction between genes and the environment. Let us assume that a gene (or set of genes) caused the hominid to be attracted to his mother (an "oedipal" gene) or sister. This gene would produce recurrent mother–son and sibling incest and few fit offspring (between 40 and 50%). The "oedipal" gene would grow ever rarer and ultimately disappear. But now assume that a "xenophilic" gene emerged which made the hominid avoid all relatives and look for a mate elsewhere. Although the offspring of such xenophilic gene would be healthy, matings would be rare and this gene would also disappear. A set of mutations would therefore emerge and survive: a genome of compromise that would create incest avoidance (see also Bengtsson, 1978).

But because the strategic benefits of inbreeding depend on certain situations, we must expect that first cousin marriages will be prescribed in cases where the costs of outbreeding are very high—that is, in small-scale, nonstratified groups, such as hunter-gatherers, slash-and-burn agriculturalists, and horticulturists (Van den Berghe, 1979). Even in such groups, most people will not follow the prescription. Leach (1962:153) has stated that "preference" of marriage to a first cousin is merely a verbal formula and does not at all correspond to the facts. A group of scientists at Princeton (Kundstadter et al., 1964), using a computer simulation, concluded that matrilineal cross cousin marriage (with the mother's brother's daughter) cannot exceed 27–28% of all marriages, even if everybody wants to abide by the preference rules (under the demographic conditions posited for the simulation). Because there are no known cases of preference rules for all four first cousins at the same time (even those for two are very rare), we can assume that first cousin marriage is rare for demographic reasons even when it is preferred.

These conclusions jeopardize Murdock's famous fifth statement: "incest taboos, in their application to persons outside of the nuclear family, fail strikingly to coincide with nearness of actual biological relationship" [This quote and subsequent quotes are reprinted from Murdock, G. P. *Social Structure*. Copyright 1949 by Macmillan Publishing Co., Inc., renewed 1977 by George Peter Murdock, p. 286]. Murdock's evidence, however, begins at second cousins: "In approximately one fourth of our tribes, for example, certain second cousins are subject to rigid marital prohibitions while first cousins of particular types are allowed or even encouraged to marry [p. 287]." Yet matings between second cousins are biologically irrelevant, and culture can play with them arbitrarily. Murdock points out that although the biological relationship is identical for all four first cousins (father's brother's daughter, father's sister's daughter, mother's sister's daughter, mother's brother's daughter), rules of marriage distinguish among them. The problem with this argument is that, as has been shown by Alexander (1974) and Greene (1978), the four cousins are identically related to ego only if the certainty of paternity is not taken into account. Otherwise, the degree of relatedness is not identical:

1. Mother's sister's daughter—highest
2. Father's sister's daughter—intermediate
3. Mother's brother's daughter—intermediate
4. Father's brother's daughter—lowest

Greene has calculated that cross cousin marriages—(2) and (3)—are, on average, less inbred than parallel cousin marriages—(1) and (4). Moreover, among parallel cousins, marriage with father's brother's daughter is permitted in more societies than is marriage with mother's sister's daughter. Not only certainty of paternity, but also sorrorate and levirate relationships must be taken into consideration in a final analysis of first cousin marriages.

Murdock's conclusion and its supporting evidence were written under the banner of those cultural anthropologists who disbelieved the biological origin of the incest taboo. (Later Murdock [1972] "very slowly and very reluctantly" repudiated his own position.) But Van den Berghe (1979), in analyzing unilinear descent and cross cousin marriage, has shown that these two phenomena were erroneously taken to contradict kin selection theory. In a unilinear descent group, although altruism is formally limited to unilinear relatives, other relatives are brought into the group as mates. To marry your mother's brother's daughter is to marry the closest kin of your own generation who is not from your own clan. Instead of "kin altruism" we see here "reciprocity" in the alliance between unilinear groups. In Van den Berghe's words: "It represents, in effect, the simplest way of eating your kin selection cake (and thereby gaining the organizational advantages of unilinear descent) and having it too (by drawing in your 'lost' relatives as in-laws) [1979:93]." If Murdock's fifth conclusion is irrelevant, and if the biological logic of avoiding too costly inbreeding but practicing a less costly form under specific circumstances in fact conforms to actual behavior, we can declare that *incest regulations seem invariably to have one basic function: the prevention of inbreeding between relatives who share 50% (or close to 50%) of their genes.*

INBREEDING AVOIDANCE IN ANIMALS

Many anthropologists have claimed that incestuous matings are "a natural phenomenon found commonly among animals [Lévi-Strauss, 1969:18]," whereas among humans the phenomenon is rare because it is forbidden. The risks of incest, however, exist throughout the animal world, as we have seen. Recent research has convincingly demonstrated that incest is avoided or prevented in most, if not all, animal species. Let us review the evidence.

Hermaphroditic organisms, such as monoecious plants, as well as most hermaphroditic animals, practice cross-fertilization (Wilson et al., 1973:346). The main selection pressure favoring dioecy (plants housing the two sexes in different organisms) as Maynard-Smith showed, is avoidance of inbreeding (Maynard-Smith, 1978:135).

In bisexual (gonochoristic) animals, there are selective forces for and against inbreeding. The balance is usually in favor of outcrossing. Again according to Maynard-Smith (1978:140), animals might reduce the frequency of inbreeding by recognizing relatives and abstaining from mating with them or by dispersing before sexual maturity. The first strategy is rare, but Hill (1974) showed that if potential partners among deer mouse have been reared together, whether or not they are actual siblings, reproduction is delayed. The same phenomenon has been observed in many species of birds—for example, by Lorenz (1943) in greylag geese, Heinroth (1911) in Egyptian geese, and Hess (Aberle et al., 1963) in Canada geese. The favored strategy in birds is dispersal, as observed by Greenwood and Harvey (1976, 1977) in seven passerine species.

In many animals, females mature before males and thereby little or *clutch* incest is avoided (Bixler 1981b:271).

Bischof (1972a, 1972b, 1975) offers evidence mainly for mammals. Through the mechanism of *family* dissolution, the following species prevent "incest," that is, mating between parent and offspring as well as between uterine siblings: the North American opossum (Reynolds, 1952), various rodents (Eisenberg, 1966), squirrels (Eibl–Eibesfeldt, 1951), the red fox (Tembrock, 1957), the tiger (Schaller, 1967), the European boar (Gundlach, 1968), and the coati (Kaufmann, 1962). Through the mechanism of change of objects, incest is prevented in the red deer, the wapiti, and in Cervidae in general (Darling, 1951; Etkin, 1964; Altmann, 1963), as well as in the African elephant (Ewer, 1968; Hendrichs and Hendrichs, 1971), the zebra (Klingel, 1967), and the dikdik (Hendrichs and Hendrichs, 1971). Packer (1979) enumerates the species of which inbreeding is prevented by male transfer between troops: spotted hyena (Kruuk, 1972), whiptail wallaby (Kaufmann, 1974), lion (Schaller, 1972), and vicuna (Franklin, 1974).

Most of the evidence has been collected on primates. Here we have an overwhelmingly convincing mass of data derived from well-controlled field research undertaken within the last 20 years.

Itani (1972) summarizes the findings of Japanese primatologists. He concludes that in Japanese macaques, mother–son and brother–sister matings are largely prevented because young adolescent males leave the troop and assume a nomadic existence. Father–daughter mating is prevented only in cases in which a male cannot maintain his dominant status in the troop for more than 4 years. A further mechanism for preventing inbreeding is *troop fission*. In one well-documented case (Koyama, 1970), troop fission was accompanied by an exchange of young males between newly formed territorial units.

Packer (1979), who researched the prevention of inbreeding through the transfer of young males, has found this mechanism mentioned in the literature in conjunction with the following primates: the mantled howler, vervet monkeys, ring-tailed lemur, Japanese monkey, rhesus monkey, bonnet monkey, togue monkey, yellow baboon, chacma baboon, Sifaka, red-tail monkey, black and white colobus, Patas monkey, hanuman langur, purple-faced langur, and gelada baboon. Demarest (1977) has summarized the evidence on incest avoidance in nonhuman primates and compared it to the evidence on humans.

Among other researchers investigating the genus *Macaca*, Sade (1968) reported inhibitions of mother–son mating among free-ranging rhesus monkeys on Cayo Santiago. Other primatologists who reported incest avoidance among rhesus monkeys include Altmann (1962), Koford (1963, 1965) and Kaufmann (1965).

Among the baboons (genus *Papio*), Washburn and DeVore (1961), Hall and DeVore (1965), Kummer (1968), and Packer (1979) found several mechanisms to prevent incest. Among the hamadryas, even father–daughter incest is largely prevented by the mechanism of harem building by young wandering males who steal young females from existing harems before they are sexually mature.

The best description of the social system of langurs appears in Hrdy (1977b). The langur social structure, based on one-male harems and wandering male groups and takeovers, largely prevents inbreeding. Although the females in the troops are related to each other, males who must fight their way into a harem are usually the "mixing" factor. Father–daughter incest is possible in cases where a dominant male rules the troop for over 4 years. But these cases are very rare.

Gibbons (Carpenter, 1964) prevents incest because this monogamous species expels male and female adolescents from the family unit.

Among the chimpanzees, several researchers (Reynolds, 1968; Reynolds and Reynolds, 1965; Goodall, 1965, 1967a, 1967b, 1971; Albrecht and Dunnett, 1971) found both inhibition and prevention. Mother–son and brother–sister incest are very rare. Although it is difficult to identify fathers in this comparatively promiscuous species, the transfer of females from one group to another may prevent father–daughter incest (Pusey, 1979:477; 1980).

Among the gorillas, wandering males and the dominance system prevent inbreeding to some extent (Schaller, 1963; Reynolds, 1968), although the data here are much scantier than that for the species mentioned earlier. Harcourt (1979) reported transfer of females among the wild mountain gorilla.

Despite its richness, this material is still not unequivocal evidence. Fist of all, we must ask how such extensive examples of incest avoidance among primates could have remained unknown until recently. This question is easily answered: In the past, most observations of animal behavior were limited to either domesticated or zoo animals. Both of these conditions severely comprise animals' natural inclinations. For example, breeders can easily force animals to mate with close relatives simply by withholding other mates, and zoos contain a necessarily limited number of potential mates. Because our thinking about animals was influenced by the old—and false—distinction between instinct and learning, researchers concluded that if zoo or domestic animals were incestuous, they must not have "an instinct" against incest and that therefore incest avoidance must not be "natural." Also, because breeders succeeded in producing excellent specimens through inbreeding, people concluded that inbreeding did not harm "the species." They forgot, however, that breeding success required unfit specimens to be eliminated and that individual animals cannot evolve a tendency to inbreed, even one that results in "the elimination of deleterious genes," by eliminating some of its own offspring.

Second, the material presented here is not comprehensive. Wildlife observation in natural settings is a laborious, costly, and in some cases nearly impossible task (e.g., the observation of nocturnal animals, marine animals, or animals that live in high altitude foliage). The future may see more research on free-ranging animals. It may also see a greater focus on the problem of inbreeding and incest. Some publications that have been devoted specifically to animal sexuality have failed to mention the problem at all (Wendt, 1968).

Third, it is clear from the preceding material that none of the mechanisms so neatly described and systematically categorized by Bischof works with utmost precision. These mechanisms simply create a low probability of incest. Incest does occur. Thus Missakian (1973) reported that among the Cayo Santiago free-ranging rhesus monkeys, 5.4% of all mountings and copulation involved mother–son pairs. Moreover, 31% of the mother–son pairs, and 12% of the brother–sister pairs, and 12% of the brother–sister pairs, were observed mating. Alexander (1975) has pointed out, however, that each son (except one) that mated with its mother and each brother that mated with its sister was a young adolescent of 3–5 years old, with no access to other females. Even so, the incestuous matings were relatively rare. The mechanisms that render incest infrequent have evolved genetically as psychobiological predispositions. The final cause of incest avoidance is apparently the prevention of *too much* inbreeding.

THE COEVOLUTIONARY PROCESS:
INCEST REGULATIONS IN THREE INCESTUOUS DYADS

It is not sufficient to show that evolution has to deal with incest and that in animals incest is indeed avoided. We must investigate those mechanisms that made incest rare in the human species. The reader will recall that in Chapter 3 we analyzed some important methodological questions. I refer to Table 3.7, which summarizes this analysis. I now fill in the cells in Table 3.7 and illustrate how the different forms of regulations—inhibition, prevention, and prohibition—operate in three different incestuous dyads: mother–son, brother–sister, and father–daughter. Moreover, I attempt to explain the dynamics of the coevolutionary process and show how the epigenetic rules that had evolved were translated into cultural forms. In other words, I examine how origins, persistence, and functions can be distinguished and their integrated effect understood.

Mother–Son Incest Inhibition

Mother–son incest has been inhibited since the early primate past. The dependence of higher primate offspring on their mother was total—for food, locomotion, security, and learning—and lengthy. Although in some species mother substitutes (allmothering) have evolved (see Hrdy, 1977a, 1977b), an infant who loses its mother is usually doomed. Such complete dependence creates a very clear dominant–submissive relationship between mother and offspring. Sade (1968) summarized his findings among rhesus macaques as follows:

> Males who remain with their natal group are inhibited from mating with their mothers by the reverberance of the role of infant in their adult relationships with their mothers. The role of the infant is incompatible with the role of mate when the same female is the object. The mother's superior dominance is a key part of the relationship, for if the son can successfully challenge his mother's dominance, the inhibition is broken and he will mate with her. Outside of the mother–son relationship a female's superior dominance risk is not sufficient to inhibit mating, since several males mated with higher-ranking unrelated females without any reluctance [p. 36].

Similar findings were reported by Imanishi (1965), Tokuda (1961), and Missakian (1972, 1973) in macaques, Goodall (1968) in chimpanzees, and Demarest (1977) in baboons, langurs, chimpanzees, and gibbons.

If Sade (1968) and Kortmulder (1974) are right, sooner or later we can expect to find mother–son intercourse inhibited in every species that (a) lives in groups; and (b) is characterized by a complete and lengthy infant dependence on the mother.

Humans clearly meet these criteria. Indeed, in humans these criteria are not only met but moveover exaggerated. Without the group, human individuals are utterly lost, and human infants are so totally dependent on their mothers (or allomothers) that infants who are fed but receive no other attention fail to thrive (Davis, 1940, 1947; Lyons, 1978).

I have already warned against the careless application of animal data to human beings. Following Wilson (1975), I recommended against analogies and in favor of homologies—and even among homologies I recommended choosing only those that have a long phylogenetic evolution and continue uninterruptedly from nonhuman primates to humans. I think that the mother-son incest prohibition satisfies these requirements, for in humans this inhbition works on the same principles as in other primates:

1. The human infant, being, during the long process of socialization, completely dependent on the mother and submissive to her develops a neuropsychological model of its relationship with her.
2. The imcompatibility of this model with that of the sexual relationship between males and females, which involves aggression and male dominance, successfully inhibits the development of a sexual relationship between mother and son.
3. Both models are genetically predisposed but must be triggered by social and psychological conditions. Thus, if a son's ontogeny does not include dependence on and submission to his mother (e.g., if the child were separated from her and socialized by someone else), the neuro-psychological model—and hence inhibition—will not be activated. *What is genetically determined is the predisposition toward inhibition under certain conditions characteristic to the species.* The inhibition does not always work, because the characteristic conditions are not always present.

Thus we have here "a genetically determined procedure that directs the assembly of the mind"—that is, an epigenetic rule which will create a biased ethnographic curve. The rule will not eliminate mother–son incest completely, but it will make it exceedingly rare.

Must we then discard the entire psychoanalytic literature on the Oedipus complex? Certainly not, but we have to restudy it. We have to know the conditions of socialization in order to know whether the lack of inhibition is a result of the male infant's having been socialized since very early by nurses, in which case its attraction to its mother was not inhibited. Freud (1953:126–132) does not present extensive data on the early socialization of the children he studied. In that most of his cases probably came from middle- and upper-class Viennese families, among whom nurses, maids, or grandmothers were common mother substitutes, the evidence for the Oedipal theory may be based on clinical cases quite uncharacteristic of the normal socializing situation.

Van den Berghe (in press) argues that the mother–son incest inhibition is not basically different from brother–sister incest inhibition, which I called "a negative imprinting" mechanism (Shepher, 1971a, 1971b; see also earlier). "It is premised on the expectation that the avoidance is greater where both potential partners are negatively imprinted on each other, than where only one of the parties is negatively imprinted." For Van den Berghe, "mother–son incest is least common because . . . the more aggressive and promiscuous individual in the pair (son) lacks both the power to enforce his will (because he is much younger) and the desire for incest (because of the negative imprinting)."

According to Van den Berghe (in press), Freud distorted the original Oedipus story of Sophocles:

> Oedipus did not imprint against his mother because, as Sophocles tell us, he was separated from her in infancy as was raised by foster parents. The prophecy of incest was realized because the cultural norm of parents raising their own children was violated. The injunction not to tempt fate was merely a mystifying way of saying: don't buck the system. While Sophocles would probably have resisted my prosaic interpretation as threatening the grandeur of his play, I am convinced that he would have regarded Freud as an inspired crackpot.

I certainly agree with Van den Berghe's statement, but with one small amendment: for the phrase "because the cultural norm of parents raising their own children was violated," I would substitute: "because the epigenetic rule stemming from our mammalian legacy that mothers rear their own children was violated." Yet the two theories complement, rather than contradict, each other. We can better understand how they complement each other by studying the second important mechanism—prevention.

Mother–Son Incest Prevention

Mother–son incest may be prevented by removing the young male as soon as he is sexually mature. It may also be prevented by allowing him to remain in his native troop but to be subject to interferences from older males. Finally, it may be prevented if the son's sexual maturity and his mother's reproductive phase do not coincide or if the mother leaves the group. All these mechanisms operate in the primate world. The first occurs among solitary pair-bonding animals like the gibbon (Carpenter, 1964) and harem polygynists like the hamadryas baboon (Kummer, 1971) and the langur (Hrdy, 1977b). Some multimale groups species like the howler monkey (Carpenter, 1965), the rhesus monkey (Carpenter, 1942), and the olive baboon (Packer, 1979) also remove juvenile males from the troop. In some species, the male seeks to leave the troop, a process Bischof calls "emancipation and quest for autonomy." The second mechanism—interference with the juvenile's sexual activity is documented for the Japanese macaque (Imanishi, 1963), the hamadryas baboon (Kummer, 1968), and other baboon species (Hall and DeVore, 1965; Washburn and DeVore, 1961a, 1961b).

The third mechanism occurs in species where males are sexually mature for relatively long periods and females for a short period. Simonds (1974) gives the following data on the chimpanzee: male subadult stage, 6–10 years; female adult stage, 6–8 years; longevity, 24+ years; birth periodicity, 1–4 years. Only a first- or second-born male could mate with his mother. Nishida (1979) and Pusey (1979) indicate that among chimpanzees, female transfer is the main mechanism that prevents mother–son incest. Slater's (1959) analysis of demographic prevention of mother–son incest can be used for nonhuman primates, although I am not aware of an analysis of primate age structure similar to that of Slater for man.

Is mother–son incest prevented in humans? We have already seen Slater's (1959) convincing analysis of prevention by demographic givens. The fact that mothers are too old to be mates when their sons come of age is a biological fact that can be changed by cultural means. If, contrary to Slater's assumptions, the lifetime of the mother is considerably extended, demographic prevention will not work.

Male initiation ceremonies come immediately in mind in conjunction with prevention. Cohen (1964) assumes that children have fantasies of marrying their parents and siblings without being aware of the sexual connotations of marriage. He writes: "The simplest way to cope with children who are directing their sexual excitation to members of the nuclear family is to remove them physically from the family [p. 53]." Instances of removal are many: the Nyakyusa (Wilson, 1951) establish age villages for boys. English upper-class parents send their adolescent sons to boarding schools. The Andaman Islanders and the Tikopia send their adolescents to adoptive friends and kinsmen to remove then from the parents' house. The Tallensi establish a special house for adolescent boys.

Typically, physical removal is followed by a series of cermonies in which boys—especially in unilinear societies—are symbolically removed from the women's world. The ceremonies represent the transition from childhood, in which the young male lives with the females of the family—his mother and sisters. He has to be extracted from this world in order to be able to do those tasks that males usually do (Tiger and Fox, 1971; Fox, 1980).

Although demographic preventions are biological, the extrusion of adolescent boys is certainly cultural. Tiger and Fox (1971) consider the process to be part of the human "biogrammar"; that is, they confer upon it the status of an epigenetic rule. However, the biased ethnographic curve resulting from the cross-cultural investigation of the phenomenon is not convincing. Thus Cohen (1964) found in a sample of 65 cultures that initiation ceremonies, while prevalent in unilinear societies in which socialization is carried out by parents and other members of the child's descent group, are lacking in other societies. All in all, he found initiation ceremonies in only 19 cultures, less than 30% of his sample. Young (1962) found a relationship between the degree of male solidarity in the culture and male initiation ceremonies. Whiting, Kluckhohn, and Anthony (1958) linked harsh initiation ceremonies to long lactation and postpartum sex taboos. Nonetheless, Fox (1980) expresses certainty about the significance of initiation ceremonies and the extrusion of male adolescents:

> Kinship and initiation ceremonies are the social expression of the taming of these emotions [the young male's ambivalent feelings toward the old male and his own access to women] and the socializing of them. But these two sets of institutions are not free creations of the intellect. The brain is geared, wired, or what have you, to produce them in some form or other, since it is itself the product of the forces they represent. The brain faithfully reproduces a version of what produced it in the first place—or rather produced it over many millions of years of primate evolution [pp. 161–162].

Although I believe Fox is right, at present sufficient evidence simply does not exist. Thus, for the time being we do not know whether in the human case preventions are closer to inhibitions (i.e., are genetically predisposed) or closer to prohibitions (i.e., are cultural inventions).

Mother–Son Incest Prohibition

We might ask why mother–son incest would have had to be prohibited, given that most males did not want to mate with their mothers, and the minority that may have wanted to were probably incapable of it. Prohibition might have developed in this way:

1. Prohibitions are consciously elaborated cultural rules and could have appeared only after humans had developed a symbolic system of communication. By that time, inhibition and prevention had rendered mother–son incest so rare that its avoidance was viewed as part of the natural order. As many informants of anthropologists have declared, and as Levy-Bruhl (1963:231) aptly stated:

> *L'etude des temoignages etablira, qu'en effet l'inceste, a leurs yeux, est avant tout quelque chose d'anormal, d'insolite, de contre nature, qui porte malheur, en un mot, une "transgression".*

Non pas . . . un acte moralement condamnable, mais un acte inhabituel et contre nature, que revèle une mauvaise influence en train de s'exercer, comme celui de la chevre qui mange ses excrements. . . .

[The study of witnesses establishes that in effect incest, in their eyes, is above all something abnormal, unprecedented, against nature, something that brings disaster, in short a "transgression."
It is not . . . a morally condemnable act, but an unusual and unnatural act, which, by being practiced, reveals a bad influence, like the goat that eats its own excrement.]

2. Because people could not tolerate even a few exceptional cases— precisely because they were so monstrously exceptional—they prohibited them.
3. Later, when the concept of the order of nature received religious sanction, incest prohibitions were incorporated into the moral and religious order.
4. Prohibition seemed successful and absolute because mother–son incest was also both inhibited *and* prevented. In fact, the prohibition probably did no more than eliminate a very few exceptional cases.

We can see the truth of this argument if we compare the prohibition of mother–son incest with prohibitions that have not been prepared for and buttressed by both inhibitions and prevention. For example, nepotism is forbidden in bureaucratic systems of modern, universalistic societies. But the success of rules prohibiting nepotism is spotty. There are so many transgressions that loopholes have appeared in the legal system to accomodate them. Other relatively unsuccessful prohibitions extend to premarital and extramarital sex and to ritual food taboos. (For similar arguments, see Bixler, 1981b, and Van den Berghe, in press.)

The coevolutionary process has thus been completed. Biological evolution gave rise to an epigenetic rule, a genetically predetermined procedure that worked in what was statistically an overwhelmingly prevalent social situation: mothers rearing their sons. In the majority of cases, mothers did socialize their sons themselves, but culture created new "culturgens"—for example, social situations in which mothers did not socialize their sons: queens who did not have time for such everyday activities, upper middle-class mothers who were too busy with shopping and philanthropic activities, and prostitutes who had to supply their clients. In those cases, the inhibition did not work. Yet the exceptional cases of incest contradicted the natural order that had been perceived by humans, and therefore culture had to proscribe. Thus culture supplemented what nature had prepared—biological and cultural evolution worked together.

Brother–Sister Incest Inhibition

Let us now inquire into the second incestuous dyad—that of brother and sister. Brother–sister mating is as genetically harmful as mother–son mating and is as likely to be inhibited. We found a paradigm of brother–sister inhibition in the kibbutz research and in the sim-pua marriage. Because kibbutz children reared together in small peer groups are genetically unrelated, researchers could discover how the inhibition works: not through some mystical "voice of the blood," but, again, *through a genetically determined predisposition to be imprinted against those with whom one has been cosocialized and with whom one has had close physical contact during early childhood.* This imprinting against feeling erotic attraction makes kibbutz children completely avoid "incest." Yet the kibbutz situation is the statistically prevalent social situation for uterine or full siblings in the primate world and probably in the entire mammalian world. For birds, Lorenz (1943) has found in greylag geese, Heinroth (1911) in Egyptian geese, and Hess (Aberle *et al.*, 1963) in Canada geese that pair formation is not possible between siblings reared together, although it is quite possible for siblings reared apart. We have less evidence of brother–sister avoidance among primates, perhaps because of a lack of interest among researchers and because of the difficulty of following sibling pairs over time. Nevertheless, Goodall (1971) witnessed avoidance of brother–sister incest in chimpanzees. Demarest (1977) has evidence on macacas, gibbons, and baboons. In Chapter 5, we saw the human evidence.

Although Kortmulder (1974) and Van den Berghe (in press) hold that mother–son and brother–sister inhibition both originate in the same mechanism—namely, the inhibition of aggression and dominance—I think that the two are basically different even though they both function to inhibit inbreeding.

In mother–son dyads, we have an adult and a dependent, submissive juvenile. For such situations, Kortmulder's aggression–dominance inhibition is right. But for siblings, the inhibitions are quite different. A brother is usually dominant over and aggressive toward his sister, especially if he is older. The human male is usually stronger than the female of comparable age, and he therefore has the "dose" of dominance and aggression needed to mate with her. If sexual intercourse or erotic attraction are avoided, it is because of negative imprinting, as explained in Chapter 5. In fact, my original explanation

(Shepher, 1971b:235–237) included a neurophysiological mechanism very similar to that of Demarest (1977:334–337), albeit much less elaborate.

Demarest, relying on the works of Sokolow and Pribram, comes to the following conclusion:

> We are in a position to explain the lowering of intensity during socialization of both aggression and sexual attraction. The amygdala has strong neural connections with the preventicular area. It is therefore possible that the electrical changes caused by novelty are carried from the amygdala to the preventicular area and disequilibrate receptors in a selective fashion creating feelings of sexual attraction, fear, or aggression, depending on the amount of novelty in the situation [p. 336].

It is not clear whether Demarest distinguishes between the two inhibitions (mother–son, brother–sister), although there is some indication that he does, as he emphasizes that both aggression and sexual attraction are lowered. The lowering of aggression stands at the core of the mother–son incest prohibition, the lowering of sexual attraction at the core of brother–sister incest inhibition. What Demarest describes is, obviously, the essence of an epigenetic rule. It is no wonder that Lumsden and Wilson (1980, 1981) took the case of sibling incest avoidance as the archetype of epigenetic rules.

There is, however, another and more important difference between mother–son and brother–sister sexual activity. Mother–son incest is inhibited by a pattern almost universal among mammals, a pattern not easily interfered with. Sibling incest is inhibited by a pattern that is not necessarily universal and is more easily disrupted: If a brother and sister are a sufficient number of years apart in age (probably more than 4) the inhibition mechanism does not work. If, for instance, children are spaced every 3 years, and the first two children are sons and the third are spaced every 3 years, and the first two children are sons and the third a daughter, the elder brother and his sister will be exempt from the inhibition if only because he will have passed the critical period by the time she is born. The inhibition may also be disrupted by separating siblings or by interfering with their childhood sex play.

Brother–Sister Incest Prevention

The mechanisms that prevent mother–son mating also prevent mating between full siblings, although probably less effectively. But "in the beginning" there was likely less interference than in recorded history, and we can assume the brother–sister inhibition preceded culture. Humans emerged from their hominid past subject to both types of incest inhibition.

Demographic prevention was less effective for brothers and sisters than for mothers and sons simply because the age difference between the sexes was smaller. Peripheral males who returned to their native groups could mate with their sisters if sexual attraction between them was not inhibited. Nevertheless, inhibition and the various preventive mechanisms effectively rendered brother–sister incest very rare.

Brother–Sister Incest Prohibition

Prohibition of brother–sister incest resembled that of mother–son incest. Once people started adding prohibitions to existing inhibitions and preventive mechanisms, the prohibitions had to be extended to even younger ages. This extension resulted in the separation of siblings and hence weakened the formation of inhibitions, which in turn, strengthened attraction, which prompted more and more elaborate prohibitions such as avoidance taboos. Other symbolic patterns, such as unilinear descent, intensified this process. Thus, if in a matrilinear descent group the sisters were "sanctified" by carrying the name of the lineage as well as its economic and symbolic values, the prohibitions would grow stronger than in a patrilinear group, where sisters became outsiders by leaving the patrilineage. We have to remember that in patrilineal societies wives usually live with the husband's family, and in matrilineal societies that pattern coexists with the pattern of a husband living with his wife's family or a nephew living with his mother's brother upon marriage (Van den Berghe, 1979). Thus the cultural evolution of the brother–sister taboo in a group like the Trobriander or the Ashanti would be as follows:

1. Incest is rare because of inhibition and prevention.
2. Avoidance of sex between brother and sister becomes part of the natural order.
3. Rare, "monstrous" transgressions are prohibited.
4. Prohibitions are extended to earlier ages.
5. Interference with cosocialization of siblings weakens inhibition.
6. Erotic attraction between siblings becomes more frequent.
7. Sterner prohibitions result in avoidance rules.
8. Matrilineal descent rules corroborate avoidance rules.
9. The entire process reaches a state of equilibrium in which people

experience guilt feelings about sibling incest, and the punishment for incest is death.

In patrilineal descent groups the process was probably different, because the sister who married an outsider left the family early. But avoidance rules and strict punishment of sibling incest can also develop in a patrilineal descent group; they are simply less common. Goody (1956) found these differences of frequency between patrilineal and matrilineal descent groups, although he explained them in terms of the two systems' different attitudes toward women (see later, Chapter 10).

A third difference between mother–son and sibling incest is that whereas there is only one kind of mother, there are three kinds of siblings: (a) uterine—having the same mother but different fathers; (b) uterine—agnatic or full siblings—having the same mother and father; and (c) agnatic—having the same father but different mothers.

If my theory is correct, we can assume that among uterine and full siblings, incest would be more severely inhibited than among agnatic siblings, unless the mothers live in the same household. Unfortunately, distinctions between different sorts of siblings in the ethnographic literature are very rare. The Bible mentions two cases of agnatic sibling incest (Abraham and Sarah, Amnon and Tamar). Van den Berghe and Mesher (1980) indicate that royal sibling marriages in seven African kingdoms (Monomotapa, Ankole, Bunyoro, Buganda, Zande, Shilluk, and Dahomey) were between agnatic half-siblings. This was probably the case, too, in the famous Egyptian and Hawaiian marriages, since the kings were highly polygynous. We can only infer the degree of inhibition in a culture from counting transgressions (the greater the inhibition, the fewer the transgressions) or from gauging the strictness of its prohibitions (the stricter the prohibitions, the lower the inhibition). This last inference is exactly the opposite of that used by Ember (1975) (see Chapter 6).

Father–Daughter Incest Inhibition

As we have seen (p. 95), father–daughter incest is the only form of incest that "pays" genetically compared to outbreeding. I therefore predicted that we would find father–daughter incest to be more common that than sibling incest, and, in fact, evidence of the inhibition of the former dyad is extremely scanty. Why?

First of all, for such a dyad to be inhibited, it must be distinguishable from other male–female dyads. Both mother–son and sibling dyads are made distinguishable because of parturition, lactation, and the long duration of socialization. The inhibitions in these cases develop during the long cohabitation of the two sexes of the dyad. But a father–daughter dyad may not be distinguishable from other male–female pairs. For example, in a relatively promiscuous group, like that of the chimpanzee, where almost every adult male has approximately the same chance to mate with every female in heat, the father–daughter dyad is indistinguishable, although research indicates that female adolescents leave the troop (Nishida, 1979; Pusey, 1979, 1980). The same can be said about a multimale group such as a yellow baboon or rhesus troop. Only in a one-male troop, like that of the hamadryas or gelada baboon or langur, is it possible to distinguish a father–daughter dyad from other male–female pairs. There the alpha male and any adolescent female in his harem constitute a father–daughter dyad. But this situation holds true only if the dominant male maintains his dominance long enough for his daughters to reach sexual maturity.

Hrdy (1977b) describes langur females who solicit "stolen," "adulterous" copulation with males who haunt the outskirts of their troop. Her explanation is very interesting:

> One explanation for these adulterous solicitations is that females are acting so as to pass on the genetic benefits of outbreeding to their offspring. This explanation is consistent with the finding that the highest incidence of extratroop adultery, in a small number of hours of observation, was reported for the School troop, which was politically the most stable of the troops studied at Abu and for this reason probably the most inbred. In most troops, given the pattern of male take-overs about once every few years, a relatively constant influx of new genetic material is virtually assured. But in the case of the School troop, Harelip had managed to remain in residence for at least five years (based on the composition of the troop when first encountered in 1971). This male with the defective lip probably fathered a young adult female and one, or possibly two, juvenile males who shared this defect, as well as other animals in the troop under five years of age. Therefore, solicitation of extratroop males by a young School troop female could reflect a bias among langurs against situations that would lead to close inbreeding. The fact that Harelip consistently interfered with attempts by young females, suspected of being his daughters to copulate with males outside the troop could be explained if these females (whose progenitive opportunities might be fewer than Harelip's) had relatively more to lose from a pairing of deleterious genes in their offspring than Harelip did [This quote and subsequent quotes are reprinted from Hrdy, Sarah B. The Langurs or Abu, 1977, Harvard University Press. pp 137, 140].

In a footnote, Hrdy adds corroborative material on multimale groups (rhesus and Japanese macaques), in which it was found that *none* of the alpha males maintained his dominant position for more than 4 years. (It would be helpful if we had an explanation of the mechanism behind such behavior. No such explanation is yet available.) Bixler (1981b) quotes an unpublished paper by J. L. Hoogland on father–daughter incest avoidance a among prairie dogs.

Another research that the inhibition of father–daughter incest is problematic lies in the different parental investment of the sexes. Because the male invests considerably less in his offspring than the female, he spends less of his time with them. An analysis of parental care for the species *Macaca sylvana* by Lahiri and Southwick (1966) yielded the data shown in Table 7.4:

TABLE 7.4
Time Spent with Mother, with Dominant Male, and with Peers in *Macaca sylvana*

Age	With mother	With dominant male	With other adults and juveniles	Play
	Way in which time spent (%)			
0–4 weeks	82	7.5	5.7	5.6
4–8 weeks	72.9	7.6	1.9	17.6
8–12 weeks	51.5	8.1	.9	39.6

The difference between the parental investment of the sexes in the infant is obvious. Even the gradual emancipation of the infant from its mother does not significantly increase the parental investment of the male, but rather the time spent in individual play.

Although in humans the father's investment is higher than it is in most primate species, it is still much lower than the mother's. If the division between hunting and gathering was an important stage in hominization, hunting males probably could not spend a lot of time with their children. Fathers were also dominant to all their children. Mothers, too, were dominant to their children, but fathers' dominance over their daughters was consistent with successful mating. Nevertheless, in spite of the scarcity of evidence, Bixler (1981b:273) thinks it probable that father–daughter incest was also inhibited. He admits that even if it were, the inhibition was one sided: The daughter was more inhibited than the father.

Father–Daughter Incest Prevention

Slater (1959) pointed out that for demographic reasons father–daughter incest was subject to fewer preventive measures than mother–son incest. The reason is that females mature sexually 2–3 years earlier than males. But demographic factors probably did prevent father–daughter incest to some extent. In cases where one-male hominid groups took over females from other groups, the sudden appearance of a new dominant male and the abduction of immature females might both have prevented father–daughter mating.

We do not know whether such primeval hordes with one-male harems actually existed. Nor do we know whether there was constant fighting among the males for possession of harems, which would have resulted in frequent rotation of dominance positions. Even if such a pattern at one time held, it probably ended before hunting became a cooperative venture. One-male harems are compatible with scavenging or with individual hunting, but certainly not with cooperative hunting. Thus early hominids entered a new period of social existence with father–daughter incest hardly inhibited and only partly prevented. Some fathers (hunting necessarily resulted in more recognizable fathers; see Shepher, 1978) occasionally committed incest with their daughters, mainly when they were unable to acquire additional wives. Only at this stage was father–daughter incest first prohibited.

Father–Daughter Incest Prohibition

Why was father–daughter incest prohibited? If it is true that the dynamics of prohibition lead it to work on rarities, the element of rarity was in this case less conspicuous. Father–daughter incest was an alternative for outmating if the age structure within the family permitted it and if an absence of additional wives made it worthwhile. The problem was that cooperative hunting was incompatible with a situation in which one male mated with several females while his hunting partners remained solitary. Moreover, one can assume that by this evolutionary stage, symbolic thinking was sufficiently evolved for humans to be able to envision the future: A father's interest was in securing the cooperation of a younger hunter who, when the father was too old to hunt, could offer help. This is a recurrent theme with Australian hunters (Hart and Pilling, 1960; Yengoyan, 1968) and in Nyae Nyae and !Kung San (Lee and DeVore, 1976; Marshall, 1976). Apparently fathers imposed prohibitions on incestuous mating with their daughters because of their own dire need, *not of outside alliance*, but of partners for their most important enterprise.

Here we have the first instance of a prohibition being a more decisive factor rather than simply an addition to existing and successful inhibition and prevention. The ultimate shaping of the human family probably did not take place until the stage of cooperative hunting, the stage at which the parental investment of the human male reached a comparatively high rate. When the mate finally became attached to the mother–offspring group, and father–daughter incest was prohibited, the principles of descent and alliance that Fox (1975, 1980) considers the final stage of hominization coalesced, and the hominization process was complete.

Yet father–daughter incest remained distinct from mother–son and sibling incest in that its regulation relied heavily on prohibition. Not subject to considerable inhibition and prevention, as were the other two dyads, fathers and, to a lesser extent, daughters were exposed to temptation whenever their group's internal arrangement happened to be conducive—that is, when it lacked additional female mates for fathers and outside males to mate with daughters.

In analyzing the origin of incest regulations, one need not presuppose a human family creating these regulations to preserve itself. On the contrary, incest regulations created the human family. Of course, the family, once in existence, benefited tremendously from them.

PERSISTENCE OF INCEST REGULATIONS

Why do incest regulations survive? Their basic function, or final cause, is ostensibly the prevention of close inbreeding. But geneticists tell us that close inbreeding might be less harmful for highly inbred populations than for those with low average inbreeding coefficients (Alexander, n.d.). During the long history of humankind there certainly have been instances of small isolated and highly inbred populations. Such populations exist today in many parts of the world (Bodmer and Cavalli-Sforza, 1976:381–383). Yet the rigor of incest regulations has not varied with the inbreeding coefficients of the isolated groups. (We are talking here only about the core incestuous dyads: mother–son, sibling, and father–daughter.) Incest regulations must therefore survive because they have additional value. We now turn to these additional values or secondary functions.

Secondary Functions: Maintenance of the Nuclear Family

Secondary functions are not necessarily less important than primary functions. Once incest regulations had eliminated close inbreeding, attention was drawn to their more immediate, day-to-day benefits. Most social scientists agree that incest regulations function to benefit the family in its primary task of socializing the young (even if some—e.g., Levy, 1955—deny the universal existence of the nuclear family). Alliance theorists (primarily White) may deny that family integration is the basis of incest regulations, but they do not deny their beneficiary impact.

Freud, Malinowski, Seligman, Murdock, and Parsons analyzed the functions of the incest taboo in detail. Their arguments are of great value *if we accept that incest regulations did not come into being to maintain the preexisting order of the nuclear family.* If we do *not* accept this, we use a group selectionist argument par excellence and end up maintaining that incest regulations are the result of purely cultural evolution. This argument contains a logical contradiction: If the nuclear family is based on a system of four double roles (as Parsons, Bales, Zelditch, and many others have claimed), this system could not have come into being without the prior existence of incest regulations, which originated elsewhere.

The best illustration of such a situation that I know of comes from a French chivalric legend adapted by the Middle High German poet Hartman von Aue (ca. 1165–1210) and rendered into modern prose by Thomas Mann in his novel *Der Erwäehlte* (published in English in 1951 as *The Holy Sinner*). This is the story of a "Great Pope," Gregorius of the Rock, who, according to the story, was born to Wiligis and Sybilla, twin children of the Prince of Flanders and Artois. The two children were so beautiful and noble that they could not conceive of finding other suitable mates, and they fell in love and begot a son. Aware of their terrible sin, they listened to the advice of a wise courtier. Wiligis took the cross and set out on a long journey to the Holy Sepulchre, but he died en route. His wife–sister bore the child and, following the courtier's advice, put the child out to sea in a case when he was 17 days old. The child was found by a fisherman on one of the Channel Islands and was adopted by Abbot Gregorius, who baptized him and gave him the name Gregorius. At the age of 17, the fact of his adoption was revealed to him, whereupon he left the monastery, became a knight, and returned to the Continent. He landed at Brugge, which was the last remaining city of the princedom of Flanders and Artois, the rest having been conquered by the Prince of Burgundy, who had tried in vain for the hand of Sybilla. Gregorius defeated the Prince in a duel and married Sybilla, who bore him two daughters. Three years later he discovered that he had mated with his own mother and begot two daughter–sisters. After a 17-year penance, during which time Gregorius lived on a solitary rock in the sea, he was elected Pope, through a divine revelation to one of the noble Romans. The two daughters, who had been named *Stultitia* (stupidity) and *Humilitas* (humility), were brought by their mother to the Pope. She confessed her terrible sins to him, only to find out that the Pope was her son–husband.

Let us examine the roles of the dramatis personae:

Wiligis:	brother and husband to Sybilla
	father, uncle, and brother-in-law to Gregorius
	grandfather and uncle to Stultitia and Humilitas
Sybilla:	sister and wife to Wiligis
	mother, aunt, and wife to Gregorius
	mother, grandmother and, grandaunt
	(grandfather's sister) to Stultitia and Humilitas
Gregorius:	son, nephew, and brother-in-law to Wiligis
	son, nephew, and husband to Sybilla
	father, brother, and cousin (mother's brother's
	son) to Stultitia and Humilitas
Stultitia and Humilitas:	granddaughters and nieces to Wiligis
	daughters and granddaughters to Sybilla
	daughters, sisters, and cousins (father's sister's
	daughters) to Gregorius

Although this list is not exhaustive (it does not include role sets unfamiliar to Western society), none of the roles coincides with the four role sets of the normal nuclear family (husband–father, wife–mother, brother–son, sister–daughter). If roles are not just names, but expectations of certain forms of behavior and relationships, the possibility for chaos if obvious. Incest regulations which created the human family also helped to maintain it and therefore have persisted regardless of the degree of inbreeding of populations.

Secondary Functions: Alliance of Groups

Although the alliance theorists, especially White, tried to explain all the core dyads, only father–daughter incest regulations actually fit to some extent with alliance theory. Parsons and Murdock, who tried to synthesize family socialization theory with the alliance theory, realized that the younger generation is "channeled out" through incest regulations, but they did not distinguish the origin of the regulations for each dyad separately.

There is no doubt that a secondary function of incest regulations is to *prevent the isolation of the nuclear family*, but whether such regulations created alliances remains an open question.

Even the father–daughter incest prohibition probably originated in the father's need for cooperation from younger males and not necessarily from the need for alliances. Once, however, this prohibition was firmly established, it (and regulations of other incestuous dyads) fused the cooperation and alliances of families and wider social units.

Both secondary functions are cultural in origin and can be explained by group selectionist arguments. Problems arise only if one argues that family organization, socialization, or the creation of alliances *were themselves the origins* of incest regulations.

Secondary Functions: Extensions of the Incest Taboo

All the classic texts on incest theory pay close attention to the "extensions of the incest taboo." From the mid-nineteenth century onward, marriage regulations have been considered such extensions, because classificatory kinship terms lead people to think that identical kinship terms for different individuals extend incest taboos accordingly. For example, if two relatives are called by the same kinship term *sister*, even if one is actually a first or second cousin, the incest taboo on the sister is believed to extend to the cousin. But because taboos are symbolic cultural norms, they can be extended without limit. Thus, among the Nyae-Nyae San (Marshall, 1976), incest taboos are extended to persons who have the same name as the tabooed person yet are completely unrelated to ego. But norms are different from actual behavior. If a Nyae-Nyae San is prohibited from marrying a girl because she is called !U like his mother, he nevertheless knows the precise difference between the relationships of the two women to him as well as the predictable reaction from members of his society if he mates with either.

If we accept that incest regulations have evolved in order to prevent close inbreeding through mechanisms of inhibition, prevention, and, later, prohibition, and that *some* of these regulations became taboos, then extensions of those taboos to people who are less closely related or unrelated are possible, but irrelevant to the topic. Relevant to the topic, however, is whether the unlimited symbolic creativity of a culture contradicts biology.

I do not think that it does. We have seen earlier (p. 103) that Murdock's fifth conclusion is irrelevant because from second cousin outward culture cannot contradict the basic biological function. But Murdock's fourth conclusion preserves the proper relationship of biology and culture: "Our fourth conclusion is that incest taboos tend to apply with *diminished intensity* [my emphasis] to kinsmen outside of the nuclear family, even though they are designated by the same kinship terms as primary relatives [1949:286]." The reader will recall that I assumed that the power of a theory lies in its ability to predict actual behavior. *If Murdock's fourth conclusion is verified by his own cross-cultural data, and if his fifth conclusion is irrelevant, then the thesis of inbreeding prevention as the final cause of incest regulations, including taboos, is proven.* We can find additional evidence for the irrelevance of extensions of the incest taboos. Schneider (1976:151) states that in some cultures, like the Etoro in New Guinea, homosexual relations are included among the incest taboos, which, he argues, shows that the taboos are wholly cultural and not at all biological in origin. If this were true, we would expect that (*a*) despite their reproductive sterility, homosexual relations would be included in incest taboos with the same frequency as heterosexual relations; and (*b*) transgressions of homosexual incest taboos would be punished as severely as those of heterosexual taboos.

I do not know of many cultures in which homosexuality is included in incest taboos, nor does Schneider provide additional examples. I cannot know what would happen had the Etoro boy whom Schneider mentions engaged in fellatio with his father rather than with his uncle, but I assume that the Etoro would have been more upset if the boy had made love to his mother or if the father had slept with his daughter.

THE EVIDENCE

In the introduction to this chapter, I predicted (*a*) the differential frequency of committed incest in the various incestual dyads; (*b*) the differential opposition of the sexes to incest; (*c*) the specific situations in which incest will occur; and (*d*) the increasing cultural variability of norms regulating sexual intercourse between partners who are less related than the core incestuous dyads.

In order to present evidence for the first prediction, we should have data on total committed incest (without distinguishing among incestuous dyads). Unfortunately, this seems to be practically impossible. Sexual activity is conducted in private, especially when it is specifically tabooed. In addition, we have the problem of definition, as is illustrated by the following quote from *Father–Daughter Incest* (Herman, 1981):

> Our definition of incest reflected a predominantly psychological rather than a biological or social concept of the taboo. Incest was defined to mean any sexual relationship between a child and an adult in a position of paternal authority.
>   We further defined a sexual relationship to mean any physical contact that had to be kept a secret [p. 70].

Similar definitions abound in books and articles on this subject (for a comprehensive bibliography, see Bixler, 1981c; Van den Berghe, in press; Willner, 1975).

Table 7.5 summarized the frequencies that this author was able to find in the literature. If we accept the definition of incest as sexual intercourse with a relative $r \geq 0.25$, the alarming frequencies of the "incest epidemic" (*Newsweek*, November 30, 1981, p. 68) shrink considerably. Thus I tend to agree with

TABLE 7.5
Estimates of General Frequency of Incest

Source	Frequency	Sample
Kinsey *et al.* (1953)	4.00	General females
Gebhard *et al.* (1965)	9.00	Sex offenders
Gebhard *et al.* (1965)	2.00	Control groups
Armstrong (1978)	12	Child abuse (estimate)
Forward and Buck (1978)	5.00	Estimate
Hughes (1964)	(335)	England and Wales, crime statistics
Maisch (1968)	(436)	West Germany, crime statistics, 1965
Maisch (1968)	(111)	West Germany, crime statistics, 1965
Maisch (1968)	.0009	New Zealand, crime statistics
Maisch (1968)	.00051	Canada, crime statistics
Maisch (1968)	.00069	Scotland, crime statistics
Maisch (1968)	3.6	of all criminals in the British commonwealth 1900–1930
Weinberg (1955:39)	.00011	United States, 1930
Riemer (1936)	.000673	Sweden
Meiselman (1978:31)	1.00–2.00	Estimate
Bixler (1981a–c)	.03	Estimate on data of Meiselman
Finkelhor (1980)	2.00	Sample of 796 college graduates (see Bixler, 1981:278)
Van den Berghe (in press)	.05	Estimate on Meiselman's sample

Note: Incest is defined as sexual intercourse with a relative, where genetic relatedness exceeds .25.

Bixler (1981c) that, in general, incest—as I define it—is still a rare phenomenon. As to the frequency distribution among different incestuous dyads, we have to rely on a few will-documented publications (Table 7.6). The picture is uniform: Father–daughter incest is by far the more frequent; mother–son incest is the rarest, never exceeding 2% of the cases. Thus, even if we accept Meiselman's (1979:31) liberal 2% estimate of the overall occurrence of incest, we come to the conclusion that mother–son incest is extremely rare (.02 × .02 = .0004; that is, 4 cases in 10,000). Father–daughter incest occurence can be estimated at 1.6% (.80 × .02) in the population, and brother–sister incest at about .0036 (.18 × .02; that is, about 4 cases in 1000).

Much additional evidence exists from samples that do not fit entirely with our classification. Maisch (1968:70) investigated 78 cases brought before German courts. As his interest was in the aggressor–victim relationship, he omitted brother–sister incest. He found 34 father–daughter and 3 mother–son cases, the rest being stepfather–stepdaughter (32), father–son (4), mother–daughter (1), and grandfather–granddaughter (4) cases. He also quoted Masters (1963) and Caprio and Brenner (1964) to support the claim that father–daughter incest is the most frequent, sibling the next most frequent, and mother–son the rarest. Riemer (1940) came to the same conclusion.

Meiselman (1978) surveyed the very extensive psychiatric literature. Assuming that brother–sister incest was less tabooed than father–daughter incest, she expected to find a higher frequency of the former. But in her own sample father–daughter cases outnumbered sibling cases by 3.5 to 1. The same pattern was found by Greenland (1958), Kaufman, Peck, and Tagiuri (1954), Sloane and Karpinski (1942), and Schachter and Cotte (1960). Only one investigator, Kubo (1959), found a 1:1 ratio.

Thus my first prediction has been verified: Differential parental investment results in different psychological mechanisms in the different incestuous dyads,

TABLE 7.6
Frequency Distribution of Incest among Different Dyads

| Source | Percentage of total | | | N |
	Mother–Son	Brother–Sister	Father–Daughter	
Weinberg (1955)	1	18.69	80.31	198
Seemanova (1971)	.7	44.7	54.7	161
Willner (1975)	1.3	15.18	83.52	1317
Justice and Justice (1979)	1.86	8.41	89.71	107

which are reflected in the differential occurrence of committed incest in those dyads.

My second prediction was that, because females lose more than do males, females will resist incest more than males. Evidence for the second prediction seems to be overwhelming. In Maisch's (1968) German courts study, females constituted 91% of the victims and 9% of the aggressors. Maisch found that females try to refuse, are generally the ones to interrupt the relationship, and, in almost all cases, are the source of complaint.

Weinberg's (1955) sample is not classified by aggressors and victims. In his analysis, "Initiation of Incest" (pp. 118–120), all the father–daughter initiators were males, and the females always tried to refuse. In brother–sister cases as well, the aggressor was male and the protestor female (p. 154). He found that sisters do not resist sex with their brothers if they have fallen in love after a long childhood separation (pp. 159–160), but that in very few brother–sister cases is the female the seducer (p. 169). Even the rare mother–son cases include some episode in which the mother rejects her son's sexual advances (p. 170). Armstrong (1978) reported only on female victims, because her aim was to protest the sexual abuse of women, especially by their fathers. The book is based on interviews with 183 women; material from a few men was omitted. Because of the intentional bias of Armstrong's selection, I cannot rely on these cases, although they do support my second prediction.

Forward and Buck (1978) also present females as victims, but their group of aggressors, although primarily fathers, includes elder brothers as well. In general, their chapters on father–daughter and brother–sister incest present males as aggressors and females as victims. The only case of mother–son incest they describe is one of mutual yearning and satisfaction between a frightened young divorcee and her 13-year-old son. Meiselman (1968) found in her sample of 58 cases that 47 were reported by females and 11 by males and that females usually felt themselves to be victims. She states that in the majority of cases, incest is initiated by males.

J. L. Herman (1981) presents extensive evidence for my second prediction. Males are initiators of incest, females try to avoid it. Males are offenders, females are victims. Interestingly, however, in surveying the different theories of incest, Herman declares: "The biological theory also fails to explain why the barrier to father–daughter mating might be weaker than the barrier against the mating of mother and son . . . . If the incest taboo is understood, then, as a biological law, there is nothing in the operation of the law itself to explain the asymmetrics in its observance by males and females [p. 52]."

Geiser (1979) found that 92% of the children involved in incest were females and that 97% of the adult offenders were males. As most cases of incest are father–daughter cases, this finding is plausible. The Lolita complex seems to be a legend (Herman, 1981).

Females are not only the victims; they usually resist, especially upon reaching adolescence. Meiselman (1979) has found that girls break away from incestuous relations at pubescence. Herman (1981) reports that girls become assertive and rebellious, running away from home or seeking an unrelated male protector, and even getting pregnant by one, in order to evade the incestuous relationship. Maisch (1972) found that 44 of 50 girls involved in a long-term incestuous relationship broke off the relationship by the age of 18.

All in all, women seem unwilling in the overwhelming majority of instances, although rare exceptions occur in mother–son, older sister–younger brother pairs and, more rarely, in older brother–younger sister pairs.

We have already seen that females are more careful and reluctant to enter even a normal sexual relationship than are males because of the higher parental investment in offspring. In the case of incest, the reluctance seems to be much stronger, definitive, and effective. Thus my second prediction has been verified.

The third prediction must be divided into two parts. First, my genetic analysis predicted that isolation will induce people to commit incest. Incest "pays" if there are no available alternative mates. Second, I argued that inhibitions develop in statistically prevalent social situations; if those situations are not present, incest will occur.

Bagley (1969:502–512) has cited an entire series of cases form different countries in which isolation is the central factor. In Sweden, according to Riemer (1936), incest (mainly between father and daughter) occurs primarily on isolated farms which are "not part of the wider social system of communities." In many of these cases, the wife and mother has died or grown ill, leaving the father without a sexual partner.

Sometimes a family's isolation is social rather than physical. In disorganized urban areas, according to Bagley, some families withdraw from the community and develop deviant norms. Mormons were persecuted in Utah in the late nineteenth century; if a particular Mormon family were also isolated from other Mormon families, father–daughter incest was common.

Another form of isolation occurs when one child is mentally defective and therefore incapable of finding a mate outside the nuclear family. Weinberg (1955:47) has talked about mentally defective daughters and sisters who were "forced back to their families for their social outlets [p. 48]." Weinberg also has emphasized isolation as conductive to incest: "Many incest participants depended upon the family socially and emotionally. Isolated from other contacts, some could not cultivate new relationships. Hence, these participants were very dependent emotionally on the family [p. 110]."

Self-imposed social isolation also occurs in cases of social superiority. In the famous cases of incestuous dynasties in ancient Egypt and Hawaii and among the Incas of Peru, no worthy mates could be found outside the immediate families (Van den Berghe and Mesher, 1980). This was especially true for the females; the males were usually polygynous. Van den Berghe (in press)· summarizes the case of royal incest as follows:

> Royal incest then becomes the ultimate conclusion of a female strategy of hypergyny. What is a poor princess to do? She has almost no way to go but down, unless she is lucky enough to find a king for a husband. Her brother happens to be the nearest king, and perhaps the only one worthy of her if she was born in the monarchy at the apex of an imperial system (as was the case for both Inca and Ancient Egypt).

Thus, the first part of the third prediction has been documented. Documentation of the second part requires brother–sister and mother–son cases.

On the sibling incest question, Weinberg (1955) offers a very convincing contrast between cosocialized and separated sibling pairs (although his conclusions are wrong):

> Sibling incest frequently was transitory, hence the sibling participants did not behave like marriage partners. But six pairs of siblings, who were separated from early childhood and who became mutually attached, did contemplate marriage. Three pairs of siblings legalized and three did not legalize the marriage. One brother insisted on marriage to evade the draft. He was not prosecuted because he was drafted into the army. Another brother refused to marry the sister although he was willing to support the child. Since the sister looked forward to the marriage, she became irritated and refused to speak further to her sibling lover. In a third case, the siblings quarreled and "broke up." Apparently, when siblings lack common family training, they lack guilt about incest with each other, and can consider each other as elegible marriage partners [p. 159].

Weinberg's more extended description of some of these cases shows clearly the great difference between ordinary inhibited behavior and the separated siblings' extraordinary uninhibited behavior (pp. 134–136). Moreover, according to Weinberg, the average age of the brothers was 24.0 years and that of the sisters 19.3 years. The difference, 4.7 years, is longer than the critical period of negative imprinting. We have seen that in the kibbutz "incest avoidance" does not work if the children were separated during the critical period, regardless of whether they are later in the same peer group. Lastly, in conjunction with the royal incest marriages, we can safely assume that princes and princesses were socialized separately, which again would have broken down inhibition, facilitating the royal incest marriages.

It is far more difficult to find evidence for the association between an absence of inhibition and mother–son incest. Most sources try to conclude something about the mothers from cases which have been published and find the mothers "emotionally remote" or "very dominant," yet we know almost nothing about the earlier preincestuous relationship between mother and son. Remoteness or excessive dominance might indicate that the mother did not or could not socialize her son, but they are far from conclusive evidence. The only couple Weinberg describes (1955) does present such a picture: The mother was a prostitute and alcoholic with several illegitimate children, and another woman helped her in the house (pp. 210–215). Although it is not explicitly stated, it is clear that the mechanism of inhibition could not develop under such circumstances. A case involving separation of mother and son during the son's early childhood was reported by Bender and Blau (1937) and Bender and Geugett (1952). Admittedly this is far from decisive evidence, but we have to take into account that mother–son cases are extremely rare. Even rarer are analyses that account for socialization patterns prior to the incestuous relationship.

My fourth prediction was that we shall find increasing cultural variability of norms regulating sexual intercourse between partners who are less related than the core incestuous dyads. Murdock (1949) verifies this prediction in the following passage, which I have already quoted in part:

> Incest taboos tend to apply with diminished intensity to kinsmen outside of the nuclear family, even though they are designated by the same kinship terms as primary relatives. From the point of view of a male Ego, the prohibitions against sexual intercourse and marriage with an own mother, sister, and daughter are the strongest of all incest taboos. Other relatives may fall under an equally severe ban, but analysis of our data reveals no instance where a relative outside the nuclear family is more stringently tabooed than one within it. The reverse, however, is often the case. Of the handful of ethnographers who give adequate nformation on the differential intensity of incest taboos, all report for their respective tribes that, for example, the taboos apply more strongly to own than to "classificatory" sisters, to half sisters than to cousins, to first than to second or remoter cousins, and so on. It must not be assumed, however, that the diminution in intensity is the same in all directions, for inequality in this respect is the rule [p. 286].

The whole anthropological literature supports this conclusion of Murdock.

TABLE 7.7
Premarital Intercourse and Marriage Permitted or Prohibited according to Consanguinity[a]

	Premarital intercourse		Marriage	
	Permitted	Prohibited	Permitted	Prohibited
Aunt–nephew	3 (2.4)	121 (97.6)	8 (23)	348 (97.7)
Uncle–niece	3 (2.6)	111 (97.4)	12 (5.1)	221 (94.9)
First-cousin parallel	2 (1.3)	144 (98.7)	23 (5.5)	390 (94.5)
First-cousin cross	25 (25)	75 (75)	144 (35.8)	258 (64.2)

Source: Murdock (1949:286).
[a]Horizontal percentages are in parentheses.

On the question of variability, Murdock, in his Table 80, provides useful data. The table, reproduced here as Table 7.7, presents a list of relatives and the number of cultures in which premarital intercourse and marriage with those relatives is permitted or forbidden. Thus, when we move from uncle–niece and aunt–nephew relationships ($r = .25$) to first cousin realtionships ($r = .125$), the variability increases. (The difference between parallel and cross cousins has been explained earlier [p. 103].)

SUMMARY

I started this lengthy chapter with eight propositions. Let me summarize the findings.

Incest, a specific case of reproduction, underwent evolutionary change. Lower organisms practice asexual reproduction, higher organisms sexual reproduction. Among the latter, most organisms prefer outbreeding. The amount of inbreeding tolerated depends on the general strategy of the organism. Too close inbreeding—incest—is avoided by most plants and animals because it brings about increasing homozygosity, a usually dangerous situation from the evolutionary point of view.

In the human case, a genetic analysis of comparisons between incestuous matings and outbreeding indicates specific benefits of incest, in some cases and in some situations. The analysis predicts the differential frequency of committed incest in the various incestuous dyads, as well as the occurrence of incest in cases of isolation. An analysis of the costs and benefits shows that regulations had to evolve to prevent inbreeding between persons related by an r of between .50 and .25.

Different mechanisms result from the epigenetic rules that evolve in the different dyads. Statistically prevalent social situations characteristic of our species exist in which mother–son and brother–sister incest become inhibited. But there is a conspicuous lack of evidence for father–daughter incest inhibition. Different preventive measures have evolved, seemingly both biologically and culturally, and cultural evolution also supplements prohibitions to remove the few cases that emerge in spite of the existing inhibitions and preventions. I hope that, by my detailed analysis of the coevolutionary process, I have convinced all those who doubted the necessity of prohibitions so long as inhibitions and preventions existed.

I emphasized the distinction between the basis function of incest regulations—the removal of too much inbreeding—and the secondary functions which explain their persistence. The origin of incest regulations is precultural, to be found in the inhibitions. I pointed out that these precultural origins were complemented by the cultural prohibitions, completing the coevolutionary process that has rendered committed incest a rare phenomenon.

Finally I brought evidence to verify four specific predictions. First, regarding differential frequency in the various dyads: Father–daughter incest is by far the most common, brother–sister incest intermediate, and mother–son incest the rarest. Second, regarding differential opposition: Females resist incest far more than do males. Third, regarding specific social situations: Incest occurs in cases of actual or socially imposed isolation; it occurs when the statistically prevalent social situations are absent, because the inhibition mechanisms do not work. Fourth, regarding cultural variability: The variability increases when we move away from the core incestuous dyads.

Many scientists have concentrated their analysis on the secondary functions of incest: the preservation of the nuclear family, the facilitation of the socialization process, the avoidance of the isolation of the nuclear family, the creation of economic and political alliances between families, the understanding of the symbolic meaning of kinship. Most of these scientists wrote when the comparative primatological evidence was not available. They asked questions that were different from the questions I asked. In the following chapters, I shall compare their theories with the sociobiological theory in order to show the place of the secondary functions of incest in the general picture of coevolutionary theory.

The corporal leads his soldiers to shooting training. Their performance is horribly inept. The corporal angrily scolds his recruits, then, after one of them again misses the target, he takes the rifle from the soldier's hand and yells:
"Fools, you can't shoot. Give me this rifle and look!"
He aims and shoots nonchalantly. But he misses. For a minute he gets confused, but then angrily points to one of the soldiers:
"That's how you shoot!"
And so on. Finally . . . his ninth shot hits the target. He proudly strikes his chest:
"And that is how I   shoot!"

* * *

The ninth shot is still delayed. The corporal's hands are still trembling, but his eyes probably see the target a little more clearly.
—F. KARINTHY
Igy'irtok ti [That's How You Write]

FREUD AND
THE FAMILY–SOCIALIZATION SCHOOL

By far the most influential theory in the incest literature is that proposed by the family–socialization school. Following Sigmund Freud, scholars of this school—Malinowski, Seligman, Murdock, and Parsons—explained the origin, persistence, and functions of the incest taboo in terms of its beneficial, even indispensable, functions in maintaining the social structure of the human family and in making the process of socialization possible.

SIGMUND FREUD—*TOTEM AND TABOO*

Almost without exception, the scholars in the family–socialization school drew heavily on Freud. Even if they did not agree completely with his theses, they usually accepted his assumptions on human sexuality. I shall limit myself here to describing Freud's theory of incest. Presenting his comprehensive theory of human sexuality is a task too ambitious for this chapter.

Freud's main focus was on religion. This was the period of deep interest in primitive religion. Frazer's voluminous *Totemism and Exogamy* (1910), Lang's *The Secret of the Totem* (1905), Wundt's *Völkerpsychologie* (1906), as well as the publication of authentic ethnographies on Australian aborigines—Spencer and Gillen, 1899, 1904; Mathews, 1897, 1905; Howitt, 1904—directed public interest among Western intellectuals to problems of totemism. Freud probably

135

felt committed to showing that the young theory of psychoanalysis had something important to contribute to the question of primitive religion.

Freud's theory of incest is included in four essays published originally in the Viennese periodical *Imago* under the title "Über einige Übereinstimmungen im Seelenleben der Wilden und der Neurotiker" ["Concerning Some Parallels between the Psychic Life of Savages and Neurotics"]. The essays were published in 1912 and 1913 and then collected in a book entitled *Totem und Tabu* (1950), published in 1913. This book later formed Volume 10 of Freud's *Gesammelte Schriften*.

Interestingly enough, the nuclear family plays only a marginal role in Freud's analysis. He assumes the existence in the primal horde of a "one-male harem" that relegates the young males to the periphery. The young males conspire against the old despot, their father, and kill him. After the patricide, the covenant between the murderous brothers introduces mother–son and brother–sister incest taboos, but nothing further is known about the nuclear family. The clan that develops from the adelphic community is based on clan-totemic exogamy and is a much more extensive exogamic unit than the nuclear family. The clinical literature describes specific Central and Eastern European nuclear families but it emphasizes the Oedipal aspect and hardly mentions brother–sister or father–daughter incest. The entire analysis focuses on the male; the female's point of view is virtually neglected.

On the significance of incest regulations in socialization, we must consult some of Freud's other publications. The psychosexual development of the ego and superego are explored but the father of the family–socialization school essentially neglected the effect of incest taboos on the origin or persistence of the family or on the socialization process. These functions were elaborated by his disciples.

Freud's basic assumption is that the sexual attraction of males to females (libido) is omnipresent, ever active, and, if not properly checked, destructive. In other words, if incest is not prohibited, it will be the rule. Hence the necessity of the patricidal brothers establishing the taboo. But what was wrong with the one-male harem of the tyrannical primal father? Freud rejects the biological explanation of any pressure toward eliminating inbreeding, claiming that the horror of incest is present among nonblood relatives such as sons-in-law and mothers-in-law. He completely rejects Westermarck's idea of inhibition (see page 47).

Admitting that incest taboos came into being in the dim past, Freud has trouble explaining how these taboos have survived to the present. He invokes the concept of the "collective mind" in which "mental processes occur just as they do in the mind of the individual." Freud finds consolation in the fact that he is not alone in using "this bold procedure," but he is extremely unhappy about this solution:

> Before I bring my remarks to a close, however, I must find room to point out that, though my arguments have led to a high degree of convergence upon a single comprehensive nexus of ideas, this fact cannot blind us to the uncertainties of my premises or the difficulties involved in my conclusions. I will only mention two of the latter which may have forced themselves on the notice of a number of my readers.
>
> No one can have failed to observe, in the first place, that I have taken as the basis of my whole position the existence of a collective mind, in which mental processes occur just as they do in the mind of an individual. In particular, I have supposed that the sense of guilt for an action has persisted for many thousands of years and has remained operative in generations which can have had no knowledge of that action. I have supposed that an emotional process, such as might have developed in generations of sons who were ill-treated by their father, has extended to new generations which were exempt from such treatment for the very reason that their father had been eliminated. It must be admitted that these are grave difficulties; and any explanation that could avoid presumption of such a kind would seem to be preferable . . .
>
> Without the assumption of a collective mind, which makes it possible to neglect the interruptions of mental acts caused by the extinction of the individual, social psychology in general cannot exist. Unless psychical processes were continued from one generation to another, if each generation were obliged to acquire its attitude to life anew, there would be no progress in this field and next to no development. This gives rise to two further questions: how much can we attribute to psychical continuity in the sequence of generations? and what are the ways and means employed by one generation in order to hand on its mental states to the next one? . . . A part of the problem seems to be met by the inheritance of psychical dispositions, which, however, need to be given some sort of impetus in the life of the individual before they can be roused into actual operation [This quote and subsequent quotes are reprinted from *Totem and Taboo* by Sigmund Freud. Translated by James Strachey. W. W. Norton & Company, Inc., New York, N. Y. Copyright 1950 by Routledge & Kegan Paul, Ltd.; copyright renewed 1978 by Alix S. Strachey. 1950:157–158].

What exactly are the "inherited psychical dispositions" that Freud attributes to the individual? In the original German, the expression used is *durch die Vererbung psychisher Dispositionen* (1913/1950:146); thus there cannot be any doubt that Freud is thinking of *genetic inheritance*. But if this is so, what place do deliberate prohibitions have in his scheme? If a predisposition toward feeling guilt is inherited, and if it has only "to be given some sort of impetus" in the individual, why was Westermarck wrong in speaking of "an innate aversion to sexual intercourse between persons living very closely together from early youth [1891:32]"? An innate aversion certainly cannot depend on the condition of "living very closely together" unless it is an *inherited disposition*, like what Freud posits. Freud is negligent about the sort of "impetus" needed to activate his inherited disposition toward guilt; his analysis is also problematic with respect to the necessity for prohibition and the reaction of horror that attends incest. Freud's and Westermarck's positions were not irreconcilable, as Fox (1962, 1980) would succeed in establishing many years later.

Despite the title of Freud's book, it is not clear whether he had in mind *taboos*—deliberate, cultural prohibitions—or, rather, *innate dispositions toward feeling guilt* about certain kinds of events (for a parallel analysis, see Fox, 1980; Chapter 3).

BRONISLAW MALINOWSKI

By far the most influential statements about incest can be found in Malinowski's writings. Malinowski had a profound impact on British social anthropologists and other incest theoreticians. Malinowski's theory can be found in *Sex and Repression in Savage Society* (1927), *The Sexual Life of Savages* (1929), and his article on "Culture" in the *Encyclopedia of the Social Sciences* (1931).

Malinowski's (1927) *Sex and Repression in Savage Society* is an early powerful criticism on Freud's Oedipus complex as a theory of psychosexual development. By systematically comparing modern Western society with the Melanesian Trobrianders, Malinowski proves that the Oedipus complex does not exist among the Trobrianders and is therefore culture bound rather than universal.

> Comparing the two systems of family attitudes briefly, we see that in a patriarchal society, the infantile rivalries and the later social functions introduce into the attitude of father and son, besides mutual attachment, also a certain amount of resentment and dislike. Between mother and son, on the other hand, the premature separation in infancy leaves a deep, unsatisfied craving which, later on, when sexual interests come in, is mixed up in memory with the new bodily longings, and assumes often an erotic character which comes up in dreams and other fantasies. In the Trobriands there is no friction between father and son, and all the infantile craving of the child for its mother is allowed gradually to spend itself in a natural spontaneous manner. The ambivalent attitude of veneration and dislike is felt between a man and his mother's brother, while the repressed sexual attitude of incestuous temptation can be formed only towards his sister. Applying to each society a terse, though somewhat crude formula, we might say that in the Oedipus complex there is the repressed desire to kill the father and marry the mother, while in the matrilineal society of the Trobriands, the wish is the marry the sister and to kill the maternal uncle [pp. 80–81].

> By my analysis, I have established that Freud's theories not only roughly correspond to human psychology, but that they follow closely the modification in human nature brought about by various constitutions of society. In other words, I have established a deep

correlation between the type of society and the nuclear complex found there. While this is in a sense a confirmation of the main tenet of Freudian psychology, it might compel us to modify certain of its features, or rather to make some of its formulae more elastic. To put it concretely, it appears necessary to draw in more systematically the correlation between biological and social influences; not to assume the universal existence of the Oedipus complex, but in studying every type of civilization, to establish the special complex which pertains to it [pp. 81–82].

Thus Malinowski accepts Freud's notion of sexual attraction within the family as part of human nature, but he calls for better understanding of the interaction between the biological and social influences. Malinowski believes that the biological given is the sexual attraction but that the expression of the attraction depends on the social system.

In his celebrated *Sexual Life of Savages* (1929), Malinowski makes an important methodological contribution. After giving a detailed description of the incest rules in Trobriand society, he explains:

What I wish to make clear, by confronting the gist of native statements with the results of direct observation, is that there is a serious discrepancy between the two. The statements contain the ideal of tribal morality; observation shows us how far real behavior conforms to it. The statements show us the polished surface of custom which is invariably presented to the inquisitive stranger; direct knowledge of native life revels the underlying strata of human conduct, moulded, it is true, by the rigid surface of custom, but still more deeply influenced by the smouldering fires of human nature. The smoothness and uniformity, which the mere verbal statements suggest as the only shape of human conduct, disappears with a better knowledge of cultural reality [pp. 425–426].

The significant differences between normative and actual behavior are underscored through several examples (pp. 423, 425, 443, 456).

Malinowski's theoretical approach is summarized in his 1931 article:

However great may be the sexual liberty allowed, in no human society are young people permitted to be entirely indiscriminate or promiscuous in experimental love making. Three main types of limitations are known: the prohibition of incest, respect for previous matrimonial obligations and the rules of combined exogamy and endogamy. The prohibition of incest is with a few significant exceptions universal. If incest could be proved to be biologically pernicious, the function of this universal tabu would be obvious. But specialists in heredity disagree on the subject. It is possible, however, to show that from a sociological point of view the function of incest tabus is of the greatest importance. The sexual impulse, which is in general a very upsetting and socially disruptive force, cannot enter into a previously existing sentiment without producing a revolutionary change in it. Sexual interest is therefore incompatible with any family relationship, whether parental or between brothers and sisters, for these relations are built up in the presexual period of human life and are founded on deep physiological needs of a non-sexual character. If erotic passion were allowed to invade the precincts of the home it would not merely establish jealousies and competitive elements and disorganize the family but it would also subvert the most fundamental bonds of kinship on which the further development of all social relations is based. Only one erotic relationship can be allowed within each family, and that is the relation between the husband and wife, which although it is built from the outset on erotic elements must be very finely adjusted to the other component parts of domestic cooperation. A society which allowed incest could not develop a stable family; it would therefore be deprived of the strongest foundations for kinship, and this in a primitive community would mean absence of social order [This quote and subsequent quotes are reprinted from Malinowski, B. "Culture" *Encyclopaedia of the Social Sciences*, Vol. 4. E. R. A Seligman, ed. Copyright 1932, renewed 1959 by Macmillan Publishing Co., Inc. pp. 629–630].

Here we have the clear crystallization of Malinowski's theory: Incest taboos have an important sociological function. The sexual impulse is socially disruptive and would destroy the fundamental bonds of kinship (within the nuclear family) on which all social development is built. If you allow incest, you destroy the family, the kinship system and, consequently, the social order.

This is a classical functional explanation: The nuclear family is the strongest foundation of the social order, and, because without it humans could not have survived, they could not allow incest. Although Malinowski does not use the word *origin*, he implies it by claiming that any society that allowed incest would disintegrate. Extending the incest taboo to the clan serves the same purpose: "exogamy is dissociating the disruptive and competitive element from workaday cooperation [p. 630]."

Although Malinowski distinguishes among incestual dyads in his ethnography, he pools all three types in his theory and thereby evades an important query: If incest itself is upsetting to the social order, why do the Trobrianders react so differently to the transgression of different incestual prohibitions? Mother–son incest is regarded with real horror among the Trobrianders, but they easily discussed the possibility of its occurrence all the while regarding it as immoral, unnatural, and highly improbable. Brother–sister incest, on the other hand, is not only horrible to them, but intolerable and upsetting to contemplate—the worst thing that can possibly happen. Father–daughter incest, although the father is not a kinsman to the matrilineal Trobriander, does occur. It "is not only illegal and improper, but it is viewed with definite moral repugnance," though without horror and without a sense of its unnaturalness. In *Sex and Repression in Savage Society* (1927), Malinowski explains the different perceptions of mother–son and brother–sister incest but does not touch upon the father–daughter problem. If the origin of the incest taboo is to maintain the social order, then one would expect the severity of social reactions to be directly proportional to the perceived degree of threat of the various incestual transgressions. In the case of the father–daughter incest, would jealousy and competition between a mother and daughter of the same kinship unit prove less upsetting than that between a father and son of different kinship units in the case of mother–son incest?

BRENDA Z. SELIGMAN

Another prominent British anthropologist, Brenda Z. Seligman, added to the family–socialization theory. A student of Malinowski, Seligman devoted three long articles to the problem of incest (1929, 1932, and 1935). These articles are concerned largely with Westermarck—the first two cite him several times, the third is exclusively devoted to disputing his 1934 article. It is worthwhile to recall that Westermarck, in his monumental *History of the Human Marriage* (1891), claimed that incest is inhibited to prevent inbreeding (as discussed here in Chapter 4). Seligman argues that were Westermarck correct, it would be impossible to explain prohibitions that arbitrarily divide first and second cousins with the same biological relationship to ego into marriageable and unmarriageable categories. Seligman rejects Westermarck's theory of both inbreeding and inhibition.

Seligman explicitly states that she is not concerned with the biological problems of inbreeding (1935:76). Instead, her work on incest combines a sociological and psychological explanation, the first of which is contained in her 1929 paper:

> The study of the family has shown the tendency to rivalries that arise within it, which are inherently human. Such situations do not occur in the other branches of the animal kingdom, because the young mature more quickly and are physically capable of fending for themselves when they reach sexual maturity. The adoption of the incest law helps to preserve harmony within the family group over periods when these rivalries might otherwise become acute. The parent–child type is the fundamental incest law, but the brother–sister type is an auxiliary to it, and the two laws function together and may be regarded as having developed together. The main function of these laws is to keep distinct throughout life and the parent–child relationship and the brother–sister relationship, and not to allow either to be changed to one which is entirely distinct in actual life (whatever may be the attitude of the unconscious), *i.e.* that of mate. It may here be mentioned that all marriage ceremonies have value in that they accentuate the fact that marriage (the social form of mating) sets up a new relationship. The parent–child type of incest taboo may be defined from the sociological point of view as the *law which prevents one person from mating with two others who stand to one another in the relationship of parent and child.* The value of the parent–child relationship is seen in the stabilized behaviour pattern it preserves, shown as respect for the elder generation. The brother–sister type of incest does not

produce a distinct behaviour pattern. It would seem that in some societies the temptation to this form of incest is so great that the brother–sister relationship is only preserved by strict etiquette and avoidance, while in other societies these forms are not observed. The value of the brother–sister relationship (protected by this incest law) is the opportunity that is offers for the cultivation of comradeship and mutual aid [This quote and subsequent quotes are reprinted from Seligman, B. A. "The Incest Barrier." *Journal of the Royal Anthropological Institute*, 1929, 59. With permission from the Royal Anthropological Institute of Great Britain and Ireland. pp. 268–269].

Seligman's psychological explanation is given in the 1932 paper:

> Civilization is seen in the capacity of man to live in organized groups. To this end natural impulses become modified for social gains.
> The family, the first human group, became consolidated by the acceptance of incest barriers.
> These barriers were not consciously formulated, but arose, not specifically to check the lust of the *pater familias*, but in the production of a harmonious family group, and actually changed it from a natural to a social group.
> The sanction for the incest barrier is primarily the persistence through childhood of the infant's belief in the omnipotence of the parents, later developed into a religious attitude and consolidated by rites expressive of ancestor worship.
> The persisting family is a social group with such survival value that other societies which may have ignored the incest barrier have died out. The family group is the pattern on which all other groups are formed [p. 276].

Seligman accepts the Freudian notion of childhood sexual attraction to the parent but rejects his theory of primal parricide; she accepts Malinowski's emphasis on the nuclear family as central but cannot follow him when it comes to brother–sister incest and exogamy. (Both Malinowski and Seligman have trouble with brother–sister incest.)

The main argument of the family–socialization theory is based on the following claims:

1. The socialization process requires a long period of dependency of the child on its parents, especially its mother.
2. The basic behaviors between parents and children are authority and respect, without which socialization itself would be impossible.
3. The basic behaviors between spouses involve given and take, and "from the point of view of status, the husband and wife together form the elder generation and are bound together by mutual duties and responsibilities [1929:241]."
4. Therefore, a sexual relationship between mother and son and/or father and daughter would upset the status system of the family and would destroy both family stability and socialization.

Despite problems which Seligman discusses and which I shall point out in what follows, this theory gives a plausible explanation with respect to parent–child incest. In contrast, brothers and sisters may have a give-and-take relationship and equal social status (in terms of generational identity which Seligman considers the most important determinant of status). What, then, is to prevent them from incest?

Seligman answers by postulating that a father who renounced his sexual rights to his daughter would not confer these rights on his sons. Seligman also writes that the brother–sister prohibition "may have a biological value" in preventing a union of two physically immature partners (1929:246). She does not, however, mention its possible biological value in preventing inbreeding.

Seligman badly needs to explain the brother–sister incest taboo, because otherwise she cannot support her contention that exogamy is an extension of brother–sister incest, and not vice versa. She writes at length about the problem of extension only to show that

> for the internal relations of the clan itself, exogamy is of no special value, but the relationship pattern carried over from the family, which engenders the respect for the seniors, is of immense value. . . . They are part of the price man pays for culture, but he frequently finds a way of turning even such restrictions to his advantage; he demands as a right those women who are not prohibited to him by law [1929:272].

Here we run into Seligman's continual confusion of sexual intercourse with marriage. Although she emphasizes that incest taboos are the basis of marriage regulations (exogamy), she continually states that incest taboos prohibit *marriage*. The confusion is even more blatant when Seligman criticizes R. W. Fortune (1932) (see Chapter 9, in what follows), an important member of the alliance school. Fortune, following Tylor (1888), claims that incest taboos originated to create alliances between groups or families. Seligman considers Fortune's idea a sound sociological explanation for the brother–sister incest barrier except for the fact that respect for virginity is not innate. She argues that even if daughters and sisters were to marry outside, the only reason for family members to avoid sleeping with them would be if virginity were a precondition of marriage. When Seligman needs to do so, she rediscovers the difference between sexual intercourse and marriage.

Seligman is not afraid to face difficulties (except on the question of inbreeding). One such difficulty is father–daughter incest.

> Whether promiscuous mating will satisfy the sexual needs of the adult male or not, the adult female requires a more permanent union. Where conditions of life are hard, those women who have not secured a partner to help feed and protect them during the later stages of pregnancy, and the infancy of the child, are unlikely to rear their offspring. Thus a woman needs a more or less permanent union, *i.e.* marriage with one man, and it is

difficult to imagine how she can obtain this except by means of sexual attraction and services mutually rendered. In the picturesque descriptions of the matriarch that have so often been made, we are shown furtive lovers who visit independent women and return to work in the households of their sisters, but we are never told what is the force that keeps them in the service of their sisters or drives them away from their mates [1929:240].

Seligman's notion essentially coincides with the theory of parental investment, according to which the father ordinarily invests less in the child than does the mother. Seligman also feels that father–daughter incest would pose less of a status reversal than would mother–son incest, and she quotes Ginsberg to that effect. (Substantiating evidence may appear in the many cases of fathers marrying females of their daughters' age.) Seligman finds refuge in the concept of status. This is surprising in light of her ambitious goal: "It is obvious that if there is any general law underlying all marriage prohibitions it must be founded on human emotions and reactions; *it must be biologically sound and have a social value so great as to have become a human institution* [1929, p. 238; my emphasis]." Yet her tone is more sombre at the beginning of her third article: "It may be that it is impossible to explain or to trace the origin of any human custom that is universal; perhaps the most we can do is to correlate it with certain other conditions. No sociological theory of incest can be proved or disproved. The incest laws and the family are so intimately associated that it is difficult to imagine the one without the other [1935:75]." Seligman paid too much attention to prohibitions, taboos, and status, and too little attention to real behavior, and, as a result, her intellectual effort reached an impasse.

George Peter Murdock

European scholars have not been the only proponents of the family-socialization theory. The American G. P. Murdock also supports family-socialization in his theory epoch-making *Social Structure* (1949, Chapter 10). Murdock tests his hypotheses on a sample of 250 societies: "An acceptable theory of incest taboos and their varying incidence in different societies must, in the first place, be consistent with the known facts and, in the second, provide a satisfactory explanation for all or most of them [p. 284]." Murdock begins by describing the known facts, which can be summarized as follows:

1. Prohibition of sexual intercourse or marriage between mother–son, father–daughter, and brother–sister is universal.
2. Incest taboos do not apply universally to any relative of the opposite sex outside the nuclear family.

3. Incest taboos are never confined exclusively to the nuclear family.
4. Incest taboos tend to apply less intensely to kin outside the nuclear family, even when they are designated by the same kinship terms as primary relatives.
5. Incest taboos applied to people outside the nuclear family fail strikingly to coincide with nearness of biological relationship.
6. Incest taboos correlate highly with purely conventional groups of kin.
7. Compared to other sexual prohibitions, incest taboos and exogamous restrictions are characterized by a peculiar intensity and emotional quality.
8. Violations of incest taboos do occur.

Having thus set the stage for finding a theory, Murdock tests and eliminates one theory after another. He rejects inbreeding theory because (a) according to his authorities (quoted in Sumner and Keller, 1927), inbreeding is not harmful; (b) some primitives do not understand biological paternity; and (c) incest taboos beyond the nuclear family do not coincide with nearness of biological relationship. Murdock then rejects the instinct theory, which he attributes to Lowie (1920/1949) rather than to Westermarck, to whom he ascribes a habit formation theory. (Murdock was probably unaware that Westermarck originated instinct theory; he used the fifth American edition [1921] of Westermarck's book.) He also misunderstands Westermarck's basic assumption about habit formation, arguing that among the Angmagsalik Eskimos, children brought up together marry. But Murdock primarily takes issue with Freud's "vast body of clinical evidence" demonstrating incestuous wishes. "The only other theory of the origin of incest taboos which deserves serious consideration is that of Freud [1949:291]." Although Murdock accepts Freud's explanation for the universality of the incest taboo, he finds it inadequate for explaining why the taboo extends beyond the nuclear family:

> In addition to accounting for the emotional quality of incest taboos, Freud's theory explains the universality of incest avoidance by relating it to a universal condition of human social life, the nuclear family. It does not, however, account for the extension of such taboos beyond the immediate family nor for their diverse application in different societies. It does not even suggest why they are so regularly a part of culture. Many if not most Freudian mechanisms and their products, e.g., regression, the displacement of aggression, projection, and sadistic behavior, are ordinarily opposed or at best barely tolerated by culture. Incest avoidance, on the other hand, universally receives the approval of society and is specifically incorporated everywhere in sanctioned cultural norms. Though helpful, Freudian theory alone is incapable of accounting for the facts revealed by ethnographers. Moreover, without detracting in the slightest from Freud's extraordinary insight into individual psychology or from his revolutionary contributions

in this field, we must admit that his ventures into cultural theory are little short of fantastic [1949:292].

An additional function of the incest taboo is the "diffusion of culture." Taking the idea from one of his students, Murdock declares that every family is a distinct social unit with a distinct culture, and incest taboos compel individuals to marry beyond the nuclear family to spread the nuclear family culture and combine it with a spouse's. This cultural diffusion would promote social solidarity (the basic idea of alliance theory). One can explain the extension of incest taboos by behavioral psychology's principle of "stimulus generalization": Because remote relatives physically resemble the forbidden nuclear relative, they are similarly to be avoided. But why are some relatives forbidden and others, with the same degree of relationship to ego, not forbidden?

Murdock then suggests his synthesis:

> It thus appears that a complete scientific explanation of incest taboos and exogamous rules emerges from a synthesis of the theories of four separate disciplines that deal with human behavior. Psychoanalytic theory accounts for the peculiar emotional quality of such taboos; for the occurrence of violations, which neither an instinct hypothesis nor Westermarck's acquired aversion explains; for the diminished intensity of taboos outside of the nuclear family; and for the universal occurrence of incest avoidance tendencies which serve as a basis for cultural elaboration. Sociological theory demonstrates the social utility of both intra-family and extended incest taboos and thus accounts for their universality. Psychological behavior theory reveals the mechanism by which extension occurs and that by which social utility becomes translated into custom, thus supplying an essential part of the reasons for both the universality and the variety of extended taboos. Cultural anthropology, finally, contributes to our explanation the varied conditions of social structure and usage which channelize generalization or produce discrimination, and thus accounts for the differential incidence of exogamous rules and extended incest taboos, for their correlation with conventional groupings of kinsmen, and for their lack of correspondence with nearness of actual biological relationship.
>
> Without any one of these four systems of social science theory an adequate explanation is impossible. All previous hypotheses concerning incest taboos have drawn upon only one or at most two of the relevant disciplines, and have thus failed to account for significant segments of observed fact [p. 300].

But he remains unsatisfied with an interpretation that is only "reasonably complete." The methodological barrier remains:

> The portion of our composite hypothesis which concerns the reasons for the universality of intra-family incest taboos cannot be subjected to independent test by any methods at our disposal, since the very universality of both the taboos and the family organization with which they are associated deprives us of independent variables to correlate [pp. 300–301].

In sum, Murdock looked for origins but found only functions. He failed to distinguish among incestuous dyads and confused avoidance, taboo, and prohibition. He did, however, make progress in explaining the correlates of exogamous prohibition.

TALCOTT PARSONS

Talcott Parsons does not fit neatly into the family–socialization school. In an article in the *British Journal of Sociology* (1954), Parsons tried to synthesize Freudian family–socialization theory with Tylor's alliance theory. The article grew out of a lecture Parsons delivered in London in January 1954. This year was a high point for structural–functional sociology. Parsons' books written alone and in collaboration with Bales and Shils—*The Social System* (1951), *Toward a General Theory of Action* (1952), *Working Papers in The Theory of Action* (1953)—had conquered one university after another. His book with Bales, *Family, Socialization and Interaction Process* (1955), was in press, and it was to be the first application of Parsonian theory to one of the "social institutions." It was to be followed by a whole series of books on economy, politics, stratification, values—the entire realm of human society.

Parsons's (1954) handling of incest was different from anything up to that point. He realized that "in recent years there has been a revival of interest in the problem of what features are common to human societies everywhere and what are the forces operating to maintain these common features" and that "societies operate only in and through the behavior of persons, and personalities on the human socio-cultural level are only possible as participants in systems of socially interactive behavior, as these are related to the needs of human organisms [p. 115]." He would acknowledge the existence of "two biological bases of differentiation: sex and generation," which may be regarded as "points of reference" of a "type of social organization that is general in small groups [1954:102]."

Parsons deliberately assumes that the incest taboo is part of the constitution of the family itself (1954:102, Footnote 3), but does not see that in doing so he is contradicting his own basic criterion of a nuclear family: the enduring mother–offspring bond. The mother–offspring bond clearly *does not need* the incest taboo as part of its constitution and at the least it does not need all *three* forms of it. Parsons's second assumption, that the *sociological* father must be from outside the mother's descent group, is also questionable in light of the evidence from many matrilinear cultures. The *biological* father must be from outside the mother's descent group, but Parsons does not state this.

Parsons integrates the results of Zelditch's cross-cultural study and Bales's small group research (both in Parsons and Bales, 1955) with Freud's theory of psychosexual development. The Zelditch–Bales research resulted in the formulation of a four-role system built along two axes: the instrumental-expressive and the leader–follower. Freud's four person nuclear family fits into the scheme.

	Leader	Follower
Instrumental	Father	Son
Expressive	Mother	Daughter

Parsons explains this scheme as biological, the result of the long dependence of the human infant and the "universal fact that women are more intimately concerned with child care than are men [1954:103]." The two leaders form a coalition strengthened by their heterosexual bond. They also have a monopoly on heterosexual relationships.

Parsons accepts Freud's theory of psychosexual development and his belief that "the infant is polymorph perverse" whose eroticism can extend toward any object. To maintain the four-role scheme, the mother directs the child, and the "child's erotic attachment is the 'rope' by which [the mother] pulls him up from a lower to a higher level in the hard climb of 'growing up' [p. 111]." Parsons continues:

> There seem to be three stages at which the mother is the primary object of erotic attachment of the child; these are what Freud identified as the Oral, the Anal and the Phallic phases. They correspond to three relatively discontinuous "steps" in the process of learning new levels of personality organization; new goals, and capacities for independent and responsible performance. Each one leaves a residuum of the erotic structures which have been essential in order to make the step, but which if allowed to remain active would interfere with the subsequent steps. Thus there is in all personalities, granting my hypothesis of addiction, a channel through erotic associations, right down into the lowest and most primitive strata of the Id—the most regressive parts of the personality system. These can be reactivated at any time. The connection of this situation with the problem of the probable psychological significance of incest seems to be clear.
>
> From this point of view the problem of incest fits into the larger context of the structuring of erotic motivation in the personality, over time and with reference to choice of objects. The context includes the problem of homosexuality and of the status of the perversions. The goal of socialization—with many variations but in its broad pattern universal—is to establish at least the primacy, if not the complete monopoly over other possibilities, of normal genital erotic attraction which includes choice of object outside the family, and stability of orientation to objects [pp. 111–112].

With the latency period and the development of one-sex peer groups, the children are gradually "propelled out of" the nuclear family and develop heterosexual attractions to outside partners. This process serves the function of the "self-liquidation" of the nuclear family and the creation of alliances—that is, it supports the "transfamilial structure" of the society.

Parsons acknowledges that he focuses on functions rather than the origins of incest taboos. He presumes that "once this level of analysis has been worked out the problem of origins assumes a lesser significance, but also can be approached with better hope of success [p. 115]."

Parsons' synthesis was important, but it begs a question to which Parsons himself implicitly demanded an answer. If, indeed "societies operate *only* in and through the behavior of persons, and personalities on the human socio-cultural level are *only* possible as participants in systems of socially interactive behavior, as these are related to the needs of human organisms," how is an individual motivated to deny his own needs, needs described in the Freudian theory to which Parsons subscribes? How is an individual motivated to accept the societal need for alliance? How have different sorts of repression evolved? If, indeed, "features common to human societies" are important and "the forces operating to maintain" those features are crucial, should we not look for them in the realm of biology, the realm of species-wide universals, rather than in the realm of culture, which is the realm of variability?

The list of the authors is far from exhaustive—a whole generation of sociologists and anthropologists subscribed to the family–socialization theory. Several additional contributions were particularly important: Levy (1955) criticizes Parsons for his exclusive connection of the incest taboo with the nuclear family. Coult (1963), in a methodologically elaborate article, argues that exogamous prohibitions preceded incest prohibitions and that the preexistence of the four-role system in the nuclear family and the practice of in- and out-marriage together explain all incest prohibitions. Bagley (1969), who investigated what he termed "functional incest"—that is, families who systematically commit incest—concludes that from the abnormalities of incestual families one can infer the correctness of Parsons's and Murdock's analyses.

SUMMARY

The family–socialization school focused on the most important secondary function of human incest regulations. By taking the theories on their own terms, there is much we can learn. The internal organization of the nuclear family would, indeed, face serious problems without incest regulations. As a general explanation of incest, however, the theories of the family–socialization school are unacceptable. They assume that the nuclear family preceded incest regulations. True, none of the scientists belonging to this school possessed the knowledge of primatological and paleoanthropological material that we have today. Some of them nevertheless felt the inherent weakness of their theory. Freud could not help but invoke genetic predispositions in order to solve the problem of "collective mind." Seligman recognized the asymmetry of parental investment between males and females. Parsons consciously evaded the problem of origin. Murdock reluctantly admitted doubts about his theory after 23 years (Murdock, 1972).

9

THE ALLIANCE SCHOOL

As we have seen, the family–socialization school emphasized the small group—the nuclear family—and argued that incest prohibitions arose and endured to maintain the nuclear family itself and to allow parents to socialize their children. Some members, especially Freud and Parsons, looked at the individual and emphasized the importance of personality. The incest taboo was indispensable in dealing with personality development. Parsons, the bridge between the family–socialization and the alliance schools, also acknowledged the importance of the incest prohibitions to interests of society as a whole.

The alliance school is completely group oriented. Its basic argument is that incest prohibitions serve the social function of compelling the young to look for mates outside the nuclear family. Such marriages create alliances between family groups, a network that constitutes basic social order.

EDWARD B. TYLOR

The alliance school properly begins with the publication in 1888 of E. B. Tylor's "On a Method of Investigating the Development of Institutions; Applied to Laws of Marriage and Descent." Read before the Royal Anthropological Institute in London, the article laid down the foundations for cross-cultural research in anthropology. In claiming that the development of institutions "may be investigated on a basis of tabulation and classification [p.

151

245]," Tylor wanted to prove that anthropology was no less scientific than the natural sciences, and he collected materials from, by his count, 350 societies. Tylor correlated phenomena like mother-in-law avoidance and residence patterns, teknonymy and uxorilocal residence, levirate and couvade. He criticized the old evolutionary school of Backhofen and Spencer and argued that evolutionary hypotheses must be tested with cross-cultural evidence.

Tylor was not specifically interested in the problem of incest; like so many of his contemporaries his concern was with exogamy. He concludes that exogamy is essential for the survival of primitive human groups:

> On looking at the distinction between endogamy and exogamy from this point of view, it will be seen that there is a period in the growth of society when it is a political question of the first importance. While the vast forest or prairie still affords abundant food for a scanty population, small hordes may wander, or groups of household may be set up, each little tribe or settlement cut off from the rest, and marrying within its own border. But when tribes begin to adjoin and press on one another and quarrel then the difference between marrying-in and marrying-out becomes patent. Endogamy is a policy of isolation, cutting off a horde or village, even from the parent-stock whence it separated, if only a generation or two back. Among tribes of low culture there is but one means known of keeping up permanent alliance, and that means is intermarriage.
>
> Exogamy, enabling a growing tribe to keep itself compact by constant unions between its spreading clans, enables it to overmatch any number of small intermarrying groups, isolated and helpless. Again and again in the world's history, savage tribes must have had plainly before their minds the simple practical alternative between marrying-out and being killed out. Even far on in culture, the political value of intermarriage remains. "Matrimonial alliances increase friendship more than aught else", is a maxim of Mohammed. "Then will we give our daughters unto you, and we will take your daughters to us, and we will dwell with you, and we will become one people", is a well known passage of Israelite history [This quote and subsequent quotes are reprinted from Tylor, E. B. "On a Method of Investigating the Development of Institutions, Applied to Laws of Marriage and Descent." *Journal of the Royal Anthropological Institute*, 1888, 18. With permission from the Royal Anthropological Institute of Great Britain and Ireland. pp. 267–268].

Thus for Tylor the question of exogamy is political. Exogamy is a policy of political alliances.

We should note that the entire article contains only one reference to incest. Tylor writes that incest proceeds from regulations governing exogamy. For instance, if a tribe changes its rules of descent, it also redefines the category of incestuous marriage. Although Tylor was not concerned with incest, he is widely quoted by his successors as the originator of the alliance theory of incest.

Tylor finds only one problem with his explanation—that alliance does not always prevent strife or bloodshed. Nevertheless, he maintains,

> by binding together a whole community with ties of kinship and affinity, and especially

by the peacemaking of the women who hold to one clan as sisters and to another as wives, it tends to keep down feuds and to heal them when they arise, so as at critical moments to hold together a tribe which under endogamous conditions would have split up. Exogamy thus shows itself as an institution which resists the tendency of uncultured populations to disintegrate, cementing them into nations capable of living together in peace and holding together in war, till they reach the period of higher military and political organisation [p. 268].

In its implicit assumption that incest regulations coincide with regulations governing exogamy, Tylor's initial statement differs significantly from the theories developed by his successors.

REO FORTUNE

For the prestigious *Encyclopedia of the Social Sciences* (1932), the task of describing and explaining incest was allotted to Reo Fortune. In a compact article, Fortune elaborated on Tylor. Fortune wrote that in modern society the law against incest is rarely enforced as severely as in primitive society, mainly because affinal obligations are less important. In primitive societies, consanguine groups are related only by intermarriage, and so incest becomes important:

A separation of affinal relationship from consanguineous relationship assures a wider recognition of social obligation, for the former relationship carries with it such obligations as alliance in war and cooperation in hunting and in mourning ceremonial. Any incestuous alliance between two persons within a single consanguineous group is in so far a withdrawal of their consanguineous group from the alliance and so endangers the group's survival. Because in modern society the obligations attached to affinal kinship are not extensive and those attached to consanguineous kinship are restricted, rules against incest such as those contained in the Anglican prayer book are not all enforced by the state; but incest between consanguineous kin who are still within the restricted circle of real obligation remains liable to severe penalty [This quote and subsequent quotes are reprinted from Fortune, R. F., "Incest." *Encyclopaedia of the Social Sciences*, Vol. 7, E. R. A. Seligman, ed. Copyright 1932, renewed 1960 by Macmillan Publishing Co., Inc. p. 620].

Once Fortune has defined incest as functional for group survival, he sets out to criticize alternative theories. He overemphasizes the differences between Freud and Malinowski and neglects their areas of agreement. He rejects Westermarck, claiming that "inbreeding . . . is not known to be biologically harmful except amongst stocks which are too poor to stand an accentuation of their qualities [p. 621]." Fortune also argues that "if, for example, brothers and sisters were encouraged to sexual familiarity in childhood, there is no evidence that sexual aversion would develop between them [p. 621]." He postulates that because most societies instill sexual aversion between brothers and sisters, this avoidance "functions effectively in prevention of incest."

Fortune also completely rejects family–socialization theory, claiming that it does not explain why incest regulations are expanded to wider consanguinity groups. Faulting Seligman and Freud for overstating the narrow "range of incest which is found in modern society," he points to incestuous royal marriages in ancient Egypt and Hawaii which served to stress the exclusiveness of blood lines.

Fortune does not distinguish between sexual intercourse and marriage other than to assume that exogamous—and, therefore alliance-creating—marriages are the only route to sexual intercourse. He does not distinguish among the core regulations of mother–son, father–daughter, and brother–sister incest and their extensions. A flaw in Fortune's logic is that he argues from the extensions of the incest taboo—the scope of which varies from society to society—to the universal core regulations. He also errs, I believe, in confidently advocating group functionalism. Because he finds it significant that modern society does not severely enforce incest regulations, Fortune chooses to explain the origin of these regulations by the alliance theory. He does not distinguish among different incestuous dyads and thereby loses the opportunity to prove his case, at least for the father–daughter dyad.

Leslie A. White: The Culturologist

White is the most important representative of cultural evolutionism in anthropology. White believed that once humans achieved the basic components of culture—tools, language, and symbolic thinking—their lives, behavior, and social activities were culturally determined.

> The stream of culture thus flows, changes, grows and develops in accordance with laws of its own. Human behavior is but the reactions of the organism man to this stream of culture. Human behavior—in the mass, or of a typical member of a group—is therefore culturally determined. A people has an aversion to drinking cow's milk, avoids mothers-in-law, believes that exercise promotes health, practices divination or vaccination, eats roasted worms or grasshoppers, etc., because their culture contains trait-stimuli that evoke such responses. These traits cannot be accounted for psychologically [This quote and subsequent quotes are reprinted from White, L. A. "The Definition and Prohibition of Incest." *American Anthropologist*, 1948, 50:433, American Anthropological Association].

The preceding quote is from White's long article, "The Definition and Prohibition of Incest," in the 1948 issue of *American Anthropologist*. To arrive at a theory explaining the problem of incest—a problem which he admits holds a strange fascination for humans—White uses a process of elimination. He quickly dismisses the theory of Hobhouse and Lowie, who claimed that incest avoidance is instinctive, by stating simply that societies would not find it necessary to enact strict laws against a behavior that was instinctively avoided to begin with. Moreover, asks White, what strange sort of instinct would be capable of distinguishing between cross cousins and parallel cousins (the latter usually defined as incestuous, the former preferred marriage partners)? White also dispenses easily with the inbreeding theory, arguing that (a) inbreeding does not cause degeneration, and that (b) degeneration is the cause of inbreeding, not the result of it: "If the children of brother–sister or father–daughter unions in our society are frequently feeble-minded or otherwise inferior it is because feeble-minded individuals are more likely to break the powerful incest taboo than are normal men and women and hence more likely to beget degenerate offspring [p. 417]." Moreover, argues White, primitives could not understand the laws of genetics or even the process of procreation, and even if they could, they could not dissociate genetic from environmental causes. White here lays a trap for himself in arguing that because primitives, like primates, did not understand the facts of procreation, the prohibition of inbreeding could not be found in genetic reasoning. White also points out that *the prohibition of incest preceded an understanding of paternity*. He completes his argument by drawing again upon the ethnographic fact that extensions of the incest taboo do not follow genetic lines. Freud's explanation is inadequate, in White's opinion, because he does not attempt to account for the many and varied forms of incest prohibitions. Westermarck and Durkheim are easily dismissed as well.

White introduces his own reasoning by first quoting from authorities like Frazer, Boas, Goldenweiser, and Wissler on mysterious and enigmatic nature of the incest problem. White states that those looking for an explanation in biology and psychology are on the wrong track. The right track is culturology, first hinted at by the culturological Tylor back in 1888 and elaborated by White. He compares himself, not very modestly, to Darwin:

> Important contributions to science are sometimes made "before their time", that is, before the general level of scientific advance has reached a point where widespread appreciation becomes possible. There was really very little that was novel in the work of Darwin; most if not all of the ideas and facts had been presented before. But the broad front of the cultural process of biologic thought had not advanced sufficiently prior to 1859 to make a general acceptance of this point of view possible. So it is with the problem of incest. An adequate explanation has been extant for decades. But, because the problem is a culturological one, and because the science of culture is still so young and so few scholars even today are able to grasp and appreciate its nature and scope, an understanding of incest and its prohibitions is still very limited. As culturology develops and matures, however, this understanding as well as that of a host of other suprapsychological problems will become commonplace [p. 430].

Like other animals, White reasons, humans are engaged in a struggle for survival in which cooperation and mutual aid are the most important weapons. There is some cooperation among primates, but the real need for cooperation comes with the development of speech. Human children, attracted to their parents and siblings because they are so close to each other, show an inclination toward inbreeding common to all primates but incompatible with cooperation among humans. This cooperation is founded on the existing structure of the family:

> In the evolutionary process, whether it be social or biological, we almost always find the new growing out of, or based upon, the old. And such was the case here; the new cooperative organization for food and defense was built upon a structure already present: the family. After all, virtually everyone belonged to one family or another, and the identification of the cooperative group with the sex-based family would mean that the benefits of mutual aid would be shared by all. When, therefore, certain species of anthropoids acquired articulate speech and became human beings, a new element, an *economic* factor, was introduced into an institution which had up to now rested solely upon sexual attraction between male and female. We are, of course, using the term *economic* in a rather broad sense here to include safety as well as subsistence. The human primate family had now become a corporation with nutritive and protective functions as well as sexual and incidentally reproductive functions. And life was made more secure as a consequence.
>
> But a regime of cooperation confined to the members of a family would be correspondingly limited in its benefits. If cooperation if advantageous *within* family groups, why not between families as well? The problem was now to extend the scope of mutual aid.
>
> In the primate order, as we have seen, the social relationships between mates, parents and children, and among siblings antedates articulate speech and cooperation. They are strong as well as primary. And, just as the earliest cooperative group was built upon these social ties, so would a subsequent extension of mutual aid have to reckon with them. At this point we run squarely against the tendency to mate with an intimate associate. Cooperation *between* families cannot be established if parent marries child; and brother, sister. A way must be found to overcome this centripetal tendency with a centrifugal force. This way was found in the definition and prohibition of incest. If persons were forbidden to marry their parents or siblings they would be compelled to marry into some other family group—or remain celibate, which is contrary to the nature of primates. The leap was taken; a way was found to unite families with one another, and social evolution as a *human* affair was launched upon its career. It would be difficult to exaggerate the significance of this step. Unless some way had been found to establish strong and enduring social ties between families, social evolution could have gone no further on the human level than among the anthropoids [pp. 424–425].

Families become units of cooperation, and affiliate according to their economic needs. White argues that marriage is an economic contract and families, economic units, as levirate and sororate, bride price, and dowry all indicate. Similarly, "the prohibition of incest has at bottom an economic motivation—not that primitive peoples were *aware* of this motivation, however, for they were not [p. 425]." White had discarded inbreeding theory, claiming that early humans were not aware of the facts of procreation. But if they were also unaware of the economic benefits of the incest taboo, how can such benefits explain its existence? There is obviously no answer.

White quotes various authorities to support his contention that marriage and family are economic institutions. It was not the need for sexual outlets that led to marriage and family: "Marriage *does* provide an avenue of sexual exercise and satisfaction, to be sure. But it was not sexual desire that produced the institution [p. 426]." Sexual outlets occur independent of marriage. Nor did romantic love create marriage and family: "No culture could afford to use such a fickle and ephemeral sentiment as the basis of an important institution [p. 427]."

Because incest was culturally created, it is, of course, culturally variable, with each culture defining incest differently. Although we know of no society that customarily permits marriage between parent and child, as White admits, nonetheless brother–sister marriages are sometimes permitted in royal families. White summarizes his argument:

> From psychology we learn that the human animal tends to unite sexually with someone close to him. The institution of exogamy is not only *not* explained by citing this tendency; it is contrary to it. But when we turn to the cultures that determine the relations between members of a group and regulate their social intercourse we readily find the reason for the definition of incest and the origin of exogamy. The struggle for existence is as vigorous in the human species as elsewhere. Life is made more secure, for group as well as individual, by cooperation. Articulate speech makes cooperation possible, extensive, and varied in human society. Incest was defined and exogamous rules were formulated in order to make cooperation compulsory and extensive, to the end that life be made more secure. These institutions were created by *social* systems, not by *neuro-sensory-muscular-glandular* systems. They were syntheses of culture elements formed within the interactive stream of culture traits. Variations of definitions and prohibition of incest are due to the great variety of situations. In one situation, in one organization of culture traits—technological, social, philosophic, etc.—we will find one type of definition of incest and one set of rules of exogamy; in a different situation we find another definition and other rules. Incest and exogamy are thus defined in terms of the mode of life of a people—by the mode of subsistence, the means and circumstances of offense and defense, the means of communication and transportation, customs of residence, knowledge, techniques of thought, etc. And the mode of life, in all its aspects, technological, sociological, and philosophical, is culturally determined [pp. 433–434].

The argument that primitives were not aware of the process of procreation is weak, and White's ideas about the lack of correspondence between incest regulation and genetic relatedness are limited to the *extensions* of the incest taboo rather than the taboo itself. The lack of a distinction between core taboos and the extensions, on one hand, and between the different incestuous dyads, on the other, further weakens White's argument.

White does not define the units among which cooperation is necessary. Are they nuclear families, extended families, lineages, clans? If the analogy between the nuclear family and wider social circles is sound, then incest prohibitions have to be located *within* cooperating units. White cites no evidence for economic cooperation between intermarrying units. If economic cooperation depends on intermarriage, no unit within which marriage is forbidden can cooperate within itself economically. This is obviously not the case, for there is strong cooperation both within nuclear families and lineages. White also quotes representatives of the family–socialization theory, such as Malinowski and Seligman, to prove that incest taboos function to prevent disorganization of the nuclear family and to promote cooperation within it. But he does not explain why sexual interest is disruptive within the family and yet promotes cooperation between families. White tries to solve the problem by pointing out that Malinowski and Seligman limit themselves to the "disruption and discord" that sexual appetites create, but that he emphasizes the "positive values" resulting from the same sexual appetites.

White repeatedly emphasizes that incest must be *culturally* defined. But White himself claimed that incest prohibitions preceded the recognition of paternity. If people did not understand paternity, how could they culturally define and prohibit father–daughter incest? Mother–offspring relations are recognized by nonhuman primates and mammals, as are uterine sibling relations, because these result from obvious physical acts. But if fatherhood is neither recognized nor understood, how could early humans have prohibited sexual relationships or marriage between this particular male and the daughter of a female? Moreover, without culturally defining the father role, how could social units be defined as cooperative unless they were only matrilinear, matrifocal subunits? Could such subunits be maintained in a species that evolved hunting and gathering and an elaborate sexual division of labor? And, last but not least, if ignorance of a certain factor rules out the possibility of that factor as a cause, how despite ignorance about paternity could relations between well-defined human family groups cause incest taboos?

White's argument is further weakened because he does not distinguish between sex and marriage or between incest taboos and exogamy. Although in arguing that marriage and family are economic institutions, White distinguishes between sex and marriage, he neglects this distinction when he argues that incest prohibitions were created in order to ensure exogamy. As Seligman convincingly argued, men need not abstain from sexual relations with their daughters or sisters in order to marry them off (especially if they do not understand biological paternity) unless premarital chastity is required, a rare enough phenomenon in human societies.

CLAUDE LÉVI-STRAUSS: THE STRUCTURALIST

Lévi-Strauss's monumental work on kinship systems, social structure, and mythology has had an enormous impact. The first four chapters of his famous *Elementary Structures of Kinship* (1949/1969) are devoted to the problem of incest.

Lévi-Strauss's approach to the problem of incest is more profound than that of his predecessors in the alliance school. He begins with the problem of nature and culture, pointing out that humans are both biological and social beings. Some human responses to external and internal stimuli depend wholly on biology, others on the social environment. Distinguishing between the two is not always easy: "Culture is not merely juxtaposed to life nor superimposed upon it but in one way serves as a substitute for life, and in the other, uses and transforms it, to bring about the synthesis of a new order." Lévi-Strauss is mainly interesting in determining where nature ends and culture begins, and to do so he looks to human rather than animal social organization.

Lévi-Strauss assigns the term "natural" to everything that is both universal in humans and characterized by spontaneity. "Cultural" describes everything subject to norms expressed in rules and characterized by relativeness and particularity. Thus, for him, the prohibition of incest constitutes the transition between nature and culture, because this prohibition is at the same time universal and rule proscribed, cultural, and particular. Its universality consists in that fact that no culture is totally free of marriage restrictions. Even the exceptions he enumerates are not really exceptions at all. Lévi-Strauss sums up:

> The prohibition of incest has the universality of bent and instinct, and the coercive character of law and institution. Where then does it come from, and what is its place and significance? Inevitably extending beyond the historical and geographical limits of culture, and co-extensive with the biological species, the prohibition of incest, however, through social prohibition, doubles the spontaneous action of the natural forces with which its own features contrast, although itself identical to these forms in field of application. As such,

the prohibition of incest present a formidable mystery to sociological thought. Few social prescriptions in our society have so kept that aura of respectful fear which clings to sacred objects [This quote and subsequent quotes are reprinted from *The Elementary Structure of Kinship* by Claude Lévi-Strauss, revised edition, translated by J. H. Bell, J. R. von Sturmer, and R. Needham. Copyright © 1969 by Beacon Press. Reprinted by permission of Beacon Press. p. 10].

Lévi-Strauss notes a problem. Following Levy-Bruhl, he states that although the explicit prohibition of incest is not universal, incest occurs very rarely, and that when it does it is considered a *monstrum*, spreading disgust and horror. Lévi-Strauss thus encounters problems with the concept of "rule," as modern sociologists have with the concept of "norm." Levy-Bruhl is right in claiming that incest does not occur, with or without explicit prohibitions, the rule or norm is "enacted": It defines what people are naturally inclined to do. If, however, Levy-Bruhl is wrong and explicit prohibitions are universal, the norm or rule is "proscriptive."

To crack this nut, Lévi-Strauss surveys various incest theories. He starts with the inbreeding theory, quoting Morgan and Maine who claimed that incest prohibitions shield the species from the disastrous consequences of consanguineous marriages. Lévi-Strauss acknowledges that some primitive folklores do have certain such beliefs, but he rejects the explanation, quoting East, a plant geneticist, who had shown that inbreeding maize can produce excellent results, and quoting Dahlberg (1937), a human geneticist, who had concluded that "as far as heredity is concerned these inhibitions do not seem to be justified." After admitting that homozygosity is *more* dangerous in small groups, Lévi-Strauss, again quoting Dahlberg, concludes as follows: "The economic systems of some primitive or archaic societies severely limit population size, and it is precisely for a population of such a size that the regulation of consanguineous marriages can have only negligible genetic consequences [p. 16]." If it is dangerous in small groups, how can it have only "negligible" consequences?

Lévi-Strauss considers Westermarck and Ellis as representative of the sociologists and psychologists who consider the prohibition of incest a social projection of natural tendencies and who ascribe incest avoidance to the dulling of erotic feeling by habituation. Lévi-Strauss argues that Ellis and Westermarck confuse two forms of familiarity: that between people with regular sexual contact and that between those without it. In order to know whether the latter dampens eroticism as does the former, one would need an experimental situation in which to separate the effects of habituation from prohibition, an experimental situation which, says Lévi-Strauss, does not exist.

Lévi-Strauss falls into the same trap as many of his predecessors in declaring that "there is no point in forbidding what would happen if it were not forbidden [p. 18]." Yet he himself presents two logical counterarguments: Such prohibitions can be used to prevent rare exceptions; suicide is inhibited but also prohibited. He rejects these arguments, however, claiming that suicide is completely sociogenic and foreign to the animal world, whereas incest is not.

Lévi-Strauss concludes at this point that "society expressly forbids only that which society brings about [p. 18]." He then takes up the problem of incest and exogamy:

> Considered as a social institution, the prohibition of incest has two different aspects. Sometimes it is only a prohibition of sexual union between close consanguines or collaterals, while at others this form of the prohibition, based as it is upon a definite biological criterion, is only one aspect of a broader system which is apparently without any biological basis. In many societies the rule of exogamy prohibits marriage between social categories which include near relatives, but, along with them, a considerable number of individuals for whom it is impossible to establish all but the most distant consanguineous or collateral relationships. In this case, it is an apparent caprice of the nomenclature to assimilate individuals who fall under the prohibition to biological relatives [p. 19].

He rejects the notion of writers such as Morgan and Frazer that exogamy encompasses the incest taboo because exogamous regulations are always wider than incest regulations. He discounts McLennan, Spencer, Lubbock, and Durkheim, with their theories of wife capture and blood horror. But for the essential problem of distinguishing clearly between sexual intercourse and marriage, Lévi-Strauss does not find a solution. He quotes Robert Lowie's despair at finding such a solution and returns to his leitmotif:

> The prohibition of incest is in origin neither purely cultural nor purely natural, nor is it a composite mixture of elements from both nature and culture. It is the fundamental step because of which, by which, but above all in which, the transition from nature to culture is accomplished [p. 24].

> But this union is neither static nor arbitrary, and as soon as it comes into being, the whole situation is completely changed. Indeed, it is less a union than a transformation or transition. Before it, culture is still non-existent; with it, nature's sovereignty over man is ended. The prohibition of incest is where nature transcends itself. It sparks the formation of a new and more complex type of structure and is superimposed upon the simpler structures of physical life through integration, just as these themselves are superimposed upon the simpler structures of animal life. It brings about and is in itself the advent of a new order [p. 25].

In his third chapter, Lévi-Strauss returns to the problem of incest and exogamy. Although he acknowledges Seligman's statement that exogamy would not prevent mother–son incest in patrilinear and father–daughter incest in matrilinear descent systems, he nevertheless insists that "in many cases it is the rule of exogamy which is decisive, without taking real relationships, apart from those of first degree, into account [p. 29]." In this somewhat contradictory sentence, Lévi-Strauss begins his struggle with the nature–culture dichotomy. Citing Australian and Oceanian examples, he declares that the terms "father," "mother," "son," "daughter," "brother," and "sister" are really indicators of social relations rather than biological ties. The incest prohibition, therefore, is the transition from the natural fact of consanguinity to the cultural fact of alliance. Nature prescribes mating, but culture modifies it as marriage. Thus nature imposes alliance through mating, and culture immediately defines its modalities. Therefore, sighs Lévi-Strauss with relief, "the apparent contradiction between the regulatory character of the prohibition and its universality is thus resolved [p. 32]."

But is it really? Lévi-Strauss has arrived at his final conclusion: The prime role of culture is to ensure the existence of the group. The group intervenes through incest prohibitions to ensure its own existence. Groups exist because they exchange valuables among themselves; the two most important valuables are food and women. Scarcity of food requires no proof or explanation, but scarcity of women does as the sex ratio usually ensures an equal number of males and females. Lévi-Strauss presents an interesting analysis of why women are a scarce commodity: In most primitive societies marriage is an economic contract and not simply an erotic relationship, and because disparities in wealth and status among males creates differences in demands for females, females are scarce. In his fourth chapter, Lévi-Strauss returns to Tylor and reasons that because females are the most valuable "bases" for creating alliances, a male must abrogate his privileged access to those females he wants to exchange with another group. Thus Lévi-Strauss lays the foundation for his magnum opus on kinship, which is based on the ideas of exchange and reciprocity.

Lévi-Strauss was finally more interested in marriage than incest. Writing on kinship and believing that incest regulations reside at the center of any kinship system, he commented at length on the question. His structuralist approach to kinship inevitably led him to embrace the alliance theory.

SUMMARY

The alliance school argues that incest regulations came into being in order to bind the nuclear family to wider social units and thereby to create political and economic alliances between families. The theorists of the alliance school are completely group oriented, whereas among the theorists of the family-socialization school one still can find some references to the individual and his or her motivation. For the alliance school, the maintenance of the larger social unit is the goal of social organization and the basis for social rules. This view is so pervasive that alliance theorists completely reject the arguments of the family–socialization school despite the fact that both use group functionalism as their essential theoretical approach.

Admittedly, neither White nor Lévi-Strauss possessed the information on inbreeding depression that we have today. Lévi-Strauss struggled with the problem of transition from nature and culture; White simply ignored it. The failure to distinguish among the different incestuous dyads rendered the alliance theories vulnerable to the attacks of family–socialization theorists, and Seligman made good use of the opportunity. Had the alliance theorists made those distinctions, they could have saved part of their theories by using it to explain father–daughter incest prohibitions.

As it stands, even the central argument of the alliance school—that incest regulations create alliances by enforcing exogamy—is still a matter of debate among ethnographers. Nevertheless, the alliance school has continued to gain its share of adherents (e.g., Cohen, 1978).

Obviously, if two theories completely contradict each other in trying to explain the same phenomena, something must be wrong with them. We turn now to two prominent theorists, Jack Goody and David Schneider, who analyzed the weaknesses of the family–socialization and alliance theories—Goody from the social point of view and Schneider from the cultural.

10

GOODY AND SCHNEIDER:
THE PROBLEM OF DEFINITION

Definitions have been a major problem of incest theory. Too wide a definition can blur the distinction between incest and other problems of kinship organization. Too narrow a definition can ignore the problem of "extension" of the incest prohibitions.

Goody and Schneider attack the problems of definition. Goody's approach is basically social, Schneider's cultural. Their common denominator is their acceptance of the definition of incest given by the people of the culture/society they describe. Goody and Schneider severely criticize the great schools for their shortcomings; however, they both ignore the problem of origins and settle for ad hoc specific explanations.

Goody (1956) argues with Murdock (1955) about the state of anthropology as a science. Murdock claimed that anthropology was beyond the "classificatory" stage and could proceed to the analysis of dynamic processes. Goody, on the other hand, found the terms anthropologists used to be ambiguous, full of discrepancies in understanding and evaluation. Goody turned to the *Oxford Concise Dictionary* for definitions of *incest*, *adultery*, and *fornication* and claimed that not everyone who dealt with the incest taboo was discussing the same range of phenomena. He documented this claim with quotations from Radcliffe-Brown, Murdock, and Malinowski. To elucidate the basic concepts, Goody investigated the evidence from two well-documented cultures: the Ashanti (Rattray, 1929) and the Tallensi (Fortes, 1936, 1949). He also used auxiliary material from the Trobriands, the Nuer, and his own research among the LoDagaa. In the case of the matrilineal Ashanti, Goody found a clear distinction between prohibitions of sexual intercourse with a woman of the matriclan and of the patriclan. The two transgressions bore different names, although they were both punishable by death, and both dealt with by the same tribunal. A third transgression included forms of adultery, and even sexual intercourse with one's own wife in the bush. Its punishment generally ranged from ridicule to repayment, although intercourse with a chief's wife and rape were punishable by death.

Thus, Goody found among the Ashanti three categories of interdictions: (a) sexual intercourse with a woman of the matriclan; (b) intercourse with a woman of the patriclan; and (c) intercourse with a married woman (adultery). Sexual intercourse with the mother and sister fall within the first category; father–daughter incest belongs to the second. The same system occurs among the matrilineal Trobriander (Malinowski, 1929).

The patrilineal Tallensi, although Fortes has not found them to have the concept of incest, distinguished three types of sexual offenses: (a) intercourse with a member of the same patriclan; (b) intercourse with the wife of a member of the same patriclan; and (c) intercourse with the wife of a nonclansman. Brother–sister and father–daughter incest belong to the first category. Mother–son incest belongs to the second: The son is forbidden to sleep with his mother not because she is his mother, but because she is the wife of a member of the same patriclan, in this case his own father. That is, however, not the spirit of Fortes's writing. According to Fortes, "incest with one's own mother the natives regard as a thing of such monstrous iniquity that it is ridiculous to conceive of anyone who is not mentally deranged committing it [This quote and subsequent quotes are reprinted from Fortes, M. *The Web of Kinship among the Tallensi*. Copyright 1949 by Oxford University Press. Published for the International African Institute by Oxford University Press. p. 112]." Having sexual relations with the other nuclear wives of clansmen—father's co-wives to mother, brother's wife, and son's wife—is "almost as heinous a sin and is regarded with little less horror [p. 112]." Thus the Tallensi obviously distinguish to some extent between the mother and other women who are wives of close clansmen.

Goody did not clasify these offenses according to their punishment, but pointed out that whereas the offenses of the first category (e.g., sexual intercourse with a daughter, sister, or paternal aunt) are simply disreputable, those of the second category are viewed with the horror usually attendant on incest. Goody acknowledged a difference between inner and outer lineage circles because among the latter, love relationships with the female were in fact permitted, but among the former, adultery with the wife of a remote member of the patriclan was considered the most reprehensible form of adultery.

In summarizing his findings, Goody suggested that the concept of incest be retained to designate forbidden sexual intercourse with the unilinear descent groups and that the concept of horror be dissociated from incest per se. For the second category of offenses, Goody suggested the concept of group-wife adultery because the taboo depends on the woman's married status. If the women were not married into the unlinear descent group, intercourse with her would be considered fornication and might not be punished at all. The implication is that in a matrilineal society a father might have sexual relations with his unmarried daughter or commit not heavily sanctioned adultery with a daughter who marries outside the father's clan. Another implication is that in a patrilineal society, a son can have sexual relations with his unmarried mother. No evidence on the actual occurrence of such cases is presented by Goody (or by anyone else, to the best of my knowledge).

Horror, according to Goody, is associated not with incest but with what he called "social reproduction." Because in a patrilinear society the continuity of the patriclan depends on the person occupying the category of "wife," illegal intercourse between wives and other members of the patriclan is horrifying. In a matrilinear society, however, social reproduction is secured by sisters, and therefore intercourse with a sister is horrifying. Father–daughter incest does not fall within the most horrifying category among either the Ashanti or the Tallensi, but mother–son incest does so in both societies. Goody offered the following explanation, one he preferred to the biological explanation: "In the Tallensi the mother is the closest *wife* of a clansman of *senior* generation, while in the Ashanti she is the closest *female clan member* of *senior* generation [1956:296]."

Goody's cultural explanation is flawed. He has not explained why father–daughter incest belongs to the least heinous category in both societies, why mother–son is the most heinous, and brother–sister somewhere in between. The explanation, I maintain, is biological. Moreover, as elegant as Goody's schematization is, it is neither the most comprehensive nor the most economical explanation possible. Thus, we do not know why the Ashanti punish father–daughter incest with death despite the fact that it is "only" a second grade offense, whereas among the Tallensi second grade offenses are merely disreputable. This, too, does not fit Fortes's description. Although Fortes clearly describes the difference between sibling incest and incest with clansmen's wives, he has some interesting remarks concerning sibling incest:

As has been previously mentioned, Tallensi do not designate incest between brother and sister as sinful. Whey they say it is forbidden (*kih*), as they sometimes do, they mean it rather in the sense that it is disgraceful, scandalous, and unnatural than in the narrower ritual sense. If they are asked why then it is so uncommon, considering the many opportunities and temptations that surely offer, they explain it by the intimacy of siblings in childhood and adolescence. They deny that the temptation exists. 'Look', said Sinkawol, arguing this point with me, 'my sister, is she not marriageable? And here am I, however attractive she is, I do not even notice it; I am never aware that she has a vagina; she is just my sister and someone will one day come and marry her and I will give her to him and get my cows. You and your sister grow up together, you quarrel and make it up, how can you desire to have intercourse with her [1949, p. 112]?

Among the Tallensi would the only social comment on father–daughter or brother–sister incest be disapproving gossip? Goody also has problems with the Nuer material because—except in the cases of wives of a father, a full brother, or a son—a wide range of sexual relations with other kinsmen's wives are permitted and the classic patrilinear society's horror of group-wife adultery is absent.

Goody evaluated the two leading theories of incest—family–socialization and alliance—in light of his categories. He succeeded in integrating the two theories by a brilliant application of his own typology. Although the prohibition of sexual intercourse within the unilinear kin group reflects alliance theory, because it compels members of the lineage to marry out and create alliances, the prohibition of sexual intercourse with group wives reflects family–socialization theory. The only flaw in this neat explanation is contained in following:

Let us now turn to the prohibition of intercourse with those who have married members of the descent group. This is spoken of by Seligman, Fortes and many others as incest. Yet clearly the explanations of Fortune, Levi-Strauss and others concerning marriage alliances have no bearing at all upon this phenomenon, because it is not intercourse with the women as such which is forbidden, but intercourse with them as wives of group members. Rights over their sexual services have been pre-empted by other males with whom one has prior relationships. These women are not necessarily consanguineal kin at all, with the exception of ego's mother; they are affines [1956:303].

But is ego's mother so easily excepted? Would it not be better to look beyond the fascinating cultural symmetry of the Ashanti and the Tallensi to see the universal facts of life—mating, reproduction, and socialization?

DAVID M. SCHNEIDER: FROM FACTS OF INCEST
TO THE MEANING OF INCEST

As a doctoral student at Rutgers, I found a mimeographed article hidden away in a dusty library corner. The paper was entitled "Attempts to Account for the Incest Taboo," and the date January 1956 was handwritten on it.

The 1956 article is in fact a review piece. Schneider does not pay attention to what he calls "bizarre theories," among which he includes Freud's theory on primal parricide, Durkheim's speculation on bloodshed, and Lord Raglan's belief that men once considered it to be dangerous to have intercourse with women who lived on the same side of the river. Neither does Schneider spend time on "genetically relevant considerations that have been refuted almost as often as they have cropped up." But Schneider is careful on this score: "However, it is still conceivable that there may be genetic considerations which have not yet been discovered, or an instinctual base that has not yet been scientifically demonstrated. It is impractical therefore to discard these ideas completely [p. 2]."

In the second section of his paper, Schneider minutely describes the theories of Tylor, Fortune, White, Malinowski, Seligman, Murdock, and Parsons, and points out the efforts toward synthesis by Parsons and Murdock. In the third section, Schneider raises important questions about these theories. He asks for a clear distinction among (a) the historical origin of the incest taboo; (b) its functions; and (c) the conditions for its universal maintenance. He points out that the second and third may be identical.

Schneider criticizes the Tylor–Fortune–White line for the following:

1. White uses contemporary data to prove the functional importance of the incest taboo at the time of its origin.
2. Only in contemporary society do various personal ties provide alternatives to marriage in promoting cooperation.
3. White explicitly assumes the nuclear family existed before the incest taboo and rules of exogamy.
4. White assumes that if there were no incest prohibitions all socially relevant marriages would be incestuous.

Schneider then predicts Slater's findings of 3 years later (see Chapter 6) and argues that even without incest prohibitions most people would mate outside the family. He also contends that in order to establish marriage, peaceful and normal relations must obtain between the partners' families, and these conditions are more the precondition than the result of marriage ties. Moreover, families cooperate for more reasons than marriage ties: "nasty mastodons" or saber-toothed tigers may endanger several families at once.

Schneider also notes the confusion of incest regulations with exogamous rules and points out that alliance theory is untenable because it fails to account for mother–son prohibitions in patrilineal systems and father–daughter prohibitions in matrilineal ones, as well as for various cases of divergence between prohibited marriage and permitted sexual relations. Schneider arrives here at three very important methodological rules:

> Clearly then what seems to be required is first, such a definition of the incest taboo as separates marriage from sexual relations; secondly, such a definition of the incest taboo as separates the prohibition on sexual relations among members of the nuclear family from that prohibition applied outside the nuclear family; third, that definition of the incest taboo as clearly distinguishes it and treats it as a separate problem from the maintenance or establishment of exogamic regulations [1956:13].

Schneider further distinguishes between homosexual and heterosexual relations, a very important point in his later writings. He also implies a distinction between incestuous dyads, although he does not explain why those dyads differ substantially.

Schneider criticizes family–socialization theory, pointing out that:

1. Sexual relationships do not interfere with power relationships, as the case of sexual relations between masters and slaves in the Deep South would prove.
2. The disruptive effect of sexual jealousy on the family can be eliminated by means other than incest taboo—by institutionalization, for instance.
3. There is no reason to assume that taboos actually prevent incest.

Schneider then offers an alternative:

> It might be an equally tenable position to state that these salutory and beneficial effects derive not from the taboo itself but from the real probability that few mothers would undertake to have relations with their sons, nor would many fathers with daughters, nor brothers with sisters, except in certain "pathological" cases, and that even if the taboo were not present, such relations would occur so infrequently—that is, just as infrequently as they do with the taboo—as to practically constitute no source of concern [p. 15].

He even exempts the mother–son dyad from his first argument against the family–socialization theory, indicating how incompatible the differences in power between a mother and son are to sexual intercourse and thereby anticipates findings by several primatologists a decade later. Unfortunately, Schneider neglected to draw the conclusions implicit in his critical analysis. When the following 20 years of research supplied evidence confirming several of his earlier theses, Schneider reconsidered and reached quite different conclusions.

Schneider's 1976 paper takes cognizance of recent thinking among social biologists and biosocial anthropologists (he calls Fox's writing "genetic and ethological word plays"), and indicates that the universality of incest prohibition is in serious doubt and that evidence is accumulating that most, if not all, humans tend to avoid sexual intercourse with members of the primary socialization unit. He acknowledges that Westermarck's old hypothesis has been reinstated, but he is doubtful about the genetic evidence.

Schneider's argument in the second paper again centers on clarifying concepts. He mentions homosexual relationships and states that they must be included in the definition of incest for certain Oceanian tribes. He contends that these people have a different conception of the three incestuous dyads and quotes Goody on the distinction between ingroup and outgroup sexual offenses. But his most important theoretical assumptions are the following:

1. Incest, exogamy, marriage, and kinship are much more than regulations of the breeding system.
2. Incest is a different matter for humans than for animals. For animals it is a matter of intragroup relations, for humans, a matter of intergroup relations.
3. A prohibition applies to a culturally defined, morally conceived pattern of behavior, and it is distinct from what is actually done or the rate at which it is done.

Schneider insists that prohibitions are in no way related to the general human tendency to avoid sexual intercourse with members of their primary socialization group. He claims that the famous Hawaiian and Egyptian cases are not exceptions to the universality of the incest because they were not prohibited. For a biologist, it might be sufficient to know whether an animal species inbreeds, but an anthropologist must know human social organization and culture. Ethology, he maintains, should not be confused with anthropology. Schneider abides by

Durkheim's notion that social norms partake of the moral authority, that social norms have moral as well as a practical quality. But Schneider modifies this notion, adding that a moral issue for one culture is a practical issue for another. Thus moral authority does not come out of thin air; it rests on social norms which themselves rest on moral authority, which emerges in turn from social norms. The argument is dizzyingly circular.

Schneider stops pursuing the origin of the incest taboo. In quoting Lindzey (1967) (see Chapter 6, p. 76) he accepts that the taboo's origin may be biological, but he also states that he is more concerned with its social purposes:

> The tendency for humans to avoid sexual intercourse with members of their primary socialization unit sounds, and is intended to sound, like a human tendency rather than a culturally defined, normatively governed mode of social action. For the moment I shall hold in abeyance the obvious question of how an innate human tendency can exist independent of some normative, culturally defined aspects.
> It is just this view of human behaviour as a set of tendencies, with whatever cultural or normative aspects may be associated with them treated as indistinguishable and not worth distinguishing, which moves the ethologists, primateologists and the students of evolutionary biology into high gear so that they react with all the full vigour of their newly hybridised field. Since it is all innate, some of the more vulgar ones might argue, and it is all grounded in the genes, we must look to some theory of innate tendencies which shape the socio-cultural material. For surely culture does not go against innate human nature. Or does it? Or does it shape human nature [pp. 158–159]?

Hence Schneider accuses social biology of claiming that everything is innate. This accusation was probably unsubstantiated in 1976, and it certainly is today.

The old nature–culture problem is pronounced dead. Surely no one can claim that *everything* in humans is innate or even that incest avoidance is totally innate—just as no one can argue that everything is culturally determined. Schneider implies that once biology has had its say it is no longer important; the next item on the agenda is culture. Yet not only does actual behavior—incest avoidance or its comparatively rare occurrence—follow the biological etiology of incest avoidance, but cultural prohibitions do as well. Even in the simplest animal, biological predispositions manifest themselves in actual behavior only after complex interaction with the environment. Among humans, culture, biologically evolved and species specific, is part of the biological background as well as part of the environment. Variations in interpretations of incest among different societies may be fascinating, but if we look there and nowhere else, we are merely collectors. If Schneider is interested in the *meanings* of incest, I am interested in its *meaning*. We cannot understand its meaning without considering the basic facts of human life—sex, reproduction, and socialization. Although the fact that humans are cultural animals makes their social behavior harder to understand than that of other animals, nonetheless cultural regularities do reflect basic biological predispositions, Schneider's rich ethnographic material notwithstanding. It is true that some cultures include homosexuality within their incest prohibitions, but no societies limit incest prohibition to homosexual relations while permitting all heterosexual relations.

SUMMARY

Goody and Schneider focused severe criticism on the two central schools of incest theory. Goody emphasized the exigencies of unilinear social structures that dictate the definition of incest and separate it from other prohibited sexual behaviors, like adultery and profligation. He introduces the important concept of "social reproduction." Schneider concentrated on the problem of meanings. For him, the definition of incest is specific to one culture, defining the meaning of incest for the people of that culture. Both Goody and Schneider are interested in the specific social-cultural configuration and not in the human universal of incest regulations.

Nevertheless, both succeed in delineating the basic features of incest regulations. Goody reveals the crucial difference between father–daughter incest and incest in other dyads. Schneider concludes that incest would not occur even if there were no incest prohibitions. Their resistance to the biosocial explanation, however, prevents them from pursuing their own findings to attain a more comprehensive view of incest.

11

CONCLUSIONS

Man's age old striving to know himself and his world has proved an amazingly fruitful adventure. Until the Renaissance, it was sufficient for him to know some basic tenets of philosophy, whereby he maintained the Socratic legacy. Renaissance empirical science and rationalist thinking provided a new cosmology. The Industrial Revolution furnished the scientist with unimagined technical instruments for observation and exploration, and our Atomic Age, with its scanning electron microscopes, nuclear accelerators, and super computers, has seemingly removed almost all obstacles to the expansion of the limits of knowledge.

Yet the more we are able to know, the more complicated the picture becomes: The map of human knowledge always turns out to contain more unknown than known territories.

When man thought the universe was composed of four basic elements and man himself was a composite of four humors, the possible combinations were not numerous. Today, the number of practically discernible variables is almost infinite. Those four humors have given way to 2000 different types of enzymes catalyzing thousands of complicated compounds. One such compound, DNA, has the exceptional capability of copying itself and therefore seems to us to contain in itself the secret of life. Built on seemingly simple principles, it can create formidable dimensions of variability: millions of species of living things—plants and animals—each different from the others, and some species containing millions of individuals, all different from each other. Differences

175

are coded in the language of DNA based on the same words, containing only three letters each. A single mistake in one word is sufficient to kill its bearers or their offspring or to bring on incurable maladies. The key to curing one of man's worst enemies, cancer, is somewhere in the DNA code.

One of the most characteristic traits of the human species is that of sociability. It is no wonder that the social sciences have chosen to try to understand man by studying his social life: An understanding of what human beings do together with other human beings may provide an important—possibly the most important—clue to what they are. But social life among humans is even more complicated than human physiology. Not only is each individual different from every other individual, but the constellations in which social behavior takes place are also each unique. On July 14, 1789, certain social activities took place in Paris, France, which we call a "revolution." On November 6, 1917, certain social activities took place in St. Petersburg, Russia, to which we assign the same name. But we are not sure about these two incidents being identical, and we are therefore careful to call the first the "French Revolution," and the second the "October Revolution." How can we know what motivates people to make revolutions? Were the constellations identical, or even similar? If they were, do people obey constellations blindly? Would any group of people caught in a "revolutionary constellation" launch a revolution? Or are the dramatis personae—those revolutionaries who led the masses to the Bastille or the Winter Palace—also important? What about the masses themselves?

Academic sociology grew during the first 60 years of this century into a discipline which claimed to possess a theory to explain all social action. But it turned out that research did not verify theory. New theories emerged, attention turned to methodology. Research became more and more sophisticated and complex. In *The Coming Crisis of Western Sociology*, Alvin Gouldner (1970), one of the great masters of modern social science, aptly summarizes the situation:

> From the viewpoint of much of the sociology dominant in the United States today, it is not man but society that is the measure. This conception of sociology and of society once had value, because it stressed the extent to which men are shaped by an environment of other men, are dependent upon one another, suffer from or take pleasure in one another; because it stressed that men are not simply the slaves of natural, biological or geographical forces. This view of man and society was, once, a benign antidote, at least when devoid of medieval nostalgia, to the individualistic and competitive bourgeois culture crystallizing in the nineteenth century. Today, however, the context is growingly bureaucratized, centralized, and committee-shackled Welfare–Warfare State. So, this sociology's inherent

subordination of the individual to the group serves not so much as a reminder to men of their debt to one another, but as a rationale for conformity to the status quo, for obedience to established authority, and for a restraint that makes haste slowly; it becomes a warning about limits rather than an invitation to pursue opportunities [p. 508].

An even more devastating criticism came 2 years later from Andreski (1972) who enumerated the "crimes" of academic sociology. Whereas Gouldner saw a way out in "reflexive sociology," Andreski declared that "we have no grounds for expecting any great leap forward in the study of society which would replicate the rapid advances of the natural sciences [p. 242]" (see also Eisenstadt and Curelaru, 1976).

But the natural sciences, with all their great advances, were taboo. Any reapprochement between the two disciplines was considered to jeopardize the hard-won separateness and uniqueness of the social sciences. Only a few social scientists dared cross the tabooed frontier and return to the study of man rather than society. They were ridiculed and persecuted, attacked as reactionaries, and some of them became outcasts at their universities. But their books, articles, and courses attracted more and more graduate students. Biosociology, biosocial anthropology, and sociobiology (different names were used for the same theory, according to the particular focus of the converging disciplines; sociology, anthropology, or biology) posed a challenge to institutionalized social science.

Most early publications in biosociology were, understandably, only reflections. The idea that man is an entity unto himself, that without him no social group can be understood, was so revolutionary and upsetting that exploring the ramifications of this idea took up all the energy of those writers. In addition, the idea that the wall separating humans from other animals is not impenetrable gave rise to wildly audacious speculations and unsubstantiated analogies in the new writings.

Unexpectedly, it was the field of biology—the "antidiscipline"—that offered some help in the matter. The publication of E. O. Wilson's *Sociobiology* in 1975 posed an enormous challenge to social scientists: to restudy all their previous conclusions in light of this well-organized new theory. I have tried in this book to test the hypotheses of this new theory and have used incest as the phenomenon to study. I believe I have shown that biosocial theory explains more questions about incest than any alternative theory—it explains more and explains better.

Why more? Family–socialization theory explained parent–child incest prohibitions, but encountered problems with sibling incest. Alliance theory, on the other hand, was successful with sibling incest prohibitions, but had several difficulties with parent–child prohibitions in unilineal societies. None of the theories could explain the different forms of regulations in different incestuous dyads; none could be tested through the criteria of prediction of actual behavior.

Biosocial theory was tested against predictions of five kinds of behavior. The first predicted a clear pattern of frequency in the occurrence of incest; the second, differential behavior patterns between the sexes participating in incestuous relationships; the third, the social and ecological patterns in which incestuous behavior was apt to occur; the fourth, the circumstances under which inhibitions will not be activated and incest, therefore, should occur; the fifth, the directions of social variability and the degree of harshness of social reactions against incest.

But was I entitled to use the term *prediction*? If it were possible to have people mate experimentally, as is the case with Lorenz's geese, my use of the term would be completely justified. With people, however, all researchers must settle for "quasi-predictions." It is possible to say, "I predict that we will find a certain frequency distribution and I have found it, even though my material was collected before I formulated the prediction." This "ex post facto prediction" (or "retrodiction") is the best available method for proving most aspects of human behavior, and certainly sexual aspects.

My evidence, though convincing, is certainly not exhaustive: We need better, more reliable statistics on committed incest, as well as a thorough review of the clinical material. We need clinical psychologists, psychiatrists, and social workers who would pay attention to those variables that heretofore have been neglected because no one thought them worth noticing. We need better studies of the psychological side of inhibitions and better cross-cultural research of the variability of incest regulation and punishment.

Exposing my conclusions to better evidence will either strengthen my theory or destroy it: a challenge to both the advocates and the opponents of biosocial theory.

An important feature of a good theory is its successful application to additional problems. Because incest is connected with reproduction, mating, and the family, these might be the areas for further testing. I am now certain that in my earlier writings on these topics—particularly *Women in the Kibbutz* (Tiger and Shepher, 1975)—many more facts would have brought into relief had parental investment theory been used as a theoretical framework (Shepher and Tiger, in press).

The paradigm of inhibitions, preventions, and prohibitions is not limited to incest. Probably an entire series of other behaviors can be explained by the same paradigm—for instance, homicide. If it can be shown that the same paradigm applies to homicide, one has to find the specific constellation in which inhibition is not activated. If it is true that behaviors that are both inhibited and prevented occur only rarely, and if we can find the mechanism of homicide inhibition, then we will be able to create situations in which homicide is as rare as mother–son incest.

Moreover, if we can better understand mate selection by applying parental investment theory, we might be able to apply *cultural* measures to make mate selection less hazardous and thereby minimize the number of unhappy families.

In short, by coming to a more complete understanding of human nature, we will be in a better position to influence our fate. Human nature is not only the result of millions of years of evolution, it is also "a potential array that might be achieved through conscious design by future societies [Wilson, 1978:196]." But the rich possibilities of the potential array of future designs must be based on the single assumption that human beings are part of nature. This assumption does not lead to biological determinism. On the contrary, an analysis of incest teaches us how biological epigenetic rules create an intricate network of coevolutionary processes. Culture, man's most important means of adaptation, evolves alongside the biological evolution of the species. Once a behavior pattern evolves, adaptive culture goes along with it, elaborates it, decorates it and embellishes it. Incest avoidance evolved to be an evolutionary stable strategy. It created a situation in which incestuous behavior became rare. Culture added its own influence by prohibiting the rare occurrence. If the occurrence was very rare, culture settled for ridicule; if owing to circumstances that weakened the inhibitions the transgressions threatened to be more frequent, culture applied sanctified taboos and horror.

Thus the sociobiological theory of incest is a modest contribution to coevolutionary theory that, as Lumsden and Wilson (1981) say "might seem to imply a coupling of processes that is unlikely and perhaps impossible [p. 1]." But it is not. True understanding of the human being must originate in the knowledge of all the ways—the biological and the social–cultural—that have led to the emergence of this species and to its social and cultural life. Perhaps such an understanding can lend to some solutions to humanity's greatest problems.

GLOSSARY

adelphic   (Greek: brother) involving brothers.

affinity   Term used in anthropology to indicate relatedness through marriage as opposed to consanguinity.

agnates, agnatic   Patrilineally related kin.

allele   One of several alternative forms of a gene on a specified locus on a chromosome.

allomothering   Mothering by somebody other than the biological mother.

altruism   In sociobiology any act that increases the fitness of another at some expense to the fitness of ego.

amygdala   Part of the brain's limbic system associated with arrest reaction, rage, and sexual activities.

analogy   (Greek: *analogia*—resembling) a resemblance in function and sometimes in structure which is due to convergence in evolution and not common ancestry (as distinguished from homology).

anal phase   In psychoanalysis the second stage of psychosexual development in which gratification is derived from expulsion or retention of feces.

androgynization   (Greek: *andros*—man, *gynos*—woman) the tendency to ignore sex differences, to attribute the same qualities to men and women.

angina pectoris   A heart condition characterized by occasional suffocating pain in the chest due to insufficient oxygenation of the heart muscle by the coronary arteries.

anomie   A social situation characterized by the absence of norms.

assortative mating   Not random mating; mating in which certain types are preferred as mates.

Atid   (Hebrew: future) pseudonym used by Bettelheim for the kibbutz he investigated in his *Children of the Dream*.

avuncolocal residence   (Latin: *avunculus* = maternal uncle) a residence rule in matrilineal cultures according to which the sister's son upon marriage goes to live with his mother's brother.

clan   Unilinear descent group, the founder of which is legendary—usually matrilineal (matriclan) but sometimes partrilineal (patriclan). The latter is sometimes called *gens*.

cognitive dissonance   Having beliefs or behavioral tendencies that contradict each other. According to the theory (Festinger) the subject will try to reduce the dissonance by changing the behavior or the belief.

consanguinity   Genetic relatedness through birth as opposed to affinity.

cortex (cerebral cortex)   Thin layer (2–5 mm) covering the surface of the main part of the brain (cerebrum) associated with voluntary motor functions, sensory perception, and association, as well as with interpretation, thought, memory, and learning.

couvade   A social practice by which the father expresses his identification with the mother in parturition by imitating her as though he were in labor.

cross cousins   Children of cross-sex siblings (i.e., father's sister and mother's brother).

crossing over   The process of exchange of genetic information between two homologus chromosomes.

culturgene   A relatively homogeneous set of artifacts, behavior, institutions, and mental concepts transmitted by learning among members of a society, and the holistic pattern they form.

culturology   Theoretical direction associated with Leslie A. White, according to which culture is the only definitive factor in shaping human behavior.

descent   Term used in anthropology to indicate the transfer of rights from generation to generation (see also unilineal, matrilineal, and patrilineal descent).

diaspora   (Greek: dispersion) term used to indicate the groups and places outside Israel where Jews lived after the destruction of the Second Temple.

diploid   A cell having a double set of chromosomes, as opposed to haploid. Somatic cell are diploid.

dominant (gene, allele)   The allele or gene that affects the phenotype of both the homozygote and the heterozygote.

endogamy   A rule whereby one is obliged to marry within a defined social group (also a tendency to do so without an explicit rule).

epigenetic rule   Genetically determined procedures that direct the assembly of the mind, including screening of stimuli by peripheral sensory filters, internuncial cellular organizing processes, and deeper processes of directed cognition.

estrogen   Hormone triggering the process of ovulation in the mammalian female.

ethology   The part of zoology that investigates animal behavior.

evolutionary stable strategy (ESS)   It connotes a strategy such that, if almost everyone is doing it, it would not pay a mutant something different.

exogamy   A rule whereby one is obliged to marry outside a defined social group (also a tendency to do so without an explicit rule).

Fehlleistung   (German) a slip of the tongue which reveals the unconscious.

fellatio   Oral intercourse performed on a male.

gene   A segment of the chromosome with a detectable function; a discrete unit of genetic information.

genetic fitness   The relative number of offspring of an organism as compared with the number of offspring of other organisms of the same species.

genetic load   The proportion of lethal and lethal-equivalent (causing severe impairment of health) mutations in a population.

genetrix   (Latin: feminine of genitor) she who bears the child.

genitor   (Latin: progenitor, sire) term used in anthropology to indicate the sire or biological father.

genome   A group of genes; the ensemble of the genetic material in a cell.

genotype   The genetic makeup of an organism comprising all the genes on its chromosomes.

group selection   Natural selection which works on the group as a unit.

haploid   A cell with one single set of chromosomes as opposed to diploid. Sex cells are haploid.

heterozygosity   The quality of having a different allele from each of the two parents on the same locus, distinguished from homozygosity.

hippocampus   Part of the limbic system of the brain associated with the involuntary movements, emotional reactions, and the channeling of incoming sensory inputs to other parts of the limbic system.

homology   (Greek: *homology*—agreement) a similarity in two structures due to inheritance from a common ancestor.

homozygosity   The quality of having the same allele from both parents on the same locus, distinguished from heterozygosity.

hypergyny   A rule or preference for the woman to marry a man of a higher class or caste.

inbreeding depression   A reduction in reproductive capacity and physiological efficiency brought about by inbreeding a population.

inclusive fitness   Fitness in terms of ego's offspring together with the offspring of ego's relatives.

infanticide   Killing of infants.

kibbutz meuchad   (Hebrew: the united kibbutz) one of the three largest kibbutz federations in Israel.

kiryat yedidim   (Hebrew: the village of friends) pseudonym used by Spiro for the kibbutz he investigated in *Kibbutz: Venture in Utopia* and *Children of the Kibbutz*.

latency   In psychoanalysis, the period of middle childhood, roughly from ages 6 to 12.

lethal equivalents   Genes (mutants) that cause severe impairment of health and therefore kill a certain proportion of individuals carrying them.

levirate   A social rule by which a brother is obliged to marry his brother's widow.

lineage   Unilinear descent group that has a historical founder (matrilineage, patrilineage).

locus   (Latin: place) the position of a gene on a chromosome.

mastigophora   (Latin: whip bearer) a group of protozoan organisms possessing flagellae as locomotor organelles.

matriarchy   Pattern of family based on the rule of the mother.

matrilineal (descent)   A social rule that limits transfer of rights to the female line (from mothers to daughters).

meiosis (reduction division)   A two-phase division of sex cells that result in haploid gametes having half the number of chromosomes (in humans, 23).

miocene   A geological epoch from 25 million years ago to 5 million years ago.

mitosis   Division of somatic cells in which duplication and assortment of the genetic material ensures genetic identity between parent and the two daughter cells.

non sequitur   (Latin: it does not follow) a logical mistake indicating that the conclusion drawn from the evidence is false.

ontogeny, ontogenetic   The life history of a single organism, as distinguished from phylogeny.

oral phase   In psychoanalysis, the first stage of psychosexual development in which pleasure is derived through the mouth.

parallel cousins   Children of same sex siblings (i.e., father's brother and mother's sister).

parricide (patricide)   The murder of a parent (father) by the offspring.

pater (Latin: father) term used in anthropology to indicate the sociological father, that is, the male who has the social responsibility for the children as opposed to the role of biological father (genitor), which may or may not coincide.

patriarchy Pattern of family based on the rule of the father.

patrilineal (descent) A social rule limiting the transfer of rights to the male line (from father to son).

phallic phase In psychoanalysis, stage of psychosexual development in which gratification is derived from the genitalia and from attachment to the opposite sex parent.

phenotype The observable part of the organism, as distinguished from the genotype.

phylogeny, phylogenetic The evolutionary history of a group of related organisms, as distinguished from ontogeny.

Pleistocene A geological epoch from 2 million years ago to about 10,000 years ago.

Pliocene Geological epoch from 5 million to 2 million years ago.

polyandry Stable mating of a female with two or more males.

polygynandry A rare form of human mating system in which a group of males (usually brothers) marry a female and later add more females; exists mainly in the subhimalayan region of India.

polygyny Stable mating between a male and two or more females.

positive feedback system A chain of reactions in an organism in which increase of one factor causes increase in another factor which again causes increase in the first and so on.

presenting The act of the female turning the genitalia toward the male inviting him to sexual intercourse.

primates The zoological order that includes prosimians (like the lemur), monkeys, apes, and man.

primatology Part of the science of zoology, the subject matter of which is the study of primates.

prolactine Hormone triggering the formation of milk in the mammalian female.

protista A separate kingdom of organisms like protozoa, algae, and fungi.

protozoa An organism consisting of one cell (unicellular), usually considered a part of the animal kingdom.

recessive (gene, allele) The allele or gene that does not affect the phenotype of heterozygote; it affects only the homozygote.

reinforcement An act or procedure of following the conditioned stimulus by the unconditioned stimulus.

rite de passage (French) a term introduced by van Gennep for a rite celebrating the transition of a person from one important phase in his life cycle to another.

sex ratio Number of males in a population multiplied by 100 divided by the number of females in the population ($SR = 100M/F$).

stimulus satiation Adaptation of the nervous system to a recurrent stimulus, as a result of which the intensity of the reaction decreases with the increase of the frequency of the stimulus.

teknonymy A social rule by which a parent is named by the name of his offspring.

unilinear descent A descent rule in which descent is counted through either the males or the females.

uterine Descending from the same mother.

uxorilocal (Latin: *uxor*—wife) a rule whereby a man upon marriage is expected to live with his wife and her relatives in their place.

vir (Latin: man) term used in anthropology to indicate the man who is formally married to the woman.

virilocal   A rule whereby a woman is expected upon marriage to live with her husband and his relatives in their place.

Volkerwanderung   (German: wandering of peoples) a phase of European history starting with the penetration of Germanic tribes around 200 B.C. and ending with the fall of the Roman Empire.

xenophilic   Loving strangers.

Yaara   (Hebrew: to the forest) pseudonym used by Shepher for the kibbutz he investigated.

REFERENCES

Aberle, D. F. *et al.*
   1963   The Incest Taboo and the Mating Patterns of Animals. American Anthropologist 64: 253–266.
Abernethy, Virginia
   1974   Dominance and Sexual Behavior: A Hypothesis. American Journal of Psychiatry 131: 813–817.
Adams, N. S., and J. V. Neel
   1967   Children of Incest. Pediatrics 40:50–62.
Albrecht, H., and S. C. Dunnet
   1971   Chimpanzees in Western Africa. Munich: Piper.
Alexander, R. D.
   1974   The Evolution of Social Behavior. Annual Review of Ecology and Systematics 5:325–383.
   1975   The Search for a General Theory of Behavior. Behavioral Sciences 20:77–100.
   1977   Natural Selection and the Analysis of Human Sociality. *In* The Changing Scene of the Natural Sciences. Special Publication of the Academy of Natural Sciences. Pp. 283–337.
   1979   Darwinism and Human Affairs. Seattle: Washington University Press.
   n.d.   Incest, Culture and Natural Selection. Unpublished manuscript.
Altmann, M.
   1962   A Field of the Sociology of Rhesus Monkeys *Macaca mulatta*. Annals of the New York Academy of Sciences 102:338–435.
   1963   Naturalistic Studies of Maternal Care in Moose and Elk. *In* Maternal Behavior in Mammals. H.L. Rheinhold, ed. New York: John Wiley & Sons.
Andreski, Stanislav
   1972   Social Sciences as Sorcery. Harmondsworth: Penguin.
Ardrey, R.
   1961   African Genesis: A Personal Investigation into the Animal Origin and Nature of Man. New York: Atheneum.

1966 The Territorial Imperative. New York: Atheneum.
1970 The Social Contract: A Personal Inquiry into the Evolutionary Sources of Order and Disorder. London: Collins.
1976 The Hunting Hypothesis: A Personal Conclusion concerning the Evolutionary Nature of Man. New York: Atheneum.

Armstrong, Louise
1978 Kiss Daddy Goodnight—A Speak-Out on Incest. New York: Hawthorn Books.

Atkinson, J. J.
1903 Primal Law. London: Longmans.

Backhofen, J. J.
1861 Das Mutterrecht. Stuttgart: Krais and Hoffmann.

Bagley, Christopher
1969 Incest Behavior and Incest Taboo. Social Problems 16:505–519.

Barash, David P.
1977 Sociobiology and Behavior. New York: Elsevier.
1979 Sociobiology: The Whispering Within. Glasgow: Fontana/Collins.

Barkow, Jerome H.
1978 Evolution and Human Sexuality. In La sexualite humaine: Textes fondamentaux. Claude Crepault and Joseph Leoy, eds. Montreal: Presse de l'Universite de Quebec.

Barlow, George W., and James Silverberg, eds.   ʼ
1980 Sociobiology: Beyond Nature/Nurture. Boulder, Colorado: Westview Press.

Barrai, I., L. L. Cavalli-Sforza, and M. Mainardi
1964 Testing a Model of Dominant Inheritance for Metric Traits in Man. Heredity 19:651–668.

Bateson, P. P. G.
1978 Early Experience and Sexual Preferences. In Biological Determinants of Sexual Behavior. J. B. Hutchinson, ed. London: John Wiley & Sons.

Beach, Frank A.
1951 Instinctive behavior: Reproductive activities. In Handbook of Experimental Psychology. S. S. Stevens, ed. New York: Wiley.

Ben-David, J., ed.
1964 Agricultural Plannings and Village Community in Israel. Paris: Unesco.

Bender, L., and A. Blau
1937 The Reaction of Children to Sexual Relations with Adults. American Journal of Orthopsychiatry 7:500–518.

Bender, L., and A. E. Geugett
1952 A Follow-Up Report on Children Who Had Atypical Sexual Experience. American Journal of Orthopsychiatry 22:825–837.

Bengtsson, B. O.
1978 Avoiding Inbreeding: At What Cost? Journal of Theoretical Biology 73:439–449.

Bettelheim, B.
1969 Children of the Dream. New York: Macmillan.

Bigelow, Robert
1969 The Dawn Warriors. Boston: Little, Brown.

Bischof, N.
1972a Inzuchtbarrieren in Saugetiersozietaten. Homo 23:330–351.
1972b The Biological Foundations of the Incest Taboo. Social Information 2(6):7–36.
1975 Comparative Ethology of Incest Avoidance. In Biosocial Anthroplogy. R. Fox, ed. Pp. 37–67. London: Malaby Press.

Bixler, Ray H.
1980 Nature versus Nurture: The Timeless Anachronism. Merrill-Palmer Quarterly 26(2):153-

1981a Primate Mother–Son "Incest." Psychological Reports 48:531–536.
1981b The Incest Controversy. Psychological Reports 49:267–283.
1981c Incest Avoidance as a Function of Environment and Heredity. Current Anthropology 22:639–643.

Bodmer, W. F., and L. L. Cavalli-Sforza
1976 Genetics, Evolution, and Man. San Francisco: W. H. Freeman.

Brace, C. L., and A. Montague
1979 Atlas of Human Evolution. Second ed. New York: Holt, Rinehart and Winston.

Briggs, Cabot L.
1975 Environment and Human Adaptation in the Sahara. In Physiological Anthropology. Albert Damon, ed. Pp. 93–119. New York, London and Toronto: Oxford University Press.

Brown, R. W., and D. McNeill
1966 The "tip-of-the-tongue" phenomenon. Journal of Verbal Learning and Verbal Behavior 5:325–337.

Burnham, Jeffrey T.
1975 Incest Avoidance and Social Evolution. Mankind 10:93–98.

Burton, Robert
1973 Folk History and the Incest Taboo. Ethos 1:504–516.

Campbell, Bernard
1976 Humankind Emerging. Boston: Little, Brown.

Caplan, Arthur L., ed.
1978 The Sociobiology Debate. New York: Harper & Row.

Caprio, Fr. S., and D. R. Brenner
1964 Sexual Behavior. New York: Citadel.

Carpenter, C. R.
1942 Sexual Behavior of Free-Ranging Rhesus Monkeys: Periodicity of Oestrus, Homo-Sexual, Auto-Erotic and Non-Conformist Behavior. In Naturalistic Behavior of Non-Human Primates. C. R. Carpenter, ed. Pp. 319–342. University Park Press, Pennsylvania: States University Press.
1964 A Field Study in Siam of the Behavior and Social Relations of the Gibbon. In Naturalistic Behavior of Non-Human Primates. C. R. Carpenter, ed. Pp. 145–271. University Park Press, Pennsylvania: States University Press.
1965 The Howlers of Barro Colorado Islands. In Primate Behavior. I. De Vore, ed. Pp. 250–292. New York: Holt, Rinehart and Winston.

Carter, C. O.
1967 Risks to Offspring of Incest. Lancet. February 25, p. 436.

Caspari, E.
1963 Selective Forces in the Evolution of Man. American Naturalist 97:5–14.

Cavalli-Sforza, L. L., and W. F. Bodmer
1971 The Genetics of Human Populations. San Francisco: W. H. Freeman.

Chagnon, N. A., and W. Irons, eds.
1979 Evolutionary Biology and Human Social Behavior. North Scituate, Massachusetts: Duxbury.

Chance, M. R. A.
1962 Nature and Special Features of the Instinctive Social Bonds of Primates. In Social Life of Early Man. S. L. Washburn, ed. London: Methuen.

Clutton-Brock, T. H., and P. H. Harvey, eds.
1978 Readings in Sociobiology. San Francisco: W. H. Freeman.

Cohen, Morris R., and Ernest Nagel.
1934 An Introduction to Logic and Scientific Method. New York: Harcourt Brace.

Cohen, Y. A.
  1964 The Transition from Childhood to Adolescence. Chicago: Aldine.
  1978 The Disappearance of Incest Taboo. Human Nature 7:27–28.
Constantine, L. L. and J. M. Constantine.
  1973 Group Marriage. New York: Macmillan.
Coult, Allan D.
  1963 Causality and the Cross-Sex Prohibition. American Anthropologist 65(2):266–278.
Count, Earl W.
  1958 The Biological Basis of Human Sociality. American Anthropologist 60:1049–1085.
  1973 Being and Becoming: Human Essays on the Biogram. New York: Van Nostrand Reinhold.
Crook, John H.
  1980 The Evolution of Human Consciousness. London: Clarendon Press
Crow, J. F., and M. Kimura.
  1970 An Introduction to Population Genetic Theory. New York: Harper and Row.
Curtis, H.
  1970 Biology. New York: Worth.
Dahlberg, G.
  1937 On Rare Defects in Human Populations with Particular Regard to In-Breeding and Isolated Effects. Proceedings of the Royal Society of Edinburgh 58:213–232.
Daly, M., and M. Wilson
  1978 Sex, Evolution and Behavior. North Scituate, Massachusetts: Duxbury Press.
D'Aquili, Eugene
  1972 The Biological Determinants of Culture. Module 13, McCaleb Module in Anthropology, Addison-Wesley Modular Publications, 1–29.
Darling, F. F.
  1951 A Herd of Red Deer. London: Oxford University Press.
Davis, Kingsley
  1940 Extreme Social Isolation of a Child. American Journal of Sociology 45:554–565.
  1947 Final Note on a Case of Extreme Isolation. American Journal of Sociology 50:430–433.
Davis, Kingsley, and Wilbert A. Moore.
  1945 Some Principles of Stratification. American Sociological Review 10:242–249.
Dawkins, Richard
  1976 The Selfish Gene. Oxford: Oxford University Press.
Demarest, William J.
  1977 Incest Avoidance among Human and Nonhuman Primates. In Primate Biosocial Development: Biological, Social and Ecological Determinants. Suzanne Chevalier-Skolnikoff and Frank E. Poirier, eds. Pp. 323–342. New York and London: Garland Press.
DeVore, I., ed.
  1965a Male Dominance and Mating Behavior in Baboons. In Sex and Behavior. Frank Beach, ed. New York: John Wiley & Sons.
  1965b Primate Behavior. New York: Holt Rinehart and Winston.
DeVos, George A.
  1975 Affective Dissonance and Primary Socialization: Implications for a Theory of Incest Avoidance. Ethos 3:165–172.
Dickemann, Mildred
  1979 Female Infanticide, Reproductive Strategies and Social Stratification: A Preliminary Model. In Evolutionary Biology and Human Social Behavior: An Anthropological

Perspective. N. A. Chagnon and W. G. Irons, eds. Pp. 321–367. North Scituate, Massachusetts: Duxbury Press.

Dickerson, E. E., *et al.*
1954 Evaluation of Selection in Developing Inbred Lines of Swine. Bulletin of the Agricultural Experiment Station 551:60–120.

Durham, William H.
1976 The Adaptive Significance of Cultural Behavior. Human Ecology 4:89–121.
1979 Toward a Coevolutionary Theory of Human Biology and Culture. *In* Evolutionary Biology and Human Social Behavior: An Anthropological Perspective. N. A. Chagnon and W. G. Irons, eds. Pp. 39–58. North Scituate, Massachusetts: Duxbury Press.

Durkheim, E.
1963 Incest: The Origin and Nature of the Taboo. New York: Lyle Stewart. (First ed. 1897.)
1952 Suicide: A Study in Sociology. London: Routledge and Kegan Paul.

Dyke, B., and W. T. Morrill, eds.
1980 Geneological Demography. New York: Academic Press.

East, E. H.
1938 Heredity and Human Affairs. New York:

Edholm, Otto G.
1978 Man—Hot and Cold. London: Edward Arnold.

Eibl-Eibesfeldt, I., von.
1951 Beobachtungen Zur Fortpflanzungsbiologie und Jugendentwikelung des Eichhörnchens. Zeitschrift fur Tierpsychologie 8:370–400.

Eisenberg, J. F.
1966 The Social Organization of Mammals. *In* Handbuch der Zoologie, Band 8. G. H. Helmeck *et al.*, eds. Pp. 1–83. Berlin: Gruyter.

Eisenstadt, S. N.
1956 Ritualized Personal Relations. Man 96:90–95.

Eisenstadt, S. N., and M. Curelaru
1976 The Form of Sociology—Paradigms and Crises. New York: John Wiley and Sons.

Elkes, Joel
1968 Mental Disorders: Biological Aspects. International Journal of the Social Sciences 10:139–149.

Ember, Melvin
1975 On the Origin and Extention of the Incest Taboo. Behavior Science Research 4:249–281.

Engels, F.
1905 Origins of the Family, Private Property and the State. Chicago: Kerr. (First ed. 1884.)

Etkin, W., ed.
1964 Social Behavior and Organization among Vertebrates. Chicago: University of Chicago Press.

Evans Pritchard, E. E.
1951 Kinship and Marriage among the Nuer. Oxford: Clarendon Press.

Ewer, R. F.
1968 Ethology of Mammals. Lonson: Logos Press.

Falconer, D. S.
1976 Introduction of Quantitative Genetics. New York: Ronald Press. (First ed. 1960.)

Festinger, L., and D. Katz, eds.
    1953   Research Methods in the Behavioral Sciences. New York: Holt, Rinehart and Winston.
Finkelhor, D.
    1980   Sex among Siblings. Archives of Sexual Behavior 9:171–194.
Fortes, M.
    1936   Kinship, Incest and Exogamy of the Northern Territorities of the Gold Coast. In Custom Is King. L. H. D. Buxton, ed. Pp. 239–259. London: Hutchinson.
    1949   The Web of Kinship among the Tallensi. Oxford: Oxford University Press.
Fortune, R. F.
    1932   Incest. In Encyclopedia of the Social Sciences 7. E. R. A. Seligman, ed. Pp. 620–622. New York: Macmillan.
Forward, Susan, and Craig Buck
    1978   Betrayal of Innocence: Incest and its Devastation. Los Angeles: J. P. Tarcher.
Fox, Robin
    1962   Sibling Incest. British Journal of Sociology 13:128–150.
    1967a   In the Beginning: Aspects of Hominid Behavioral Evolution. Man 2:415–433.
    1967b   Kinship and Marriage. Harmondsworth: Penguin.
    1967c   Totem and Taboo Reconsidered. In The Structural Study of Myth and Totemism. Edmund Leach, ed. Pp. 161–178. ASA Monographs 45. London: Tavistock.
    1968   Incest, Inhibition and Hominid Evolution. Paper presented at the Wenner-Gren Symposium Burg Wartenstein.
    1972   Alliance and Constraint: Sexual Selection in the Evolution of Human Kinship. In Sexual Selection and the Descent of Man 1871–1971. B. Campbell, ed. Pp. 282–331. Chicago: Aldine.
Fox, Robin (ed.)
    1975a   Biosocial Anthropology. London: Malaby Press.
    1975b   Primate Kin and Human Kinship. In Biosocial Anthropology. Robin Fox, ed. Pp. 9–35. London: Malaby Press.
    1980   The Red Lamp of Incest. New York: E. P. Dutton.
Frances, Vera, and Allen Frances
    1976   The Incest Taboo and Family Structure. Family Process 15:235–244.
Franklin, W. L.
    1974   The Social Behavior of the Vicuna. In The Behavior of Ungulates and Its Relation to Management, Vol. 1. V. Geist and F. Waltner, eds. Pp. 477–487. Morges, Switzerland: IUCN Publications.
Frazer, J. G.
    1910   Totemism and Exogamy, London: Macmillan.
Freud, Sigmund
    1910   [Three Contributions to the Theory of Sex] (A. A. Brill, trans.). New York: Dutton.
    1950   Totem and Taboo. New York: Norton. (First ed., 1913.)
    1953   Three Essays on the Theory of Sexuality. In The Standard Edition of the Complete Psychological Works of Sigmund Freud. London: Hogarth; Macmillan. Vol. 7:123–245. (First ed., 1905.)
    1961   The Ego and the Id. In The Standard Edition of the Complete Psychological Works of Sigmund Freud. London: Hogarth; New York: Macmillan. Vol. 19:12–63. (First ed., 1923.)
Gebhard, P. H. et al.
    1965   Sex Offenders. New York: Harper & Row.

Geiser, R. L.
1979 Hidden Victims: The Sexual Abuse of Children. Boston: Beacon Press.
Giraud-Teulon, A.
1874 Les origines de la famille. Geneva-Paris: Cherbuliez-Sandozet, Fischbacher.
Goethe, F. W.
1944 Faust. Basel: Verlag Birkhausen.
Goodall, J.
1965 Chimpanzees of the Gombe Stream Reserve. *In* Primate Behavior. I. DeVore, ed. Pp. 53–110. New York: Holt, Rinehart and Winston.
1967a Mother–Offspring Relationship in Free Ranging Chimpanzees. *In* Primate Ethology. D. Morris, ed. Pp. 287–347. London: Weidenfold and Nicholson.
1967b My Friends the Wild Chimpanzees. New York: National Geographic Society.
1968 The Behavior of Free-Living Chimpanzees in the Gombe Stream Reserve. Animal Behavior Monographs 1(3):161–311.
1971 In the Shadow of Man. London: W. Collins.
Goodale, J. C.
1971 Tiwi Wives: A Study of Women of Melville Island, North Australia. Seattle: University of Washington Press.
Goody, J.
1956 A Comparative Approach to Incest and Adultery. British Journal of Sociology 7:286–305.
Gough, K. E.
1959 The Nayars and the Definition of the Marriage. Journal of the Royal Anthropological Institute 89:23–34.
Gould, J. L., and C. G. Gould
1981 The Instinct to Learn. Science 81 2(4):44–50.
Gould, Julius, and William L. Kolb, eds.
1964 A Dictionary of the Social Sciences. New York: The Free Press.
Gouldner, Alvin W.
1970 The Coming Crisis of Western Sociology. New York: Basic Books.
Granit, Ragnar
1963 Recurrent Inhibition as a Mechanism of Control. *In* Progress in Brain Research. G. Moruzzi, A. Fessard, and H. H. Jasper, eds. Pp. 23–37. Vol. 1: Brain Mechanisms. Amsterdam: Elsevier.
Greene, Penelope J.
1978 Promiscuity, Paternity and Culture. American Ethnologist 5:151–159.
Greenland, C.
1958 Incest. British Journal of Delinquency 9: 62–65.
Greenwood, P. J., and P. H. Harvey
1976 The Adaptive Significance of Variation in Breeding Area Fidelity of the Blackbird. Journal of Animal Ecology 45:887–898.
1977 Feeding Strategies and Dispersal of Territorial Passerines: A Comparative Study of the Blackbird. Ibis 119:528–531.
Gregory, M. S., and A. Silvers
1978 Sociobiology and Human Nature. San Francisco: Jossey-Bass Publishers.
Gundlach, H.
1968 Brutfürsorge, Verhaltensontogenese und Tagesperiodik beim Europäischem Wildschwein. Zeitschrift fur Tierpsychologie 25:955–995.
Hall, K. R. L., and I. DeVore.
1965 Baboon Social Behavior. *In* Primate Behavior: Field Studies of Monkeys and Apes. I.

DeVore, ed. New York: Holt Rinehart and Winston.

Hamburg, D. A., and E. McCown
1979 The Great Apes. Menlo Park, California: Benjamin/Cummings.

Hamilton, W. D.
1964 The Genetic Evolution of Social Behavior. Journal of Theoretical Biology, 7:1–52.
1970 Selfish and Spiteful Behavior in an Evolutionary Model. Nature 228:1218–1220.
1972 Altruism and Related Phenomena, Mainly in Social Insects. Annual Review of Ecology and Systematics 3:193–232.

Harcourt, A. H.
1979 The Social Relations and Group Structure of Wild Mountain Gorilla. In The Great Apes. D. A. Hamburg and E. R. McCown, eds. Pp. 187–192. Menlo Park, California: Benjamin/Cummings.

Hart, C. W. M., and H. R. Pilling
1960 The Tiwi of North Australia. New York: Holt Rinehart and Winston.

Hartl, Daniel L.
1977 Our Uncertain Heritage Genetics and Human Diversity. Philadelphia: J. B. Lippincott.

Hartung, J.
1976 On Natural Selection and the Inheritance of Wealth. Current Anthropology 17:607–622.
1982 Polygyny and Inheritance. Current Anthropology 23:1–12.

Heinroth, O.
1911 Beitrage zur Biologie, Namentlich Ethologie und Psychologie der Anatiden. Verhandlungen des V. Internationalen Ornithologen-Kongresses. Berlin. Pp. 652–654.

Hendrichs, H., and N. Hendrichs
1971 Dikdik und Elefanten Munich: Piper.

Herman, J. L.
1981 Father–Daughter Incest. Cambridge, Massachusetts: Harvard University Press.

Herzog, Elizabeth
1966 The Chronic Revolution: Births Out of Wedlock. Clinical Pediatrics 5:130–135.

Hill, J. L.
1974 Peromyscus: Effect of early pairing in reproduction. Science 186:1042–1044.

Hobhouse, L.
1912 Morals in Evolution. London: Chapman and Hall.

Homans, G. C., and D. M. Schneider
1955 Marriage, Authority and Final Causes. Glencoe, Illinois: Free Press.

Houriet, Robert
1971 Getting Back Together. London: Abacus.

Howell, Nancy
1976 The Population of the Dobe Area 'Kung'. In Kalahari Hunter-Gatherers. R. B. Lee and I. DeVore. Pp. 137–151. Cambridge, Massachusetts: Harvard University Press.

Howitt, A. W.
1904 The Native Tribes of South East Australia. London and New York: Macmillan.

Hrdy, Sarah B.
1977a Infanticide as a Primate Reproductive Strategy. American Scientist 65:40–49.
1977b The Langurs of Abu. Cambridge, Massachusetts: Harvard University Press.
1981 The Women That Never Evolved. Cambridge, Massachusetts: Harvard University Press.

Hughes, Graham
1964 The Crime of Incest. Journal of Criminal Law 55:322–331.

Huxley, A.
  1932 Brave New World. London: Chatto and Windus. [Reprinted New York: Harper and Row, 1969.]
Imanishi, Kinji
  1963 Social Behavior in Japanese Monkeys Macaca fuscata. In Primate Social Behavior. C. H. Southwick, ed. Pp. 68–82. New York: Van Nostrand.
  1965 The Origins of the Human Family. In Japanese Monkeys. S. A. Altman and K. Imanishi, eds. University of Alberta Emory.
Itani, Junichiro
  1972 A Preliminary Essay on the Relationship between Social Organization and Incest Avoidance in Nonhuman Primates. In Primate Socialization. Pp. 165–171. New York: Random House.
Jacquard, Albert
  1974 The Genetic Structure of Populations. Berlin, Heidelberg and New York: Springer Verlag.
Johanson, D. C., and M. A. Edey
  1981 Lucy—The Beginning of Humankind. New York: Simon and Schuster.
Jonas, D. F.
  1976 On an "Alternative Paleobiology" and the Concept of Scavenging Phase. Current Anthropology 17:144–145.
Justice, B., and R. Justice
  1979 The Broken Taboo. New York: Human Sciences Press.
Kaffman, Mordecai
  1977 Sexual Standards and Behavior of the Kibbutz Adolescent. American Journal of Orthopsychiatry 47:207–216.
Kaufman, I., A. L. Peck, and C. K. Tagiuri.
  1954 The Family Constellation and Overt Incestuous Relations between Father and Daughter. American Journal of Orthopsychiatry 24:266–277.
Kaufmann, J. H.
  1962 Ecology and Social Behavior of the Coati (Nasua marica) on Barro Colorado Islands, Panama. University of California Publications in Zoology 60:95.
  1965 A Three-Year Study of Mating Behavior in a Free-Ranging Band of Rhesus Monkeys. Ecology 46:500–512.
  1974 Social Ethology of the Whiptail Wallaby. Animal Behavior 22:281.
Kinsey, A. C., et al.
  1953 Sexual Behavior in the Human Female. Philadelphia: W. P. Saunders.
Kitagawa, E. M.
  1981 New Life-Styles: Marriage Patterns, Living Arrangements, and Fertility outside of Marriage. Annals of the American Academy of Political and Social Science 453:1–27.
Klingel, H.
  1967 Soziale Organization und Verhalten Freilebender Steppenzebras. Zeitschrift fur Tierpsychologie 24:518–624.
Koford, C. B.
  1963 Rank of Mothers and Sons in Rhesus Monkeys on Cayo Science 141:356–357.
  1965 Population Dynamics of Rhesus Monkeys on Cayo Santiago. In Primate Behavior. I. DeVore, ed. Pp. 160–175. New York: Holt, Rinehart and Winston.
Kortmulder, K.
  1974 On Ethology and Human Behavior. Acta Biotheoretica 23(2):55–78.
Koyama, N.
  1970 Changes in Dominance Rank and Division of a Wild Japanese Monkey Troop in Hrashiyama. Primates 11:335–390.

Kruuk, H.
 1972 The Spotted Hyena: A Study of Predation and Social Behavior. Chicago: University of Chicago Press.
Kubo, S.
 1959 Researches and Studies on Incest in Japan. Hiroshima Journal of Medical Sciences 8:99–159.
Kummer, H.
 1968 Social Organization of Hamadryas Baboons. Chicago: University of Chicago Press.
 1971 Primate Societies. Chicago: Aldine.
Kunstadter, Peter, et al.
 1964 Demographic Variability and Preferential Marriage Patterns. American Journal of Physical Anthropology 21:511–519.
Kurland, J. A.
 1979 Paternity, Mother's Brother and Human Sociality. In Evolutionary Biology and Human Social Behavior. N. A. Chagnon and W. Irons, eds. Pp. 145–180. North Scituate, Massachusetts: Duxbury Press.
Lahiri, R. K., and C. H. Southwick
 1966 Parental Care in Macaca sylvana. Folia Primatologica 4:257–264.
Lang, A.
 1905 The Secret of the Totem. London: Longman.
Larsen, R. R.
 1974 Rules of Inference When Arguing from Animal to Man. Paper presented at the meeting of the Animal Behavior Society, University of Illinois.
Lawrence, Douglas H.
 1968 Discriminative Learning. In The International Encyclopedia of the Social Sciences. Vol. 9:143–148.
Leach, Edmund R.
 1962 The Determinants of Differential Cross-Cousin Marriage. Man 62:238.
Leakey, R. E., and R. Lewin
 1977 Origins. New York: Dutton.
Lee, Richard B., and I. DeVore
 1968 Man the Hunter. Chicago: Aldine.
 1976 Kalahari Hunter-Gatherers. Cambridge, Massachusetts: Harvard University Press.
Lerner, I. M.
 1968 Heredity, Evolution and Society. San Francisco: W. H. Freeman.
Lévi-Strauss, C.
 1969 [The Elementary Structure of Kinship] (translated by J. H. Bell, J. R. von Sturmer, and R. Needham). Boston: Beacon Press. (First ed. 1949.)
Levy-Bruhl, L.
 1963 Le Surnaturel et la Nature dans la Mentalite Primitive. Paris: F. Alcan (First ed. 1931.)
Levy, Marion T.
 1955 Some Questions about Parsons' Treatment of the Incest Problem. British Journal of Sociology 6:277–285.
Li, C. C.
 1962 Population Genetics. Chicago: University of Chicago Press. (First ed. 1955.)
Lindzey, Gardner
 1967 Some Remarks Concerning Incest, the Incest Taboo, and Psychoanalytic Theory. American Psychologist 22:1051–1059.
Livingstone, F. B.
 1980 Cultural Causes of Genetic change. In Sociobiology: Beyond Nature/Nurture. G. W.

Barlow and T. Silverberg, eds. Pp. 307–329. Boulder, Colorado: Westview Press.

Loffler, Von Lorenz G.
1972   Inzest und Exogamie. Homo 23:351–365.

Lorenz, Konrad
1943   Die Angeborenen Formen Möglicher Erfahrung. Zeitschrift fur Tierpsychologie 5:235–409.
1960   King Solomon's Ring. London: Pan Books Ltd. (First ed. 1952.)
1966   On Aggression. New York: Harcourt Brace and World. (First ed. 1963.)

Lowie, R. H.
1933   The Family as a Social Unit. Papers of the Michigan Academy of Science, Arts and Letters 18:5369.
1940   In Introduction to Cultural Anthropology. New York: Rinehart.
1949   Primitive Society. London: Routledge and Regan Paul. (First ed. 1920.)

Loy, James
1971   Estrous Behavior of Free-Ranging Rhesus Monkeys (*Macaca mulatta*). Primates 12(1):1–31.

Lubbock, Sir John
1874   The Origin of Civilization and the Primitive Condition of Man. London: C. Knight.

Lumsden, C. J., and E. O. Wilson
1980   Gene–Culture Translation in the Avoidance of Sibling Incest. Proceedings of the National Academy of Sciences 77:6248–6250.
1981   Genes, Mind and Culture. Cambridge, Massachusetts: Harvard University Press.

Lyons, Andrew P.
1978   Wild Man and Beast Children. Paper presented at the Tenth International Conference of Anthropological and Ethnographic Science, New Delhi.

Maccoby, E. E., T. M. Newcomb, and E. Hartley, eds.
1958   Readings in Social Psychology. (Third ed.) New York: Holt, Rinehart and Winston.

Maine, Sir Henry Summer
1874   Ancient Law. New York: C. Scribner.

Maisch, H.
1968   Inzest. Hamburg: Rowohlt.
1972   Incest. New York: Stern and Day.

Malinowski, B.
1927   Sex and Repression in Savage Society. New York: Meridian.
1929   The Sexual Life of Savages. New York: Harcourt Brace and World.
1931   Culture. *In* Encyclopaedia of the Social Sciences, Vol. 4. Seligman, E. R. A., ed. Pp. 621–646. London: Macmillan.

Mann, T.
1951   Der Erwaehlte. Oldenburg: S. Vischer Verlag. [The Holy Sinner, New York: Knopf.]

Marshall, Lorna
1976   The !Kung of Nyae Nyae. Cambridge Massachusetts: Harvard University Press.

Masters, R. E. L.
1963   Patterns of Incest. New York: Julian Press.

Mathews, R. H.
1897   The Totemic Division of Australian Tribes. Journal and Proceedings of the Royal Society of New South Wales 31:272–285.
1905   Ethnological Notes on the Aboriginal Tribes of New South Wales and Victoria. Journal and Proceeding of the Royal Society of New South Wales 38:272–381.

Maynard-Smith, John
  1971   The Origin and Maintenance of Sex. *In* Group Selection. G. C. Williams, ed. Chicago: Aldine Atherton.
  1978   The Evolution of Sex. Cambridge: Cambridge University Press.
Mayr, Ernst
  1970   Population, Species and Evolution. Cambridge, Massachusetts: Harvard-Belknap.
Mead, Margaret
  1968   *In* International Encyclopedia of the Social Sciences, Vol. 7. p. 115. New York: Macmillan and The Free Press.
Meiselman, Karin C.
  1978   Incest. San Francisco: Jossey-Bass.
Merton, Robert K.
  1949   Social Theory and Social Structure. Glencoe, Illinois: The Free Press.
Middleton, R.
  1962   Brother–Sister and Father–Daughter Marriage in Ancient Egypt. American Sociological Review 27:603–611.
Missakian, Elizabeth A.
  1972   Genealogical and Cross-Genealogical Dominance Relations in a Group of Free-Ranging Rhesus Monkeys (*Macaca mulatta*) on Cayo Santiago. Primates, 13:169–180.
  1973   The Timing of Fission among Free-Ranging Rhesus Monkeys. American Journal of Physical Anthropology 38:321–624.
Morgan, L. H.
  1877   Systems of Consanguinity and Affinity in the Human Family. Washington, D.C.: Smithsonian Institution.
Morley, F. H. W.
  1954   Selection for Economic Characters in Australian Merino Sheep, IV: The Effect of Inbreeding. Australian Journal of Agricultural Research 5:305–316.
Morris, Desmond
  1967   Primate Ethology. Chicago: Aldine.
  1971   The Human Zoo. New York: Dell.
  1973   The Naked Ape. New York: Dell.
Morton, N. E., J. F. Crow, and H. J. Muller
  1956   An Estimate of Mutational Damage in Man from Data on Consanguinous Marriages. Proceedings of the National Academy of Science 42:855–863.
Murdock, G. P.
  1949   Social Structure. New York: Macmillan.
  1955   Changing Emphases in Social Structure. Southwestern Journal of Anthropology 11:361–370.
  1962–
  1967   Ethnographic Atlas. Ethnology. 1–6.
  1972   Anthropology's Mythology. Proceedings of the Royal Anthropological Institute of Great Britain and Ireland for 1971. Pp. 17–24.
Newsweek
  1981   Incest Epidemic. November 30, p. 68.
Nishida, Toshisada
  1979   The Social Structure of Chimpanzees of the Mahale Mountains. In The Great Apes. D. A. Hamburg and E. McCown, eds. Menlo Park, California: Benjamin/Cummings.

O'Neal, Joseph M.
  1977   When Are You Going to Make Me a Grandmother? An Explanatory Look at Pronatalist Pressure in Social Networks. Paper presented at the 76th Annual Meeting of the American Anthropological Association, Houston, Texas.
Packer, C.
  1979   Inter-troop Transfer and Inbreeding Avoidance in *Papio anubis*. Animal Behavior 27:1–36.
Parker, Seymour
  1976   Precultural Basis of the Incest Taboo: Toward a Biosocial Theory. American Anthropologist 78:285–305.
Parsons, T.
  1951   The Social System. Glencoe, Illinois: Free Press.
  1954   The Incest Taboo in Relation to Social Structure and the Socialization of the Child. British Journal of Sociology 5:101–107.
Parsons, T., and Robert F. Bales
  1955   Family Socialization and Interaction Process. Glencoe, Illinois: The Free Press.
Parsons, T., and Edward A. Shils, eds.
  1952   Toward a General Theory of Action. Cambridge, Massachusetts: Harvard University Press.
Parsons, T., Robert F. Bales, and Edward A. Shils
  1953   Working Papers in the Theory of Action. Glencoe, Illinois: The Free Press.
Peter, Prince of Greece and Denmark
  1963   A Study of Polyandry. The Hague: Mouton.
Pusey, Ann
  1979   Intercommunity Transfer of Chimpanzees in Gombe National Park. *In* The Great Apes. D. A. Hamburg and E. R. McCown, eds. Pp. 465–479. Menlo Park, California: Benjamin/Cummings.
  1980   Inbreeding Avoidance in Chimpanzees. Animal Behavior 28:543–552.
Rabin, I. A.
  1965   Growing Up in a Kibbutz. New York: Springer.
Rattray, R. F.
  1929   Ashanti Law and Constitution. Oxford: Oxford University Press.
Reynolds, H. C.
  1952   Studies on Reproduction in the Opossum (*Didelphis virginiana*). University of California Publications in Zoology 52:223 sq.
Reynolds, V.
  1968   Kinship and the Family in Monkeys, Apes and Man. Man 3:209–223.
Reynolds, V., and F. Reynolds
  1965   Chimpanzees of the Budongo Forest. *In* Primate Behavior. I. DeVore, ed. Pp. 368–425. New York: Holt, Rinehart and Winston.
Richerson, P. J., and R. Boyd
  1978   A Dual Inheritance Model of the Human Evolutionary Process. Journal of Social and Biological Structures 1:127–154.
Riemer, Svend
  1936   Die Blutschande als Soziologisches Problem. Monatschrift der Kriminalbiologie 27:86.
  1940   A Research Note on Incest. American Journal of Sociology 45:566.
Robertson, A.
  1954   Inbreeding and Performance in British Friesian Cattle. Proceedings of the British Society of Animal Production 1954. Pp. 87–92.

Robinson, H. G., S. C. Woods, and A. E. Williams
   1980   The Desire to Bear Children. *In* The Evolution of Human Social Behavior. J. S. Lockard, ed. Pp. 87–105. New York: Elsevier.
Rosenfeld, E.
   1958   The American Social Scientist in Israel: A Case-Study in Role Conflict. American Journal of Orthopsychiatry 28:563–571.
Ruse, Michael
   1979   Sociobiology: Sense or Nonsense. Doordrecht: D. Reidel.
Sade, D. S.
   1968   Inhibition of Son–Mother Mating among Free-Ranging Rhesus Monkeys. Science and Psychoanalysis 12:18–38.
Schachter, M., and S. Cotte
   1960   Etude Medico-Psychologique et Social de l'Inceste, dans la Perspective Pedo-Psychiatrique. Acta Pedo-Psychiatry 27:139–146.
Schaller, G. B.
   1963   The Mountain Gorilla. Chicago: University of Chicago Press.
   1967   The Deer and the Tiger. Chicago: University of Chicago Press.
   1972   The Serengeti Lion: A Study of Predator–Prey Relations. Chicago: Univeristy of Chicago Press.
Schneider, David M.
   1956   Attempts to Account for the Incest Taboo. Unpublished paper.
   1972   What is Kinship all About? *In* Kinship Studies in the Morgan Centennial Year. P. Reining, ed. Pp. 32–63. Washington, D.C.: Anthropological Society of Washington, D.C.
   1976   The Meaning of Incest. The Journal of the Polynesian Society 85:149–169.
Schull, E. J., and J. V. Neel
   1965   The Effects of Inbreeding on Japanese Children. New York: Harper & Row.
Schwartzman, John
   1974   The Individual, Incest, and Exogamy. Psychiatry 37:171–180.
Second Abstracts of British Historical Statistics
   1971   Cambridge. University Press.
Seemanova, Eva
   1971   A Study of Children of Incestuous Matings. Human Heredity 21:108–128.
Seligman, Brenda A.
   1929   Incest and Descent: Their Influence on Social Organization. Journal of the Royal Anthropological Institute 59:231–272.
   1932   The Incest Barrier: Its Role in Social Organization. British Journal of Psychology 22:250–276.
   1935   The Incest Taboo as a Social Regulation. The Sociological Review 27:75–93.
   1950   The Problem of Incest and Exogamy: A Restatement. American Anthropologist 52:305–316.
Shepher, Joseph
   1969   Familism and Social Structure: The Case of the Kibbutz. Journal of Marriage and the Family 31:568–573.
   1971a   Mate Selection among Second-Generation Kibbutz Adolescents and Adults: Incest Avoidance and Negative Imprinting. Archives of Sexual Behavior 1:293–307.
   1971b   Self Imposed Incest Avoidance and Exogamy in Second Generation Kibbutz Adults. Ann Arbor: University Microfilms.
   1977   Introduction to the Sociology of the Kibbutz. (In Hebrew.) Tel-Aviv: Hamidrashah Hachaklaith.
   1978   Reflections on the Origin of the "Human Pairbond." Journal of Social and Biological

Structures 1:253–264.

Shepher, Joseph, and L. Tiger
In   Kibbutz and Parental Investment—Women in the Kibbutz Reconsidered. Small
press   Groups: Social-Psychological Processes, Social Action and Living Together. P. A.
         Hare *et al.*, eds. London: John Wiley and Sons.

Shepher, Joseph *et al.*
1977   Female Dominance and Sexual Inadequacy. Research report submitted to the 76th
         Annual Meeting of the American Anthropological Association, Houston, Texas.

Shoffner, R. N.
1948   The Reduction of the Fowl to Inbreeding. Poultry Science 27:448–452.

Simonds, Paul E.
1974   The Social Primates. New York: Harper & Row.

Slater, M. Kreiseman
1959   Ecological Factors in the Origin of Incest. American Anthropologist 61:1042–
         1059.

Sloane, P., and E. Karpinski
1942   Effect of Incest on the Participants. American Journal of Orthopsychiatry 12:666–
         673.

Spencer, B., and F. J. Gillen
1899   The Native Tribes of Central Australia. London: Macmillan.
1904   The Northern Tribes of Central Australia. London: Macmillan.

Spencer, H.
1915   Principles of Sociology. New York: Appleton.

Spiro, M. E.
1958   Children of the Kibbutz. Cambridge, Massachusetts: Harvard University Press.

Starcke, C. N.
1889   The Primitive Family in its Origin and Development. New York: Appleton.

Steadman, Lyle
1977   On Marriage, the Incest Taboo and Exogamy. Paper presented at the 76th Meeting of
         the American Anthropological Association.

Stern, Curt
1973   Principles of Human Genetics. (Third ed.) San Francisco: W. H. Freeman.

Sumner, W. G., and A. G. Keller
1927   The Science of Society. New Haven: Yale University Press.

Symons, Donald
1979   The Evolution of Human Sexuality. New York: Oxford University Press.

Talmon, Gerber Y.
1964   Mate Selection in Collective Settlements. American Sociological Review 29:408–
         491.

Tembrock, G.
1957   Zur Ethologie des Rotfuchses. Der Zoologische Garten (NF) 23:431.

Thorpe, W. H.
1964   Learning and Instinct in Animals. London: Methuen.

Tiger, Lionel
1969   Men in Groups. New York: Random House.
1975   Somatic Factors and Social Behavior. *In* Biosocial Anthropology. R. Fox, ed. Pp. 115–
         132. London: Malaby Press.
1979   Optimism. New York; Simon and Schuster.

Tiger, Lionel, and R. Fox
1971   The Imperial Animal. New York: Holt, Rinehart and Winston.

Tiger, Lionel, and J. Shepher

1975   Women in the Kibbutz. New York: Harcourt Brace Jovanovich.
Tokuda, K.
1961   A Study of Sexual Behavior in the Japanese Monkey Troop. Primates 3:1–41.
Trivers, Robert L.
1971   The Evolution of Reciprocal Altruism. Quarterly Review of Biology 46:35–57.
1972   Parental Investment and Sexual Selection. *In* Sexual Selection and the Descent of
         Man. B. Campbell, ed. Pp. 136–179. Chicago: Aldine.
1974   Parent–Offspring Conflict. American Zoology 14:249–264.
Trivers, R. L., and H. Hare
1976   Haplodiploidy and the Evolution of the Social Insect. Science 191:249–263.
Turnbull, C. M.
1972   The Mountain People. New York: Simon and Schuster.
Tylor, E. B.
1870   Researches into the Early History of Mankind and the Development of Civilization.
         London: T. Murray.
1888   On a Method of Investigating the Development of Institutions, Applied to Laws of
         Marriage and Descent. Journal of the Royal Anthropological Institute 18:245–272.
U. S. Department of Commerce
1970   Historical Statistics of the United States. Washington, D.C.: Government Printing
         Office.
Vandenberg, S. G.
1967   In Recent Advances in Biological Psychiatry, F. Wortis, ed. Vol. 9.
Van den Berghe, Pierre
1975   Man in Society: A Biosocial View. New York: Elsevier.
1977   Territorial Behavior in a Natural Human Group. Social Science Information 16:419–
         430.
1979   Human Family Systems. New York: Elsevier.
1980a   The Human Family: A Sociobiological Look. *In* Evolution of Human Social Behavior.
         J. Lockard, ed. New York: Elsevier.
1980b   Incest and Exogamy: A Sociobiological Reconsideration. Ethology and Sociobiology
         1:151–162.
In   Human Inbreeding Avoidance: Culture in Nature. Behavior and Brain
press   Sciences.
Van den Berghe, Pierre, and G. M. Mesher
1980   Royal Incest and Inclusive Fitness. American Ethnologist 1:300–317.
Wachter, K. W.
1980   Ancestors at the Norman Conquest. *In* Geneological Demography. B. Dyke and
         W. T. Morrill, eds. Pp. 85–93. New York: Academic Press.
Wagner, Roy
1972   Incest and Identity: A Critique and Theory on the Subject of Exogamy and Incest
         Prohibition. Man 7:601–603.
Wallis, Wilson
1950   The Origin of Incest Rules. American Anthropologist 52:277–279.
Washburn, S. L.
1973   The Evolution Game. Journal of Human Evolution 2:557–561.
Washburn, S. L., and I. DeVore
1961a   Social Behavior of Baboons and Early Man. *In* Social Life of Early Man. S. L.
         Washburn, ed. Pp. 91–105. Chicago: Aldine.
1961b   The Social Life of Baboons. Scientific American 204(6):62–71.
Watson, James D.

1976   Molecular Biology of the Gene. Menlo Park, California: W. A. Benjamin, Inc. (Addison-Wesley Student Series).
Webster, G., and B. C. Goodwin
   1982   The Origin of Species: A Structuralist Approach. Journal of Social and Biological Structures 5:15–47.
Weinberg, Kirson S.
   1955   Incest Behavior. New York: Citadel Press.
Weintraub, D. *et al.*
   1969   Moshava, Kibbutz and Moshav. Ithaca: Cornell University Press.
Wendt, Herbert
   1965   The Sex Life of the Animals. New York: Simon and Schuster.
Westermarck, E. A.
   1891   The History of Human Marriage. London: Macmillan.
   1921   The History of Human Marriage. (Fifth ed.) London: Macmillan.
   1934a Recent Theories of Exogamy. The Sociological Review 26:22–40.
   1934b Three Essays on Sex and Marriage. London: Macmillan.
Westoff, Charles
   1978   Marriage and Fertility in the Developed Countries. Scientific American 238(6):35–41.
White, L. A.
   1948   The Definition and Prohibition of Incest. American Anthropologist 50:416–435.
Whiting, J. W. M., R. Kluckhohn, and A. Anthony
   1958   The Function of Male Initiation Ceremonies at Puberty. *In* Readings in Social Psychology. (Third ed.) E. E. Maccoby, T. M. Newcomb, and E. Hartley, eds. Pp. 359–370. New York: Holt Rinehart and Winston.
Williams, George C.
   1975   Sex and Evolution. Princeton, New Jersey: Princeton University Press.
Willner, Dorothy
   1975   Sexual Appropriation and Social Space: Another View of Incest. Paper presented at the 74th Annual Meeting of the American Anthropological Association.
Wilson, Edward O.
   1971   The Insect Societies. Cambridge, Massachusetts: Harvard University Press, Belknap Press.
   1975   Sociobiology—The New Synthesis. Cambridge, Massachusetts: Harvard University Press, Belknap Press.
   1978   On Human Nature. Cambridge, Massachusetts: Harvard University Press.
Wilson, Edward O., *et al.*
   1973   Life on Earth. Sunderland, Massachusetts: Sinauer Associates.
Wilson, M.
   1951   Good Company: A Study of Nyakyusa Age Villages. London: Oxford University Press.
Witherspoon, Gary
   1975   Navajo Kinship and Marriage. Chicago: University of Chicago Press.
Wolf, A. P.
   1966   Childhood Association, Sexual Attraction and the Incest Taboo: A Chinese Case. American Anthropologist 68:883–898.
   1968   Adopt a Daughter-in-Law, Marry a Sister: A Chinese Solution to the Problem of Incest Taboo. American Anthropologist 70:864–874.
   1970   Childhood Association and Sexual Attraction: A Further Test of the Westermarck Hypothesis. American Anthropologist 72:503–515.

Wolf, A. P., and C. Huang
  1980   Marriage and Adoption in China 1845–1945. Stanford: Stanford University Press.
Wundt, W.
  1906   Volkerpsychologie. Leipzig: A. Krômer.
Yamaguchi, M., T. Yanase, H. Nagamo, and N. Norinoba
  1970   Effect of Inbreeding on Mortality in Fukuoka Population. The American Journal of
         Human Genetics 22:145–155.
Yengoyan, Aram A.
  1968   Demographic and Ecological Influences on Aboriginal Australian Marriage Sections.
         In Man the Hunter, R. B. Lee and I. DeVore, eds. Pp. 185–200. Chicago: Aldine.
Young, Frank W.
  1962   The Function of Male Initiation Ceremonies: A Cross Cultural Test of an Alternative
         Hypothesis. American Journal of Sociology 67:379–391.

Author Index

SUBJECT INDEX

STUDIES IN ANTHROPOLOGY

Under the Consulting Editorship of E. A. Hammel,
UNIVERSITY OF CALIFORNIA, BERKELEY